W9-CNV-320

Preferring Christ

A DEVOTIONAL COMMENTARY

and WORKBOOK

on THE RULE of ST. BENEDICT

By Norvene Vest, Oblate O.S.B.

Foreword by
D. Robert Hale, O.S.B.Cam.

SOURCE BOOKS
TRABUCO CANYON CALIFORNIA

Cover and illustrations by Denis Clarke

Typeset at St. Andrew's Abbey, Valyermo, California

First Printing June 1991
Reprinted 1993

ISBN 0-940147-14-9

Published by SOURCE BOOKS
Box 794
Trabuco Canyon CA 92678
USA

Printed and bound in the USA by KNI Inc., Anaheim CA

This book is dedicated first of all to a place: the Our Lady Undercroft at Canterbury Cathedral, where I first had the idea which eventually produced this book;

and then to a community: the monks and oblates of St. Andrew's Priory in Valyermo, California who provided the rich soil in which these seeds could take root and produce fruit;

and finally to a guide: my husband, Douglas, who teaches me daily through his un-selfconscious presence at my side the delightful art of preferring Christ in all things.

Table of Contents

Foreword

This profound yet very practical volume speaks to an urgent spiritual need. Many people are yearning for an interior life deeply rooted in God, humanly balanced and substantially founded in the Christian heritage. Norvene Vest offers a valuable resource in this regard by rendering much more accessible the spiritual wealth of the key text of the ancient Benedictine charism. These pages explore the solid, balanced wisdom of Saint Benedict`s Rule which has nourished and guided innumerable Christians for nearly fifteen centuries.

Contemporary Christians from various denominations are feeling ever more attracted to spiritual classics such as the Rule. But it is not an easy matter thoroughly to engage a text of another age. Here, Norvene is singularly qualified to help.

With her husband, an Episcopal priest, she has ministered for ten years to the spiritual life of clergy and laity of the Episcopal Diocese of Los Angeles. The importance of the spiritual classics to this ministry has long been clear to them. And as Chairperson of the Oblate Formation Committee of Saint Andrew's Priory in California (a Roman Catholic Benedictine community), she has ongoing contact with monastic life, and with those in the world who wish more directly to share in its ancient charism.

Norvene's participation in the direction of the *Benedictine Experience* programs at Bishop's Ranch, California, which draw people of several denominations, and her own long experience as spiritual director for many Christians of varied traditions, -all this has enriched her own reflection regarding Benedictine spirituality and the heartfelt spiritual needs of people today.

I remember when Norvene first shared with me the central insight which made this book possible. We were walking down a rural road beyond Bishop's Ranch, with lovely vineyards to the right and left, -a very Benedictine, sacramental setting! We were discussing the difficult issue of how an ancient text can be claimed for our own spiritual life, how to avoid a fundamentalistic approach on the one hand, and an arbitrary "adaptation" of the text to our own subjective tastes, on the other. How can we authentically engage Saint Benedict's Rule in a manner that is true to its profound insights, and also true to our own spiritual journey?

As we rounded the curve of the road, Norvene turned and said with intense enthusiasm: "The answer lies in the **way** we read the Rule. It shouldn't be studied like a book of regulations, or a school text-book. It should be read as *lectio divina!*" It was as if she had found the key to the front door of a wonderful and fascinating ancient cathedral. As true insights always are, once articulated, it was more than evident, and we monks have been reading the Rule this way for centuries. But I have never heard a monk put it that directly. And often we slip into other modes of reading, and lose contact with the deepest dimensions of the Rule's wisdom.

What precisely is the method of *lectio divina?* Basically it means that we should read the Rule as we would meditate upon Holy Scripture or a spiritual classic. This means that we should first **study** the passage very attentively in order to grasp what is there. But then we should go on to **meditate** on it at a deeper, spiritual level, in our hearts. Even then we are not halfway through the adventure. We need to go on to **pray** the text, to render it a vehicle for worship. And finally we need to enable the text to lead us into a yet deeper level of **contemplation** of the ineffable God.

This is the way the monks and the faithful have read Scripture and the great Christian spiritual writings through the ages. It is quite different from the "recreational" approach: speed-reading, skimming, then discarding and often forgetting a text. It is also quite different from anxiously studying a book for a test of a job requirement, -the approach which is drilled into us at school.

Each page of this workbook is structured to support the reader in the ancient approach of *lectio,* enabling us to explore and assimilate in a reverential and penetrating way, the riches of the Rule. If from this workbook we learn nothing other than this method of *lectio*, or if, already "knowing" it, we deepen our familiarity with it, and our seriousness in using it, we shall have gained a great deal indeed, and come to know much about a foundational element of Benedictine spirituality. In fact this volume offers a great deal beyond this. It provides numerous deep insights regarding other key elements of the wisdom of the Rule, -fruit of the author's own careful and prayerful *lectio.*

To use this method is not to force upon the Rule some foreign and artificial technique. Rather it is to have prayerful recourse precisely to the approach which Saint Benedict presupposes. *Lectio* is the way Benedictine monks endeavor to read any spiritual classic, in fact to read their very lives. It is the way that Scripture itself presupposes that all of salvation history will be meditated, that every individual life journey will be pondered and prayed. For God is present, powerfully and effectively, in Scripture, in the Rule, in the spiritual classics, and also in our lives. If we can carefully "read" that Presence, meditate that Presence, then go on to pray and contemplate that Presence, we shall be transformed.

But... Do we have time for this? Do we have the **energy**? Can we muster the attention-span? After all, we are frenetically busy, even with our "R & R" projects and hobbies. Not for nothing have we produced multi-billion dollar "entertainment" industries. In the words of T.S. Eliot, we are *distracted from distraction by distraction.* Thomas Merton notes the word's etymology: "Distraction" comes from the Latin, "Pulled apart". Our rush alienates us from our deepest center, -from that *Still point of the turning world* (Eliot). But if we can find courage and open ourselves to the grace of following through with the discipline of *lectio*, of cleaving to the Rule (or another deep, spiritual text) until we have arrived at *The heart of the matter,* -then we can finally start to heal and become transformed.

Some fourteen hundred years ago Pope Gregory the Great characterized Saint Benedict's Rule as remarkable for its **discretion**. That last term is a rich one, rooted in Scripture and the earliest Christian texts. It refers to Spirit-enabled discernment, carefulness, wise balance, deep insight. Perhaps our own age and each one of us could use more of that Benedictine discretion. We can all too easily become "charged-up", obsessed with something (it might be the latest spiritual craze). But carefully to undertake a journey that will certainly lead to the heights if we keep moving steadily, taking nourishment from the Christian wisdom of the ages, -that is something else. And so this workbook is something else.

The invitation which one hears from these pages comes from far beyond the book itself, from far beyond Saint Benedict. The source is ultimately The Beloved. And as the Rule observes, *What, dear brethren, is more delightful than the Lord's voice calling us? Behold, the Lord in His love shows us the way of life.*

D. Robert Hale, O.S.B. Cam.
New Camaldoli Hermitage
Big Sur, California

January 1991

Introduction

The purpose of this book is to make the Rule of St. Benedict more accessible to the modern lay person.

Many readers will at once recognize Benedict of Nursia as an Italian layman, who died approximately 545 A.D. at Monte Cassino, the great monastery he founded and presided over as abbot for about twenty-five years. As a Christian living in the Sixth Century, Benedict faced the collapse of the Roman Empire, and consequent warring and inflation and instability so characteristic of such periods. He also faced in a personal way the question of how the church was to survive, how Christians were to survive, indeed how civilization was to survive in such a time. He was heir to two primary responses of the Christian church: the freely given martyrdom of the first few centuries, and the search for holiness in the desert hermitages of the next few centuries.

Benedict was not particularly a theoretican. He loved God, he believed Christian life was best lived in community, and he sought practical ways to guide the brothers under his care in the daily life of holiness. He wrote the simple and short document, called merely The Rule,[1] in response to these concerns and influences. Its simplicity, its practicality, and its faithfulness to the Gospel caused the Rule to become the primary guide for monastic life (and to have wider influence, as well) for at least 1000 years. It is still in use today.

Despite the major role of Benedictine monasteries in the subsequent life of the church (and indeed, Western civilization itself), there is remarkably little written about the major emphases of the Benedictine approach to Christian life, and even less about how this might be applicable for ordinary Christians. Certainly all Christian spiritualities draw on the same basic material of the Gospels and tradition, but each has its different emphasis, its own peculiar themes.

So too, the Rule has a special way of viewing the patterns and dynamics of Christian life. The whole orientation of the Rule is to the principle that God is everywhere, all the time, and thus that every element of our ordinary day is potentially holy. Very few of us believe that and/or act on it. Benedict urges us both so to believe and so to act. It is an enormous challenge, involving life-long response, and yet it is very simple and can be begun this moment. Because the Rule is so "homely", so oriented to the opportunities of daily life as grist for the mill of Christian consecration, it has a great deal to say which is directly helpful to a Christian lay person, struggling to live the Christian life even in our contemporary, secular world.

However, the modern reader often finds the Rule hard to understand, even though it emphasizes daily life. That is because it is written within the context of the ancient monastic art of *lectio divina*, and it needs to be read in that way, if it is to be truly appreciated. *Lectio divina* literally means "divine reading", and carries the same double meaning in Latin as in English: what is being read is divine/holy, usually the Scriptures; and how it is being read is with the help of God's Spirit. In order for this "how" to happen, one slows down radically so as to open up freely.

It is the monastic insight that reading, if it be authentic, cannot be undertaken simply with the eyes and the mind. Rather, it must involve the whole person: mind, heart, body and spirit. It is reading not so much for information as for formation, that is, for encounter with the living God in this moment in such a way that one's heart catches fire and one's life is transformed.

Benedict has written the Rule in the mode of *lectio divina*, and in order best to be appreciated, it is best read in that mode. Thus, this book is designed to provide a framework for slow and simple, daily reflection, meditation and prayer on the Rule, in such a way that we are reading in the spirit of *lectio divina* a work written in that spirit.

Traditionally, *lectio divina* is understood to contain four basic steps or elements.

1. *Lectio* **(reading):** take a passage of scripture or other devotional/theological work and read aloud a few verses. The reading aloud engages the body in the reading, and already begins to draw one more deeply into the text.

2. *Meditatio* **(meditation):** allow oneself to be drawn by a particular word or phrase, pondering in the mind what it means, what was its intent.

3. *Oratio* **(prayer):** apply the meaning to the present situation in one's own life, allowing the word to penetrate the heart, evoking prayerful response.

4. *Contemplatio* **(contemplation):** turn the whole process back over to the Giver, allowing oneself to be deepened, guided, and transformed by the Spirit.

Roughly following that basic structure, the format for this book takes the following shape. Each entry is intended to correspond to one day's prayerful engagement by the reader. The day's entry has four components:

1. Text: A few verses of the Rule are provided, taken from a translation made for this commentary by Fr. Luke Dysinger, O.S.B. of St. Andrew's Priory, Valyermo. This new translation is based in part on a version of the Rule prepared in 1921 by Dom Justin McCann, O.S.B., which accompanied the first English edition of the *Commentary on the Rule of St. Benedict* by Dom Paul Delatte, O.S.B. In cases of doubtful readings we have consulted the critical edition of the Latin text of the Rule: *La Règle de Saint Benoît* edited by Adelbert de Vogüé and Jean Neufville in *Sources Chrétiennes* (Paris: *Les Éditions du Cerf* 1971-72), volumes 1-7.

It is recommended that the reader take the time to write out these verses in one's own hand, paraphrasing to be certain the text is understood. Alternatively, read the text aloud, slowly, experiencing its sound fully.

2. Comment: This component contains a few paragraphs of commentary on the selected passage, emphasizing what Benedict meant by the passage, what he was trying to get at, what he is doing here, and why. While these comments are informed by wide acquaintance with secondary sources, they are not intended primarily to be a scholarly commentary, but rather express an intuitive exploration of the basic spiritual themes here intended, as they might be most applicable to situations of contemporary readers. The central question is, what is Benedict doing here? And it is answered in a mode designed to help modern readers relate Benedict's concerns to our own.

3. Reflection: Here a shift is made, from the objective to the more personal framework. I endeavor to inquire more fully with my own heart, what might this text mean for me. This section is necessarily individual, involving my own responses to the text in light of current issues with which I am struggling. The intention is to offer an example of one contemporary lay person -- myself -- seeking to integrate the text with my life issues, exploring connections and resistances. The central question here is, how does this passage touch my own life? My response is as often evoked by a word or phrase as by the whole passage. The answer to this question involves what I am thinking and feeling now, as I relate to what I have read. It is hoped that my responses will be sufficiently "universal" that they will at least stimulate the reader's own personal interaction with the text. The reader is urged to use this as a jumping off place from which to seek her or his own integration, since the primary intention of this commentary is to provide a workbook within which the reader can become directly engaged with the Gospel in her or his life, via the medium of the Rule.

4. Prayer/Response: Finally, for each daily segment there is a blank space, under this title, in which the reader is invited specifically to become personally engaged. Perhaps that will involve taking up pen and filling in this page or the reader's own journal, with whatever responses seem evoked. Perhaps that will involve setting the book aside, closing the eyes, breathing deeply, and in quietness waiting to discover where God is leading in this connection on this day. It is, in any case, the reader's and the Spirit's own segment.

The reader is encouraged to take time with the text, even and often more than I have suggested by this format. Look up the Scripture references in the Rule and ponder them too. Wonder what Benedict is getting at: always look twice for what might be the deeper meaning, first giving him the benefit of the doubt. Ask what is being said to you today by these words. Offer it all in prayer.

Because this daily exercise may be a new experience for the reader, "interludes" are provided at the end of each major section. These interludes are intended to give practical helps for improving and strengthening the personal process of *lectio divina* upon the Rule[2] in which the reader is engaged. The "interludes" may be read all at once, or skipped altogether, as they are not specifically related to the Rule itself, but rather are intended simply as workbook aids.

Perhaps the strongest feeling that comes to me as I have undertaken this journey of *lectio divina* through the Rule, is that Benedict always keeps us focused on Christ. He quotes extensively from Scripture, sometimes in ways that at first seem confusing, but almost always in response to the fundamental question in his mind: "How can I, this day, allow myself to be drawn more deeply into the mind of Christ, that I might be more and more the one God has called me forth to be?"

Always, too, the emphasis is on God's love, in creation and especially in Christ, and the urgent, wonderful, and personal calling it is to respond to that love. It is no accident that the best-known phrase of the Rule and its summary statement is:

Prefer nothing to the love of Christ!

The transformation of our whole selves toward that preference is the Rule's goal. Amen.

The Prologue

Prologue, verses 1-2

L isten, O my son to the precepts of the master, and incline the ear of your heart: willingly receive and faithfully fulfil the admonition of your loving father; that you may return by the labor of obedience to him from whom you had departed through the sloth of disobedience.

Comment: In these first words of the Rule, Benedict communicates both a direct and personal relationship, and a sense of eager urgency. "My son" and "admonition of your loving father" make clear the sense in which the Rule is truly addressed to each one who reads or hears it; it is a personal word for each.

The phrases "listen", "willingly receive", "faithfully fulfil" and "that you may return" all convey energy and action, a kind of immediate personal application of what is here spoken.

The first word of the Rule is well-known: listen! It is interesting indeed that this Latin word ob-sculta has the same root, and indeed almost the same meaning, as the Latin word ob-oedire, which makes our English obedience. There is a very important connection between true listening and deep obedience; both suggest a turning in order to receive more fully that which is being given.

Turning is really what the whole Rule is about. It presumes the first turning, or conversion, of baptism; and it is then deeply interested in the second and lifelong turning, of daily conversion to Christ. The question always in Benedict's mind is the question of Christian maturity: "how can we live out our commitment to the Lord in daily life?" He is certain that God calls each one of us each day to respond more fully:

"If only you would listen to him today, do not harden your hearts..." (RB Prologue 10, and Psalm 95 which is the *Venite*--opening psalm--of Vigils and Morning Prayer).

His central concern is what environment and what behavior will daily "bring us back to him".

Thus Benedict begins with the practical questions of daily life.[2] He finds these clearly raised in Psalm 34:12 "Which of you wants to live to the full?" and Psalm 15:1: "Yahweh, who has the right to enter your tent, or to live (with you)?", and he allows these psalms broadly to shape his call to a life of consecration to God, a call to take seriously the (second) ongoing turning of listening obedience.

Reflection: The word is addressed personally to each one who reads or hears this prologue. Do I take that as true for me, too? I do know that I often struggle with the "sloth of disobedience", if by that is meant forgetfulness. Forgetfulness that I live even this minute in the sight of God. Forgetfulness that I am, even in this conflict or brokenness or joy or creative moment, empowered by the Spirit of God. Forgetfulness that I am, even and perhaps especially in my weakness and limitation, loved profoundly by my Christ.

And I do know that I desire life and I long to "dwell with the Lord", but I am often bewildered about how to respond to these longings. Yes, I could use a school for the Lord's service, a pattern or an environment which would help me live more fully each day in the heart of God. I am eager to see what fruit this *lectio* might produce in me. Lead on, Benedict!

Prayer/Response:

Prologue, verses 3-7

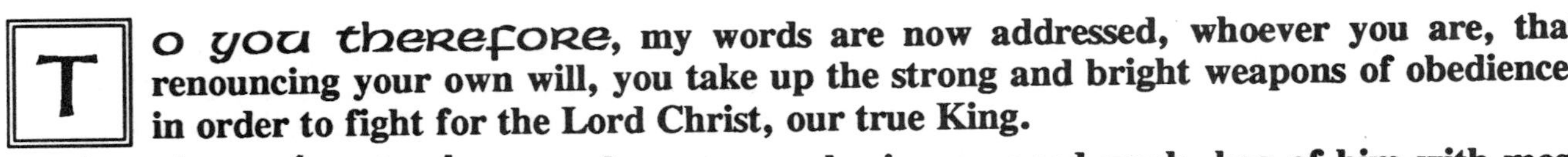

To you therefore, my words are now addressed, whoever you are, that renouncing your own will, you take up the strong and bright weapons of obedience, in order to fight for the Lord Christ, our true King.

In the first place, whenever you begin any good work, beg of him with most earnest prayer to perfect it; so that he who has now granted us the dignity of being counted in the number of his children may not at any time be grieved by our evil deeds. For we must always so serve him with the good things he has given us, that not only may he never, as an angry father, disinherit his children; but may never as a dread Lord, incensed by our sins, deliver us to everlasting punishment as most wicked servants who would not follow him to glory.

Comment: The images tumble out of Benedict's mind: King, father, manor lord, jumbled in a mixture of eagerness much like the letters of St. Peter when he seeks with such urgency to communicate to his hearers the majesty of the proferred gift and the danger of losing it. All Benedict's thought is centered upon salvation: the mystery of eternal life in God offered through Christ, and the possibility that we may refuse that glorious gift by our hard-heartedness.[3] God has extended Godself in every way: by already counting us as children, by giving us good gifts within us, by aiding us even in our prayer, by co-operating with our beginnings (responses) to bring about completion.

But the choice is ours. Not once only, but every day in every action we take, we choose to follow God to glory or not. This is what Benedict means by readiness to give up our own will: the intention to choose daily, to learn to choose habitually, to allow deepening of the disposition to choose for God. It is not that our desires are inherently bad; indeed sometimes they can be good.[4] It is rather that it is necessary to train and discipline our desires toward the truly good choices of God's glory. The consecrated life is precisely the life of such discipline, set squarely in the context of ordinary, everyday choices. It is this life which the Rule endeavors to guide.

Reflection: I love one of C.S. Lewis' metaphors for God as "a smooth inclined plane on which there is no resting," so that given our present consciousness we are all day long "sliding, slipping and falling away."[5] I experience my intention like that--I intend to experience the day entirely as God's gift, and before I am finished with breakfast, I have clutched at it, as if it were my possession, to be shaped and structured as I choose, closed off to any interruptions in my plan. Sometimes I wonder what I would say if Jesus decided to come in glory on this day....Most likely I would urge him to go away until I am better prepared; I have certain activities I wish to finish first!

And I can sense that the issue involved in my own willing is not simply a matter of conscious intention, but also a matter of my "spontaneous" responses. That is, what I truly will is revealed just as much in my habitual patterns as it is by my periodic conscious decisions. Thus, it seems likely to me that practice, moment-by-moment training of my responses in daily situations, might really bring me closer to God. When I look at it that way, how clear it is that I am not very good at habitually choosing God.

Prayer/Response:

Prologue, verses 8-13

Let us then at last arise, since the Scripture stirs us up saying: *It is time now for us to rise from sleep* (Rom. 13:11). And our eyes being open to the deifying light, let us hear with wondering ears what the Divine Voice admonishes us, daily crying out: *Today if you hear his voice, harden not your hearts* (Psalm 95:7-8). And again, *You who have ears to hear, hear what the Spirit says to the Churches* (Rev. 2:7).

And what does he say? *Come my children, listen to me, I will teach you the fear of the Lord* (Psalm 34:12). *Run while you have the light of life, lest the darkness of death seize hold of you* (John 12:35).

Comment: As is so often the case in the Rule, when he introduces a subject Benedict piles one Scripture quotation on top of another, in a way quite bewildering to the modern reader. The essential reason for this lies in the ancient way of "knowing" Scripture. In Benedict's time, even literate persons memorized large passages of Scripture, with mouth as well as mind iterating verses over and over, so that the cadences and resonances of various passages evoked one another in a manner not disconnected from context, but not primarily dependent upon it.[6]

The key here is the matter of the word and truly hearing it.

As far back as the times of the ancient Hebrews, the spoken word is understood as having an effective and inherent power of its own, which goes forth from the speaker, creating a response in those who hear. This is clear in the creation account of Genesis Chapter One, for example (God spoke and it was so!).

Benedict is bringing that concept to bear here, on the specific thing that happens every day with every Christian. God calls out (God's effective Word goes forth) each day, bringing us into immediate relationship with God in the midst of our daily activity, if we but hear. Benedict has offered these scripture passages which resonate in his deepest imagination, with the power of this daily Word. It might be well to meditate directly on these passages, as he obviously has.

Reflection: In many ways, this is my favorite passage from the Rule. Partly that is because I live in one of the continuing "Benedictine" ecclesiastical traditions (that is, the Anglican church), where Psalm 95 is chanted every morning, so that each day I do literally hear the call, "If only you would listen to him today, do not harden your hearts..." I rejoice in knowing that I belong to the community of saints, living and dead who share that call.

And partly this is my favorite because I am strengthened by the idea that God's word is effective and potent: my role is to hear it and let it reside in me and do its work; my response is already evoked in the hearing. Some days that is easy and some days hard, but no matter how it feels, I am comforted by Benedict's sense that every day God's word is here, gently calling me forth.

Prayer/Response:

nd the Lord, **seeking his own workman in the multitude of the people to whom he cries out, says again:** ***Who is it who longs for life, and desires to see good days*** **(Psalm 34:12)*?***

And if you, hearing him, answer, **"I am the one!" God says to you:** ***If you long for true and everlasting life, keep your tongue from evil and your lips from speaking deceit. Turn aside from evil and do good; seek peace and pursue it*** **(Psalm 34:13-14).**

And when you have done these things, ***my eyes will be upon you, and my ears will be open to your prayers; and before you call upon me, I will say unto you, Behold, I am here*** **(Isa. 58:9).**

Comment: We see by Benedict's continued emphasis on the words of Psalm 34 that it carries a special meaning for him. Clearly an essential element that he would impress upon us is the question and answer posed here:

(1) do you long for eternal life with all your heart and soul?

(2) I do!

So then, he continues, what is the practical and daily response/behavior that is to be made and can be made. Crucial to this response is the fear of the Lord and the disciplined moral behavior that is evoked by awed regard. (This spirit is often missing in modern experience, and is worth pondering for whatever relevance and value it might contain. There will be other opportunities in the Rule for such consideration.) An equally crucial element is the profound empowerment which happens by virtue of the Lord's active presence in our midst. The two go hand in hand.

As always, Benedict presumes that a few verses will call to our minds the whole Scriptural context. Both Psalm 34 and Isaiah 58 are concerned with the juxtaposition of human righteousness and God's glory which occurs in the life of one consecrated to God. What a lovely consideration is suggested by the first line of Psalm 34: "I will bless Yahweh at all times". For "bless" in that phrase has the same meaning as "benediction": both conveying the desire to live out the good word of God given in one's very own creation and continually renewed in the effective power of God's daily call.

Reflection: How well Benedict sets forth his goal (the yearning for Life!), the purpose of his work (to provide a sound daily framework for our generous response to that yearning), and indeed even stimulates my response by his very vigor. In reading his words, I feel my own excitement build that I am personally called to take my own life seriously enough to offer it to God. Such consecration as I understand it does not mean to withdraw from the world, but to recognize God's effective power in me and in the world in the midst of things as I find them. It is a double astonishment: (1) that it truly involves me; and (2) that God is effective within things as they are.

Prayer/Response:

Prologue, verses 19-22

What can be sweeter to us, dear brothers, than this voice of the Lord inviting us? Behold in his loving kindness the Lord shows us the way of life. Having our loins, therefore, girded with faith and the performance of good works, let us walk in his paths by the guidance of the Gospel, that we may deserve to see him *who has called us in his kingdom* (I Thess.2:12).

And if we wish to dwell in the tabernacle of this kingdom, we shall never reach it unless we run there by our good deeds.

Comment: This is the basic stuff of faith: God is the One who calls (I Thess). Humans are the ones who are called. The whole of human life can be summed up in the trusting response we make to that call. The goal of the monastic journey can be summarized by the phrase from Mt. 5:8 here alluded to: that we may deserve to see God.[7]

Notice that there is no opposition between faith and works. For Benedict, concerned with the practical questions of how best to carry out this response to God's call within the context of the given-ness of each unique life, turns immediately to the phrase "faith...and works". One without the other is empty. He never suggests that it is solely our own efforts that bring us to God,[8] for he always emphasizes that it is only the goodness of the Lord which enables us to undertake this journey at all.

Yet, he urges us on: since God does so call us, dare we refuse to respond with our whole being? We are indeed called to participate in the sweetest joy we can imagine. Let us get on with it!

Reflection: At one level, I wonder why it is necessary to say this at all in the Rule, since it is so consistently the essence of the Gospel, so completely that which I already "know". In pondering this, I remember two of my favorite ideas: the first, that the heart of the Gospel can be told in a very few words, but it takes a lifetime or longer to learn to live the truth of those words. The second is that the Bible is one of the few books we read, not because we don't know what is in it, but because we do.

In other words, the Rule is not intended primarily to inform me. Rather it is intended primarily to be formative: to give a pattern from which I can begin to apply the Gospel fruitfully to my own daily life; to set forth an ordering framework which allows my heart to be enlarged so that it can more fully resonate with the glory of Love Itself.

Sometimes when I turn to the Rule this way -- slowly and reflectively, a few verses at a time, inquiring of it from the quiet center of my spirit -- I find that I want both to weep and to laugh with the unutterable joy of what God offers me.

Prayer/Response:

But let us ask the Lord with the Prophet, saying to him: ***Lord, who shall dwell in your tent, or who shall rest upon your holy mountain?*** **(Ps. 15:1) After this question, brethren, let us hear the Lord answering and showing us the way to his tent, saying:** ***One who walks without stain and works justice; one who speaks truth in his heart, who has not practiced deceit with his tongue; one who has done no evil to his neighbor, and has not believed false accusations against his neighbor.*** **(Ps. 15:2-3)**

One who has brought the malignant devil to naught, casting him ***out of the sight*** **of his heart with all his suggestions; and has** ***taken hold of his*** **bad thoughts, while they were still** ***young, and dashed them down upon*** **Christ. (Ps.15:4, 137:9)**

Comment: In general, it is modern liturgical practice simply to avoid those sections of the Psalms or other Scripture which seem to suggest uncivilized, not to say unChristian, behavior. But Benedict is here doing with Scripture what we are seeking to do with the Rule: approach sacramentally every verse of it, even those comments that at first seem repugnant or offensive. In other words, we always first give the benefit of the doubt; we always first ask: Is there here a deeper meaning than the obvious, which can lead me more truthfully to see my own life through God's eyes?

Evidently, Benedict found such a meaning in this "offensive" 137th Psalm, for he refers to it twice in the Rule, both here and in Chapter 4 (verse 50). He understands the young who are dashed against the rock to be young temptations which are dashed at once at the feet of Christ, and thus destroyed before they have a chance to take hold in our souls. Modern psychological practice, especially in cognitive therapy, has rediscovered the wisdom of this advice. Today we are newly aware that we need not succumb to the pull of the many voices in our heads, not all of which are in our best interest. Centuries ago, Benedict asked us to consider this same possibility as a powerful dynamic of our journey toward and with God. The journey has its joy; it also has its risks. Christ is the surest foundation for both. Let us turn to him at once with whatever moves us.

At this point in the Prologue there is a mood shift, from "mercy" to "judgment". Each person is called by God, but when that call is accepted, one also accepts responsibility for one's behavior. Yet that is a responsibility which no one can truly carry; the strength is not always in us to act as we would. This matter of daily living in such a way as to deepen the mind of Christ in our whole being, even and especially where "we can't" -- that is the issue of Christian formation; that is the primary issue of concern in the Rule. Here Benedict is beginning to challenge us to accept certain disciplines which he transmits as one within the community of faith.

Reflection: What touches me today is an invitation I feel from Benedict to be attentive to, and to guide, those many "inner voices" which push and pull at me all day. I often think of these voices as "parent tapes" or other psychological jargon, but fancy names don't minimize their harassment. As I ponder Benedict's intention in his language, and my experience which I generally understand in psychological language, some connections appear.

I see that there is a connection between the likelihood that I will speak sharply to my husband, or eagerly devour the latest gossip about a "friend", and the extent to which I have let myself become "hooked" by negative inner voices. If I am feeling rotten about myself, inadequate or confused, it is very easy to distract myself with external trivia or to discharge my emotions in a harsh outburst. Perhaps I don't usually think of it as a temptation to be preoccupied with concerns that keep me from present awareness that God loves me. Yet that may be one of the main ways in which I hold God off.

And if I teach myself to be aware of such temptations in their infancy, at the very first moment they appear, and at once offer them to Christ, I sense that I might find much greater peace of mind. And perhaps also much greater genuine care for my neighbor.

Prayer/Response:

These are they (dwelling in God's tent) who, fearing the Lord, are not elated over their own good works; but knowing that the good which is in them comes not from themselves but from the Lord, they *magnify* (Ps. 15:4) the Lord who works in them, saying with the Prophet: *Not unto us, O Lord, not unto us, but unto your name give the glory.* (Ps. 115:1) In this way the Apostle Paul imputed nothing of his preaching to himself, but said: *By the grace of God I am what I am."* (I Cor. 15:10) And again he says: *He who glories, let him glory in the Lord.* (II Cor. 10:17)

Hence also the Lord says in the Gospel: *He who hears these words of mine and does them is like a wise man who built his house upon a rock: the floods came, the winds blew and beat upon that house, and it did not fall; because it was founded upon a rock.* (Mt. 7:24-5)

Comment: One reads Benedict with joy, as one discovers him to be a person who is asking serious questions about (and proposing guidelines for) the life of commitment to the Lord -- a consecrated life, in other words. There are particular issues in such a life, and one often feels without guidance for these issues. Benedict clarifies what is essential, and tells how to shape a response that is faithful. We realize at once that temptations will be an issue, but it is perhaps less clear to us that elation may equally be a problem in the consecrated life. Yet Benedict sees it as important enough to mention very early. The issue is this: how to handle the awareness that one is being used as an instrument and partner of God's own spirit.[9] The committed Christian will often find himself or herself lifted up, empowered in the strongest and most harmonious way to carry out a given work. The temptations here are very great --either to refuse altogether because of the overwhelming sense of being carried (i.e., "out of control" or "beyond one's capacity"), or to claim it as one's own, as if God had nothing to do with it.

Benedict sets this issue in two contexts: (1) the one of Psalm 15 (continuing from above) -- that fundamentally our orientation must be toward God, in fear and praise; and (2) the other of Matthew chapters 5 through 7 (the Sermon on the Mount) -- that we must, and will, do those things that astonish the world, because we belong to Christ and are founded on him.

Reflection: The quotations from St. Paul emphasize grace and glory....I could profitably spend years wondering/pondering about these two fundamental concepts of the Christian life. I imagine that Benedict is urging me to do just that -- and to live in such a way as to allow those "concepts" to be embodied in my life!

I often wonder about giving God glory. Exactly how does one undertake an action in such a way that people see it and give glory to God? It mystifies me, and I continue to wonder about it. Benedict suggests it has something to do with fear of God, and praise....But maybe the key is in the house built upon a rock. If I love Christ above all things, and try to allow that to be more and more true in the way I actually live each day, then both my actions and other people's responses will ultimately be as they should be.

Recently I had an experience that afterwards struck me as an experience of God's glory. I was making a presentation to an eager and interested group of persons, and together in that moment we had an experience of God in our midst. We all felt high and lifted up -- and also empowered to be better people. Afterward it came to me that's what God's glory is like! That realization enabled me to carry the joy of the moment with me for a time. I could offer up the whole experience, experiencing the delight of it even more because I knew it to be the touch of God.

Prayer/Response:

Prologue, verses 35-44

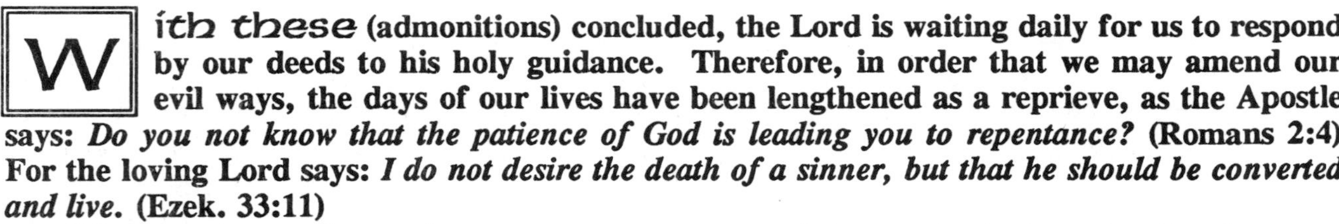

With these (admonitions) concluded, the Lord is waiting daily for us to respond by our deeds to his holy guidance. Therefore, in order that we may amend our evil ways, the days of our lives have been lengthened as a reprieve, as the Apostle says: *Do you not know that the patience of God is leading you to repentance?* (Romans 2:4) For the loving Lord says: *I do not desire the death of a sinner, but that he should be converted and live.* (Ezek. 33:11)

Since then brethren, we have asked of the Lord who is to dwell in his tent, we have heard his commands to those who are to abide there, it remains for us to complete the duties of those who dwell there. Our hearts, therefore, and our bodies must be prepared to fight in holy obedience to his commands. And let us ask God to supply by the help of his grace what by nature is hardly possible to us. And if we wish to reach eternal life, escaping the pains of hell, then - while there is yet time, while we are still in the flesh and are able to fufil all these things by the light which is given us - we must run and perform now what will profit us for all eternity.

Comment: With these verses, Benedict brings the body of his prologue to a close. The whole tone of what he has presented to us has been that of invitation. Do you wish life? Do you long to dwell in the Lord's tent? Do you hear the Lord calling out to you today?!

This invitation comes through Benedict, but clearly he means to convey that the invitation is God's own; he is just the messenger. God assures us in love that we are each invited to life, not death. Indeed, God will supply to us what is lacking in nature, so that we may respond to the invitation so generously, so consistently offered.

The invitation must receive a response. In fact, it does receive a response from each one of us, whether intentional or not. We have asked the Lord who may dwell with him, and we have heard his answer. God awaits our response. What will we do now? How important is all this to us? How much will we invest?

Benedict concludes his Prologue with a heightened exhortation to each Christian to take the baptismal promise with life-and-death earnestness. Our response to God's gift in baptism must involve a daily turning toward the Creator of all life, to claim our gift of life within God's "tent". That turning involves offering ourselves in each moment to Christ, or we might say, consecrating our lives. Consecration means here and now, with the materials -- indeed the very life -- we each one are given.

Is the longing in us so great that we will consecrate ourselves? That is the question which Benedict poses, and each of us must answer for ourselves.

Reflection: Is it more difficult for people of our time than of Benedict's to offer themselves wholly to God? It seems clear to me that such self-offering does not mean to run away to somewhere else, but to offer myself here and today, where I am. Yet in some ways, it does seem to me that it is harder to do that today than in Benedict's day. Today we feel we know so much more about "the way things are". God seems more remote and impersonal, or sort of detached from normal everyday life; or alternatively, God in Christ is often understood so personally that we lose our fear/awe regarding the hereafter. There is today a greater sense of complexity, and of the many things on earth that need doing by people. There is a greater sense of personalism, of the urgency to use individual gifts effectively. And who knows what all else....

I see that I am wandering away from the question of how I am touched by this passage. I am avoiding the real issue: will I offer myself to God today? I doubt that ever since the world began was there a time when it was "easy" to give oneself wholly to God; yet, in some ways, it is the most "natural" thing in the world to do. So, today, do I accept both the difficulty and the naturalness and plunge in? Will I simply make the offer of my life to God in this moment? I want to....As I wait, I realize I have given a big sigh...breathed out and up myself...given what I can in this moment!

Prayer/Response:

We have therefore, to establish a school of the Lord's service. In the institution of it we hope to establish nothing that is harsh or oppressive. But if anything is somewhat strictly laid down, according to the dictates of equity and for the amendment of vices, or for the preservation of love; do not therefore flee in dismay from the way of salvation, which cannot be other than narrow at the beginning.

For as we progress in this our way of life and in faith, our hearts shall expand, and we shall run the way of God's commandments with the unspeakable sweetness of love. So that, never departing from his guidance, but perservering in his teaching in the monastery until death, we may by patience participate in the sufferings of Christ; that we may deserve also to be partakers of his kingdom. Amen.

Comment: This rich text may be fruitfully reflected upon many times at length. Let us note here simply that in general it is a summary of the purpose of the ascetical program set forth in the Rule, and thus an abbreviated commentary on the purpose of Christian spiritual discipline.

Notice particularly that the school for the Lord's service is both a continuing place of learning and a place for exercise of the journeyman's skills. The spiritual life always involves learning, as well as always requiring action congruent with faith in the concrete opportunities presented by community life. Notice, too, that the basic text for this school is "his guidance" -- not primarily the Rule itself, but rather primarily the Word of the Lord, made known in Scripture and in daily revelation, and secondarily in the Rule, the abbot, and one's fellow pilgrims insofar as they are expressions of that Word.

But it is nonetheless true that one must choose where one will stand in order to follow "his guidance". For each of us there must be a place to which we are committed, and a path to which we give our obedience, or we have not truly incarnated our commitment to him. And to some extent, that means choosing something blindly, giving ourselves to something we do not fully understand, trusting that in the faithful self-offering, we will be transformed so that our understanding -- as well as our loving -- is gradually deepened and enriched.

Perhaps the most powerful of these many powerful sentences is verse 49 ("For as we progress in this our way...."). The "our way of life" is a translation of the Latin "conversatio", the third monastic vow, representing that daily conversion in response to God in the midst of life events which is at the core of the Rule. Growth involves growth in "conversatio" and in faith, that is, ever more intimate relationship with God. Benedict acknowledges that this relationship may involve fear and discipline, a darkness of vision from which one can only proceed in faith or simple obedience. But he also insists/exclaims that the relationship involves the "unspeakable sweetness of love" even in this life.

Reflection: In the past I have reflected at length upon spiritual discipline, what it is, what motivates it at best, what it is oriented toward. I have concluded that I cannot "capture" it with my mind, because it inevitably involves what I regard as opposites -- strictness and fear, as well as generosity and delight. It seems to me that at some point I must simply give up my struggle to understand, and give myself to a regimen that has been tested by others of faith.

One of the very odd things about such self-giving (submission) for a person like me is the sense in which it must involve a leap of faith. At some points along the journey, it is not permitted to me to ask "why". That is not because I cannot or do not want to ask, but because I haven't yet the capacity to receive the true answer. I have discovered that the very essence of spiritual formation is that it involves encounter and engagement with something/Someone of whom I am profoundly ignorant. It seems right that initially I test the path I wish to consider for its reasonableness and its compassion. But it is equally appropriate for me to realize that there are times in which my present "world-view" is totally inadequate for me to receive the response I seek. So I must simply continue to give myself to that which I do not understand. In such a journey, how very much I value the guides of tradition and authority which give me occasional markers to let me know others have trod here before me.

Prayer/Response:

Interlude I:

a note to the reader....

How are you doing on reading in the mode of *lectio divina*?

Perhaps you have been following Benedict's Prologue, in the format outlined here, reading the words in a daily rhythm, but not finding it easy to get into the additional rhythm of the reflection and prayer components. These occasional interludes at the end of major units of the Rule are intended to provide additional help to strengthen your process of *lectio*.

First, be aware that my reflection process is intended as a model, but not a rigid mold for your own. You may discover that the content of my reflection on any given day is simply out-of-sync with what is on your heart. Feel quite free to follow the leading of your own inclinations.

Perhaps the most important element in *lectio* is allowing yourself to be drawn by the specific words or phrases which are attracting you this day. The living word addresses each person each day. Its method is that of attraction. Some word or phrase not necessarily central to the whole passage is calling, reaching out to you, inviting your attention. That word or phrase has a particular message, integrating the theme of the passage with some specific component of your life at this moment. So the key to effective *lectio* is to listen for, and respond to, the personal attraction.

For example, in the *lectio* segment for Prologue, verses 8-13, I was attracted by the phrase "If you hear his voice today, do not harden your hearts". But perhaps as you read over the passage reflectively, a quite different phrase jumps out at you. Perhaps "It is time now..." or "ears to hear"...or something else. As you say this phrase over and over a couple of times to yourself, suddenly there comes a connection with something in your own life that you had not been aware was bothering you, or some insight will occur about an area in which you had been resisting God, or a sense of great joy will steal over you, or whatever.

The idea is to stop for a few moments, read over the text slowly and expectantly, and be attentive when something "clicks". Hear the word to you, perhaps jot down a few notes so you don't forget it, offer a short prayer, and then go on with your day. Be aware that your *lectio* will continue to nourish your heart the whole day long. Why not try it right now?

Foundational Matters

Chapter 1*: The Various Kinds of Monks, verses 1-2

It is plain that there are four kinds of monks. **The first are the Cenobites: that is, those who do their service in monasteries under a rule and an abbot.**

(*Before the chapter title, there is a parenthetical note as follows: *Here begins the text of the Rule. It is called a Rule because it directs the lives of those who obey it.*)

Comment: There is much misunderstanding and variation in opinion about who monks are and what they do, as well as what a Rule of Life is and how it is to be used. In these "Comment" sections we look closely and prayerfully at the language of the Rule itself to see what it tells us in its own terms about such questions. We ask, what is Benedict saying in his own language and emphases?

Two items of note appear here. The parenthetical phrase at the beginning was perhaps not in the earliest manuscripts, but it is a helpful reminder about the linguistic roots of the word "rule". Regula literally means "straight edge", used in the sense of a plumb line or carpenter's edge to set a measure or boundary on that which is "true", or properly aligned. The Rule serves that purpose for the community of monks -- and with Benedict's direction, it does this largely by pointing always toward the Gospel and its daily applicability.

The reference here to cenobitic monks is brief, chiefly because the balance of the Rule is addressed to them. (Unlike present literary practice, Benedict states his preference first in the list of types, rather than saving it till last.) There was in Benedict's time, and still is, a tendency to think of a solitary individual engaged in heroic ascetical feats, works of charity, or spiritual heights, as the culmination of the religious life. However, the whole mode of Benedict's Rule is to suggest something quite different: that the optimum setting for the true Christian life is in community -- in the daily, committed, face to face interaction of very different people who share a love for God. Not only does Benedict list first the cenobites (community monks, the sort for whom he writes), but in verse 13 of this chapter, he calls them "the strong kind". For all practical purposes, Benedict defines the true monk this way: as one who lives in monastic community, serving under an abbot and a rule. He goes on (after this preliminary chapter) to provide a rule for that cenobitic monk which articulates powerfully the nature of the optimum communal setting for the consecrated Christian life.

Reflection: Both rule and community are severe and constant tests of my willingness to be a part of something bigger and more important than my ego. There are days when the idea that I really belong is so exhilarating that I give myself generously and with joy; and days when I feel so grumpy that I would like to withdraw from the constant pressure of otherness and incompleteness which is so exasperatingly manifest in human interaction. I guess it is precisely that tension which makes the Rule a sound and practical ascetical system, subtle as it sometimes seems. To let my ego be given away, daily and bit by bit, but intentionally: that surely is even harder work than regular fasting! Well, Benedict, I'll walk with you a while to see what you want to teach my heart....

Prayer/Response:

The second are the anchorites - hermits: that is, those who, not in the first fervor of monastic life, but after long probation in the monastery, have learned by the help and experience of others to fight against the devil. They go forth well-armed from the ranks of their brethren to the solitary combat of the desert. They are now able to fight safely without the support of others, by their own strength and with God's assistance, against the vices of flesh and thoughts.

Comment: This short chapter sketches a brief history of the cumulative Christian wisdom about the best ways to live the consecrated life. In the first centuries after Christ, serious Christians often found themselves embracing martyrdom. After Christianity became the official religion of the Roman empire, many earnest Christians found the faith lukewarm at best "in the world", and thus chose the way of the hermit. As generations of Christians experimented and observed carefully the results of those experiments, the awareness grew that certain forms of monastic life enhance spiritual progress, and certain forms hinder it. Consensus developed that one who is serious about the Christian life "needs training, a training that aims at absorbing the wisdom and profiting from the experience of many previous generations."[10]

Benedict's Rule clarifies the emerging idea that the cenobitic or community life is at least equally important as the eremitic, or solitary, calling. The language in this paragraph reveals a great deal of his mind in this matter.

The real battle is the devil's war against God for human souls. This battle is fought in every setting on earth, but becomes particularly intense whenever a human spirit determines to turn to God. The methods of the devil are subtle and carefully designed, so that one unacquainted with these tactics in general may incorrectly interpret them as personal doubts, desires, or incapacities. In any case, two things (in addition to prayer) are very helpful in combatting these tactics: one is knowledge of them, shared by those who themselves have struggled; one is continual support of those now engaged side by side in this struggle.[11]

Living in community itself is often a source of temptation, when irritation, comparisons, and conflicts invite ego isolation from one another. Yet Benedict consistently treats such temptations as opportunities for self-giving, in the context of the community of faith.

Reflection: I often wonder whether Christian community really exists in the contemporary parish setting. Yet, I am compelled to admit that I am given opportunity to experience the support of community far more than my pride lets me see or respond to. It seems to me that true community grows only over a long time of shared intimacy and explicit acknowledgement of Christ's empowering presence. Yet I feel that I have seldom either had or taken the opportunity truly to grow in faith and love (and trials!) with other committed Christians. What might be the reasons for this -- both in me and in my environment? Even my present-day monastic friends struggle with this. For me, community is indeed a strenuous discipline -- and a gift of grace. I look forward to the hard interior work of exploring this discipline of community further with Benedict.

Prayer/Response:

Chapter 1, verses 6-9

A third and detestable kind of monks are the Sarabaites, who have been tried neither by rule nor by experience *as gold by the furnace;* (Prov 27:21) but, being as soft as lead, still keep faith with the world in their behavior, lying to God with their tonsure. Living in twos or threes, or even singly without a shepherd, they enclose themselves not in the Lord's sheepfolds but in their own. Their law consists in their own pleasures and desires: whatever they think fit or choose to do, that they call holy; and what they do not like, that they consider unlawful.

Comment: Strong language here! In Benedict's day the Roman world as it was known was falling apart. Many persons were intensely seeking roots, something that would give security and stability in a time of great change. Yet Benedict suggests that there are those who try to fool themselves -- or others -- into believing that they have found something worthwhile, but it is really a vast illusion, and a cynical one at that. When one pretends to believe in God, and is quite without inspiration, one either doesn't believe there is a God, or believes God has no power.

True commitment to God demands submission both to tradition and to authority. Both tradition and authority have their limits, but one is only qualified to speak to those limits after one has been tested in the crucible. At first and for a long time one must submit to the wisdom contained in the tradition and in the elders. One must find a good school and undergo strenuous training -- training which will often demand of us something different from what we would "freely" choose. For even our Will must be taught to recognize the good, and to choose it in daily situations.

Make no mistake: there is real and awesome power here! It is a fearful thing to fall into the hands of the living God, and while one does that gladly, it behooves one also to do it with the utmost respect and obedience.

Reflection: I hear again the phrase: "still keep faith with the world in their behavior" -- and I am indicted and humbled by it! I keep forgetting or being unaware of how deeply my most "personal" desires have been formed by this crass, egoistic, and consumptive culture in which we live. What are most damning are those moments in which I realize how utterly I am incapable of choosing for myself that which (even) is my own good. I don't yet know enough to make such choices; more profoundly, I don't yet love enough. How often am I aware of what a puny thing my loving is!

There is great comfort in the possibility that I can rest in and be formed by something I can trust which is "bigger" and wiser than I am. Something incarnated, something which belongs to the human community as God's gift. There is also great risk in the vulnerability entailed in giving myself to such tradition and authority. But perhaps the power of my need and my longing is now great enough to allow me to take that risk....

Prayer/Response:

The fourth kind of monks are those called gyrovagues, who spend their whole lives seeking hospitality in province after province, monastery after monastery, staying three or four days at a time; always wandering and never stable, they are slaves to self-will and the snares of appetite: they are in all things worse than the Sarabaites.

Of the most wretched life of all these it is better to remain silent than to speak. Leaving these behind us, therefore, let us proceed, with the help of God, to make provision for the Cenobites - the strong kind of monks.

Comment: Benedict has told us that he proposes a school for the service of the Lord, and in this chapter he makes clear that the school does call for some definite training. In this section, he gives a clue about the training -- it is a training of the Will; it is designed to liberate us from slavery to the Will. One who calls himself a monk dares not be a slave to appetite/willfulness.

"Will" is a word very narrowly conceived in our culture: we think of it as kind of an executive Will which is decisive and controlling; it almost has the features of an "iron fist". In contrast to this concept however, the main stream of Christian tradition has generally conceived Will as a thing of the heart -- not in a sentimental, flaccid way, but as a passionate harmony of one's entire being. What Benedict is opposed to is allowing oneself to be moved by the superficial forces of appetite, which prevent one's deep discovery of authentic inner necessity.

Here Benedict spells out that monks in community are the strong kind. He writes to those of us willing to explore our own experience for the ways in which community brings us into fuller life. One commentator has suggested that Benedict understands cenobites to be the "strong" kind, because they are willing to recognize, and act, on their need, their weakness, and their longing.[12] In some essential way, Christians in community belong to and supplement one another. Thus, in community it is as important to offer one's need as it is to offer one's gifts. Strength is found in the combination.

Reflection: Many times have I thought about what Will is (especially when I start a new diet), and I cannot say that I know, in the sense of knowledge that wells up out of me from within.

But I believe Benedict is right, that in order to discover (and train) my Will, I must be stable, that is "stay put". I need to stay quiet for a time, undistracted by multiple stimuli and competitions for my attention, undistracted by the noisy inner cravings that would mentally draw me here and there. I need to stay put until I enter quiet, and know the greatness of God and the terrible inadequacy of myself. I need to stay put until I have passed beyond even that, and know the enduring power of love. And there finally, I discover a depth and passion that must flow over and spend itself in compassion, charity, and adoration.

Prayer/Response:

Chapter 2: What Kind of Man the Abbot Ought to Be,

verses 1-5

An abbot who is worthy to govern a monastery must always remember what he is called, and fulfill his title through his deeds. For he is believed to hold the place of Christ in the monastery, since he is addressed by a title of His (Christ's), as the Apostle has said: *You have received the spirit of adoption of sons by which we cry, "abba, father"* (Rom 8:15).

Therefore, the abbot should never teach or enact or command anything contrary to the teaching of the Lord; rather let his commands and his teaching, like the leaven of divine justice, suffuse the minds of his disciples.

Comment: The word abbot is obviously taken from the intimate word of prayer which Jesus taught his disciples, "abba". St. Paul reminds us that we are enabled to use this word only when empowered by the Spirit, and that the nature of that empowering is to know ourselves to be children of God, and heirs of the promise made manifest in Christ. (Romans 8:15b-17)

What is Benedict up to with this "abba"? He has made two major shifts in the biblical tradition, but those shifts tell us not so much about a theology of abba, as about Benedict's idea of what a monastery is.[13] First, he calls Christ "Abba", as well as God the Father. Second, he applies the place of Christ to the one in charge of the monastery, and therefore calls him abbot.

The abbot is always to remember what his title signifies, and act accordingly. The monks believe the abbot represents Christ to them, that he exercises that spiritual parenthood which will bring them forth into the fullness of life eternal.[14] He is the mystical Head as the monks are the mystical Body of the glorified Christ, who brings all things to perfection in himself.

The abbot bears the responsibility to help form the monks into Christ's way. This spiritual formation is communicated by word and example. It is rooted in the Gospel. Humanly, it is best communicated by a guide, however, as well as a "map". The abbot is this guide.

One cannot understand the role of the abbot without understanding something of the work to be done, in taking on the "mind of Christ". True, the abbot has sole responsibility and authority, to which the monks are required to submit in willing obedience. But this responsibility carries with it the need to give life, ongoing even into eternity. The monk cannot know what this is or how to receive it, except as the abbot and the Spirit help open the spaces inside oneself which are designed as receptacle.

Reflection: How does this passage touch my life today? I realize that only recently have I begun to be aware of questions for which I am not yet capable of receiving the answers. What I must first do, is to allow a capacity to be created inside me which will permit me to discover what I seek. This is humbling and frustrating. Especially as I come to see myself as a competent adult, sometimes I resent having to slow down, turn off all my analytical apparatus and evaluation criteria, and simply submit myself to come to a new thing as a babe -- innocent, unknowing, receiving it at first all in its own terms, until I belong enough to it and it to me for creative dialogue to begin. In a sense, this is the process any artist goes through in learning a craft. It is, I think, the continuing process of becoming part of Christ.

Prayer/Response:

Let the abbot remember always that at the fearful judgment of God both his (the Abbot's) teaching and the obedience of his disciples - both of these matters - will be examined. The abbot must, therefore, know that the shepherd will be considered at fault if the father of the household *(paterfamilias)* finds that the sheep have yielded no profit. If, on the other hand, he has exercised all pastoral diligence over a restless and disobedient flock, always striving to heal their unhealthy ways; then the shepherd will be acquitted at the Judgment of the Lord, and will say to the Lord with the prophet: *I have not hidden your justice in my heart; I have declared your truth and your salvation* (Ps 40:11), *but they condemned and spurned me* (Isa 1:2, Ezek 20:27). Then at last the sheep disobedient to his care will be punished by overpowering death.

Comment: What obligation do we owe to our God? To speak forth God's truth when we know it; to listen for God's truth when we do not. (And to know the difference!) Obedience is one of three key vows to the Benedictine way of life, and Benedict's concept of obedience is rooted in the ancient notion of listening. Benedict here draws this from his Old Testament sources: both Isaiah and Ezekiel are told to speak forth the Word, for the people have refused to listen; they are disobedient and rebellious.

The whole point of the Benedictine life is to train the heart to listen for the Word that matters, and when it is heard, to allow it to take creative root in one's heart and then burst forth "giving growth to provide seed for the sower and bread for the eating" (Isa. 55:10). Thus at various cyclical points in one's life, one is either listening, nurturing or proclaiming. Each of these tasks is a kind of stewardship for God.

In order for God's whole work to be done, each must perform his or her part faithfully and at the right time, the abbot no less than the novice. No one is responsible for what the other refuses to do, but each is responsible not only to do his or her own part, but also mightily to encourage the others to do theirs. Yet finally it is God's work and God's ultimate judgment under which all rest.

It is often said that the Benedictine abbot is the *paterfamilias*, the head of the family with ultimate power and authority. However, that Roman word/concept appears only once in the Rule: here,--where it refers explicitly to God, to whom the abbot is accountable. Rather, the abbot is a father primarily in the sense of one who has nurtured the seed of God's Word in himself and now must proclaim it, thus mysteriously begetting it in his spiritual sons and daughters.

Reflection: Often do I wonder when to speak and when to listen. The analytical part of my head wants precise rules to tell me when I am at which stage. But Benedict's helpfulness to me is to point out that relationships are always better than -- or perhaps essential supplements to -- rules. To be faithful to the growing life of the Spirit in me, I do very much better when I entrust myself to a guide, who has travelled at least part of the path before me. And to be faithful to Godself, I do very much better when I continue to listen for God's own living Word, than when I think I have heard all that is necessary and stop listening/relating.

How to discern? First, I wonder when to speak and when to listen? If the answer to that is, find a guide, the next question is how to find a guide? And how to relate to a guide, once such a person is found. All this takes discernment. Again, I ask for rules, and all I get is relationship! Relationship is much harder work, and often seems very ambiguous. Perhaps the answer lies in verses 2-4 above, wherein the abbot is told to belong to Christ, and let Christ live in him. The first step is to soak myself in the gifts of God: scripture, Eucharist, tradition and human guides. I am to train my heart to listen for the Word, and to receive it gladly. Then, as Christ comes more fully to dwell in me, my questions will begin to sort themselves out more readily. This is a school Benedict is guiding. And how much I need to be a student!

Prayer/Response:

Chapter 2, verses 11-15

Therefore, when anyone receives the name of abbot he is to govern his disciples by a twofold teaching: that is, he must show forth all that is good and holy more by deeds than by words; declaring to receptive disciples the commandments of the Lord with words, but demonstrating the divine precepts to the stubborn and the simple-minded by the example of his deeds. And all of the things which he teaches his disciples are contrary (to the law of God) - it should be seen from his own actions that these are not to be done, *lest while preaching to others, he himself be found reprobate* (I Cor 9:27); and God say to him in his sin: *How is it that you recite my justice and declare my covenant with your mouth, when you hate discipline and cast my words behind you* (Ps 50:16-17)*?* And also this: *How is it that you can see a speck in your brother's eye, and not notice the plank in your own* (Matt 7:3)*?*

Comment: The Lord's commandments, those lessons about the good and the holy which come to us in the Christian tradition, these must be lived. They are empty words, unless one takes them in and allows them to form one's heart, mind, spirit, and behavior.

In ancient cultures, the main task of the parents was understood to be teaching children how to live. The orphan was not only bereft because he or she had no land to inherit, and no skills to be learned in apprenticeship, but essentially because he or she had no one to pass along wisdom: how really to live.[15] The most important gift of parents was to communicate a sense of values, their convictions about life and how it was to be practiced. This inner formation is truly a gift of life, in which every person needs the help of others.

The Benedictine abbot carries parenthood in this sense. He is so to have received what he has been taught, that he is able to pass it along through his very presence. The essence of the Christian life, represented in these passages of Scripture, is that it is not enough simply to hear the word: one must allow it to enter deeply into one's soul, shaping it and pouring forth fruitful response. The abbot cannot teach the Lord's commandments, unless he himself has been so formed and is so living. The abbot himself must be obedient to the Word, or he has nothing to teach.

A modern author puts it like this: "So few understand; because where they know, they do not obey....If Christ's words seem true, obey them with your whole strength and might. This is the way of life."[16]

Reflection: I find I am getting increasingly impatient with my urge to go on and on reading more "spiritual books". It is true there are many good ones; it is also true that fundamentally they all say the same thing, and it can be said in very few words indeed. What I am trying to teach myself is that knowledge is not worth anything until it begins to become lived knowledge.

And so I long -- with all my heart -- simply to be true to Christ, true to the one Christ calls me to be. And I sense this calls me to less rather than more. This calls me to simplicity, gentleness, prayer, silence.

Oh, I know I will always fall short. And I know that very few will see what I am doing. And I know that the nearer to Christ I am, the more appalled I shall be at my lack of charity. Even so, I long to be more drawn into the mind of Christ, and I find myself more and more allowing this longing to be my prayer.

Prayer/Response:

Chapter 2, verses 16-22

The abbot is not to make any distinction of persons in the monastery. He should not love one more than another unless he finds one better in good actions and obedience. A free-born man is not to be put before a slave who becomes a monk, except for some other reasonable cause. Although, if justice requires it, the abbot may see fit to change anyone's rank. Otherwise let each keep to his regular place, because *whether we are slaves or free, we are all one in Christ* (Gal 3:28, Eph 6:8) and serve alike in the army of the one Lord; for *with God there is no partiality among persons* (Rom 2:11).

Solely in this only are we distinguished in his sight: if we are found to surpass others in good works and in humility. Therefore, let the abbot show equal love to all and impose on all the same discipline, according to their merits.

Comment: In a sense this is a lesson in discernment. Given that wisdom of the heart and the person's inner formation are the goals of the monastic life, how is the abbot to discern who is progressing well and who is to be rewarded with positions of responsibility, authority and respect? (Benedict's evident familiarity with the Sermon on the Mount no doubt shaped his thought that all persons do indeed have their reward, but the issue is primarily that of right rewards for right motives and right actions in such a way that the Kingdom of God is drawn near.)

First and radically, the world's exterior standards -- slavery or freedom, wealth or poverty, title, education, etc -- are clearly irrelevant. Each person has an important place in Christ's body.

Second, there are nonetheless standards which we can use. Implicit here is the fact that interior dispositions do show themselves exteriorly, especially in the interactions of community. The work of the heart, the hidden action of amenability to the Spirit's graces, the evolving disposition toward the mind of Christ -- all these are manifest, for the one who has eyes to see and ears to hear. And they will be manifest in two ways particularly: (1) good works, and (2) humility/obedience. Within a very few pages, Benedict will present his thinking on both these topics (Chapters 4, 5, & 7).

But one thing more is here. The purpose of the abbot's discernment is to know how to "discipline" and give favors to all the members of the community. This discipline/favoring is to aid their ongoing formation, their ongoing conversion into the life of Christ, and to aid the whole community to become Christ's body. Each and all are called to the extraordinary communion characteristic of the members of the Body of Christ. The abbot's work is to build toward this communion, especially by noticing and nurturing the Christ-life growing inside each one.

Reflection: Benedict uses the phrase "the abbot may see fit". I wonder how I see? As my prayer deepens, I feel that many shifts occur of which I am only partly aware. Certainly some of these shifts affect my response to -- and even my basic perception of -- what is there to be seen.

I realize as I reflect on this passage that one of the key ingredients of discernment is indeed what I see -- not only where my focus is, but how superficially or deeply I am looking. For a long time, I saw only with the world's eyes; and I was impressed by wealth and power and repelled by poverty and weakness. Sadly, I have not lost such perceptions altogether.

But I sense also that I am learning to see with God's eyes. What great joy it is to notice and celebrate the Christ-life growing inside so many persons! I realize that often I see that new life in others more clearly than they do "from the inside", and it is a great encouragement for me to lift it up and help them see and celebrate it too!

Prayer/Response:

Chapter 2, verses 23-29

For in his teaching the Abbot should always observe the recommendation of the Apostle, in which he says: *Reprove, convince, rebuke.* (2 Tim 4:2) That is, he should suit his action to the circumstances, mingling gentleness with sternness; showing now the rigor of a master, now the loving affection of a father, so as sternly to rebuke the undisciplined and restless, and to exhort the obedient, mild, and patient to advance in virtue. And such as are negligent and haughty we charge him to reprove and correct. Let him not shut his eyes to the faults of offenders; but as soon as they appear, let him strive, as he has the authority for that, to root them out, remembering the fate of Eli, the priest of Shiloh. (1 Sam 2:11-4:18) Those of good disposition and understanding let him correct, for the first or second time, with words only; but such as are troublesome and hard of heart, proud or disobedient, let him chastise with bodily stripes at the very first offense, knowing that it is written: *The fool is not corrected with words* (Prov 29:19), and again, *Strike your son with a rod and you will have freed his soul from death* (Prov 23:14).

Comment: Usually in our *lectio*, it is well to turn first to those matters which disturb us or seem repugnant to our ways of thinking. In this passage, there are two such ingredients. One is the physical punishment, which nowadays is not something we condone for any reason. But the other, deeper issue is that of any punishment. In today's "democratic" and "modern" society, it is fashionable to believe that no one has any right to judge anyone else, nor to take action based on that judgment.

Benedict has dealt with the issue of what standards or criteria we may use in the immediately preceeding verses of this chapter. But here he is dealing with the more fundamental question of why use any standards at all.

In Chapter 4, he makes clear that one of the essential tools of the spiritual craft is to "Fear the day of judgment", and in this passage he demonstrates that the abbot must also live in such fear. Note that the 2 Timothy passage quoted here begins with the admonition:

"Before God and before Christ Jesus who is to be judge of the living and the dead, I put this duty to you..."

and Eli in 1 Samuel pleads with his sons:

"...if (one) sins against Yaweh, who will intercede for him?"

The point is, there is a day of God's judgment, and the abbot bears the heavy responsibility to account not only for his own actions, but for the souls of those entrusted to him. Often a sharp rebuke or blow, or even an honest verbal confrontation of the truth about what one is doing, will "bring a person to his senses". The abbot's responsibility is such that he may not refuse these useful tools for the purpose of God's work of converting love.

Reflection: There's a lot to chew over here. Part of me knows that often I really should speak to those I love plainly and honestly about what I see them doing to themselves. But that is so hard, for it involves at least two ingredients quite beyond my "control": one is that I must do it because of my deep love for that specific person (and I never am "naturally" utterly pure of heart in my loving). So I usually have to go back to my prayer for a while before I can even consider such a step.

The other is that their response is really wholly up to them and the Holy Spirit, and if I have got up my courage to speak at all, then I want the outcome to be what I desire (and I begin to get a vested interest, which causes me to try to control the result rather than simply speak what I see). Yet again am I driven back to prayer that I may truly release the situation and the person to God.

And yet I am acutely grateful when a true friend has spoken so to me, even though usually my first reaction is angry denial!

Prayer/Response:

Chapter 2, verses 30-36

The Abbot ought always to remember what he is, and what he is called, and to know that to whom more is commited, from him more is required. And he must consider how difficult and arduous a task he has undertaken, of ruling souls and adapting himself to many dispositions. Let him so accomodate and suit himself to the character and intelligence of each, winning some by kindness, others by reproof, others by persuasion, that he may not only suffer no loss in the flock committed to him, but may even rejoice in their virtuous increase.

Above all let him not, overlooking or undervaluing the salvation of the souls entrusted to him, be more solicitious for fleeting, earthly, and perishable things; but let him ever bear in mind that he has undertaken the government of souls, of which he shall have to give an account. And that he may not complain for want of wordly resources, let him remember what is written: *Seek first the kingdom of God and his justice, and all these things shall be added unto you* (Matt 6:33), and again: *Nothing is wanting to them that fear him* (Ps 34:9).

Comment: The abbot has been given the name of Christ; he is entrusted with the most precious of treasures. By his implicit reference to the passage in Luke, Benedict makes clear that the abbot is a servant, but a highly placed one -- one who "knows what his master wants". (Luke 12: 47-8) If such a one defaults, there is severe punishment indeed.

So what does the master's will call for the abbot to do? (1) He is to have great regard for the unique qualities of each one given to his charge, dealing with each according to his or her need or capacity. This goes against our modern instinct, by which, in the name of equality/fairness, we treat all the same. It takes both discernment and skill to regard and treat each according to who they are in God's eyes.

(2) He is not to allow himself to become so burdened with administrative duties that he defaults on the spiritual formation responsibilities he carries. The abbot has considerable responsibility to provide for food, clothing, housing, and security -- none of which in Benedict's time (nor often since) could be taken for granted. It is easy for us to carry these burdens so heavily that they preoccupy us and consume all our energy, especially today when our whole economy functions on the principle of relative scarcity. But here Benedict recalls the abbot (and us!) to the radical way of the Sermon on the Mount, and reminds us that there is only one fear that is important -- the fear of God. When that one fear is properly in place, all the rest falls into order. "How good Yahweh is - only taste and see! Happy the (one) who takes shelter in him!" (Ps 34:8)

Reflection: The phrases which seem most to touch me today are these: "remember who I am and what I am called" and "may not complain for want of worldly resources". It seems to me that it is very important for me to remember who I am (child of God) and what I am called (Christian). Usually I forget. In fact, recently I participated in one of those exercises in which you fill out ten slips of paper, each one completing the sentence "I am....". When I finished the exercise, I had listed ten different "identities" of myself. I did not even think to put down Christian on the list. Many days pass without my recalling that I am a baptized person and child of God. How would my days be different, if I were regularly to meditate on that identity of mine? For I do believe that it is my most important identity.

I suppose that one of the reasons I don't take it more seriously is actually because I don't think I have the resources. I am, after all, just an ordinary human creature, with the usual quota of neuroses. I get "stuck" in many ways in my days: in the blues, in physical dis-ease, in preoccupation with my activities and engagements. There is so much to occupy me, and so little to uplift me. How could I possibly take very seriously a call God gives me to become "a holy person"?! (I don't even have good language for it.) But Benedict does take it seriously on my behalf. Even more astonishing to me than his continual lack of surprise in the face of human limitation is his constant emphasis on the ultimate human vocation. He never forgets that God longs for every one of us to "dwell in his tent". Nothing is to him more precious nor more valuable than my soul. Can I say the same?....

Prayer/Response:

Chapter 2, verses 37-40 (end)

Let the abbot know that he who has undertaken the government of souls, must prepare himself to render an account of them. And whatever may be the number of the brethren under his care, let him be certainly assured that on the Day of Judgment he will have to give an account to the Lord of all these souls, as well as of his own. And thus, being ever fearful of the coming judgment of the shepherd concerning the state of the flock committed to him, while he is careful on others' accounts, he will be solicitous also on his own. And so, while correcting others by his admonitions, he will be himself cured of his own defects.

Comment: Benedict is drawing slightly here on Hebrews 13:17: "Obey your leaders and do as they tell you, because they must give an account of the way they look after your souls; make this a joy for them to do, and not a grief - you yourselves would be the losers"

In this chapter, Benedict has been establishing the authority and responsibility of the abbot. Indeed, he has actually defined monk (cenobite) as those who "do their service in monasteries under a rule and an abbot" (RB 1:2). So the abbot's role and functions are foundational to the faithfulness of the monastery to its call in Christ.

Throughout, Benedict's image of the monastic community seems very like St. Paul's image of the "Body of Christ": many members, each with own gifts and weaknesses, interdependent, drawn into being by Christ the head. While the abbot plays the incarnated role as head in Christ's name, it is always clear that the abbot too is under Christ's sovereignty. And that the abbot too is interdependent -- his life, indeed his very soul, is deeply entwined with the life of the members whom he serves.

Thus it is fitting to close this chapter with a reference to the profound importance of the daily deepening in the abbot's own conversion to Christ, as he grows in the Spirit likewise to conform his monks to the mind of Christ.

Reflection: Several years ago a (very honest) retreat participant came up to me after a conference I had conducted and said to me, "Do you dare to speak like that without every day living that way?" It was a serious question, and not an accusation, and I was touched by it, for it is exactly to the point. Sometimes I get so carried away with the beauty and the power of who I am in Christ that I forget who I am without Christ. I am so often tempted to say, "OK, Lord, now I understand. I can go it on my own for a while." And I neglect my own word of humility and obedience as I allow my energies to be focused solely on my care of and for others.

Perhaps, though, the other extreme is equally bad: to be so aware of who I am without Christ that I refuse to act when and where I am called to, because I know I can't do it alone. Obedience calls me to take authority when appropriate, even though it may cause me to carry a burden for other souls that I know I am not good enough to carry alone.

Prayer/Response:

Chapter 3, Summoning the Brothers for Counsel,

verses 1-6

As often as any important matters have to be transacted in the monastery, let the abbot call together the whole community, and himself declare what is the question to be settled. And, having heard the counsel of the brethren, let him weigh it within himself and then do what he shall judge most expedient. We have said that all should be called to council, because it is often to the younger that the Lord reveals what is best. But let the brethren give their advice with all the restraint of humility, and not presume stubbornly to defend their own opinion; but rather let the matter rest with the Abbot's discretion, that all may submit to whatever he shall consider best. Yet, even as it becomes disciples to obey their master, so does it behoove him to order all things prudently and with justice.

Comment: In the previous chapter, we recognized the abbot's responsibility to discern and act, and noted the guidance Benedict offered in that connection. This is another instance of guidance in discernment.

From a human point of view, these are astonishing verses: why should one with sole authority consult those he supervises? And in what manner do those consulted give their opinions? Not in Benedict's time nor in ours is there anything comparable to this consultation in a secular setting, and infrequently enough in religious ones. For this is a matter of listening for God's will, in the recognition and expectation that in matters affecting the life of the community, God speaks not only through Scripture and in the wisdom of the praying seniors, but also through the insights of every member of the Body. The key phrase is "the Lord reveals...". All in the consecrated community are listening (and learning to listen, a lifelong task) for what the Spirit is saying, in every context in which that voice may be heard.

Thus, so far from being an exercise in which a majority opinion is sought or defended, this is a case in which there is attentiveness, by all gathered in this moment, to internal whisperings as well as external voices, that the Spirit of God may be made manifest and then discerned and then acted upon.

The abbot is to choose that which is salubrious (health-giving) for the Body, his community.

Reflection: Learning to listen for the Will of God is quite a task. Oddly I seldom discover it in myself when I approach it directly. Usually it is revealed more readily when my approach is indirect. If I say to myself, gritting my teeth, "today I will listen for the Will of God", it rarely produces fruit. But if instead, I pray, willing to wait and be silent and give up the initiative...and if I am very attentive to each thing or person I encounter during the day, just enjoying the wonder that they are...and if I give thanks for all that is given so abundantly to me in that day (air and warm water and birds singing and good smells and a phone-call from dear Aunt Sally)..., then, unaccountably I find myself more attuned to the presence of God's Kingdom in this place and in this moment. And I think the "big decisions" are naturally and easily birthed in such a presence.

Prayer/Response:

Let all, therefore, **follow the Rule in all things as their guide, and from it let no one rashly turn aside. Let no one in the monastery follow the will of his own heart: nor let anyone presume insolently to contend with his Abbot, either within or without the monastery. But if he should dare to do so, let him be subjected to the Rule. The Abbot himself, however, must do everything with the fear of God, and in observance of the Rule: Knowing that he will have without doubt to render to God, the most just judge, an account of all his judgments.**

If it happens **that less important matters have to be transacted for the advantage of the monastery, let him take counsel with the seniors only, as it is written: *Do all things with counsel, and you will not afterwards repent of it.* (Sir 32:24)**

Comment: The cenobitic monastery is defined as monks living together under a Rule and an abbot (RB 1:2). Throughout the Rule, there is an effort to balance these three essential components of the life: the Rule, the abbot, and mutual obedience among the brothers. In each case, there are involved both an authority and responsive obedience to that authority. Both of these are matters which in our time are very elusive. Rather than trying to define authority and obedience, let us simply pay attention to the way Benedict describes them in context, and reflect on possible relevance for us. At the minimum, as used here, obedience seems to involve relinquishment of personal willfullness.

Even the abbot is to be obedient to the Rule. Perhaps the passage in Sirach from which Benedict quotes helps clarify what is intended here:

"The (one) who fears the Lord will accept his correction...

"Those who fear the Lord will have justice done them, and make their good deeds shine like a light...

"If (one) fears the Lord, evil will not come his way, again and again he will be rescued in his trials." (Sir 32: 14, 16; 33:1)

The key is fear of the Lord -- knowing that one is in fact under authority, a steward of the God of creation. Stewardship involves thought and care, but also obligation and finally freedom, for full responsibility lies with Another, whom one can call upon in time of trial for deliverance.

Reflection: I turn "obedience" over and over in my mind, wondering about it. How does it apply to my life? Perhaps the idea of stewardship does help, for it seems to involve obedience in two directions. The steward must care for that which has been placed in her charge. She must know its essential qualities and what it requires for health and optimum growth. She must be attentive and responsive to it. This careful listening to the nature of a thing or a person is a kind of obedience, and might, for example, involve watering the lawn when I would rather be reading a book.

However, another direction is involved because stewardship implies also an obedience to one who assigns or gives responsibility, a Giver. That would seem to imply first, recognizing that what I have is gift, and then caring for it accordingly. Perhaps being responsible in my care of my own body, mind, and spirit so that I am able to care for my charges. And certainly, it would involve knowing that I have help: there is someone I can call when I'm in "over my head". I don't have to know all or be everything, but just to do the best I can.

And yet I sense obedience to the Giver goes even deeper than that. Perhaps careful attentiveness to all I have been given, "charges" and capacities both included, eventually allows me to see into them so fully that I discover the mystery they embody, and find myself lost in wonder. Surely the joy and gratitude evoked at such a time are part of obedience!

Prayer/Response:

Chapter 4, The Instruments of Good Works, verse 1

In the first place ***to love the Lord God with all your heart, all your soul, and all your strength [and to love your neighbor as yourself]*** **(Matt 22:37-39; Mark 12:30-31; Luke 10:47).**

Comment: In a sense, this chapter of the Rule is an icon for the whole Rule itself; it is a summary, a window opening onto the whole vision of the life to which the Christian is called. Benedict sees the world as God's gift, not like something external and separate, but rather a gift which is filled with God longing to give Godself to us in all the moments of the day. Paradoxically, the way we best respond to God's presence within the ordinary occasions of each day is to offer each of those occasions to God. God is involved in everything; we come to know that by offering everything to God.

This work of offering, or consecrating, of every moment to God is the basic work of Christian formation. It is thus practiced and learned and deepened in us within every moment. This simple task is lifelong.

The Rule is designed to help us discover and be faithful to ways to undertake this daily task of consecration. This chapter of the Rule, in particular, is a special and privileged *lectio* of the sort we are undertaking in this book. This chapter, culled from Scripture, is a poem with rhythmic cadences in the Latin which allow it to be memorized, taking root in one's heart. Thus, it can be carried throughout the day, as a way to hold priorities before one's eyes, so as never to be separated from God. It becomes a way to bring one's grounding in prayer into one's daily actions.

It is interesting that Benedict begins with the great commandments rather than the "new commandment" -- the ones there all along, which Jesus himself lived by and passed along to us, transformed by what his life teaches us.

Perhaps we wonder how the emphasis of Benedictine spirituality can be characterized as distinct from other Christian forms. This first, central tool gives us an important clue. Benedict here offers his summary of what he learns in his prayer about how to live life. We might ask of him: what is the basic reality which you meet/encounter at the deepest point of your prayer life? We might expect an answer something like this: "I am a worm. And how astonishing, God, that you should redeem me." Yet pondering Benedict's spirit in the Rule, we sense that his answer moves in quite a different way, rushing forth like this: "Oh, God, what a wonder you are! My heart cannot encompass the Glory you give forth, and yet I rejoice to join in your praises with all the angels and saints!"

Obviously, both responses are essential to the Christian life, but they involve very different emphases. It is enormously revealing of Benedict's spirituality that this crucial list of instruments begins with these four words: LOVE THE LORD GOD!

Reflection: Love the Lord God! Sometimes I let this short phrase be my prayer word for the day, repeating it over and over to myself as I wash the dishes, drive to work, talk with associates, brush my teeth, work on the computer.

When I think of the phrase with my mind, as a command, I get confused and I don't know where to start. But when I let it be the prayer of my heart and my body, I am so comforted, because I know it to be something the Spirit does in me. I know it to be one of those "effective words" of God, whose empowering presence is taking root in me.

Prayer/Response:

Chapter 4, verses 2-9

Then, to love your neighbor as yourself. ***You are not to kill, not to commit adultery, not to steal, not to covet*** **(Rom. 13:9).** ***You are not to bear false witness*** **(Matt 19:18; Mark 10:19; Luke 18:20).** ***You must honor all*** **(I Pet 2:17). You must** ***not do to another what you would not have done to yourself*** **(Tob 4:16; Matt 7:12; Luke 6:31).**

Comment: Much might be said about loving neighbor as self, and Benedict does say much throughout the Rule as he instructs us how to receive Christ in ourselves and in others. Indeed, this loving is an essential dimension of the Benedictine way of loving God. And this in turn inevitably involves the related commandments which follow. Here Benedict is concerned as a first priority to state the practical commandments that bear immediately upon life in a voluntary community.

We notice that Benedict slightly shifts the order of presentation of the Ten Commandments.[17] In this way, he presents us with three pairs of rules, first stipulating the negative and then the positive aspect. It then reads like this:

(a) Do not steal from anyone; but more, do not even covet something another has.

(b) Do not lie about anyone; but more, honor each person's essence.

(c) Do not kill anyone; but more, do not violate their integrity and yours by adultery or even the avoidance of charity.

These are practical ways of loving one's neighbor and oneself, essential as the foundational elements of community life, summed up finally in that phrase used by Jesus in the Sermon on the Mount to capture the essence of the Law and the Prophets:

Treat others as you would like them to treat you.

Reflection: Many days I feel like a rotten person, and it is not so easy for me to value myself as God does. At such times, I am very hard to live with! The great comfort of these simple, practical rules is that one can do them. Simple intention suffices to be kind to one's neighbors, friends, family and acquaintances in this way. It is not difficult to be kind; indeed it is a great relief simply to decide such is one's intention and act upon it. Oftentimes, indeed, that is all I would ask of others for myself....They don't need to be deeply sensitive to the inner qualities of my soul, if they are simply willing to be kind. And it is helpful to remember that on this little, unostentatious basis, the Christian life is founded. Kindness is faithfulness to God in little things, on which any deeper level of commitment must be based.

Prayer/Response:

Chapter 4, verses 10-19

TO DENY YOURSELF, ***in order to follow Christ*** **(Matt 16:24; Luke 9:23).** ***To chastise the body*** **(I Cor 9:27)*:* not to seek after delicate living; to love fasting. To relieve the poor; *to clothe the naked, to visit the sick* (Matt 25:36), to bury the dead. To help in affliction; to console the sorrowing.**

Comment: Having set forth the basic commandments, Benedict turns to the central motive of this Christian life -- Christ Himself. He reflects on Peter's confession, realizing that when we know who Jesus is, it must make radical changes in the orientation and outcome of our daily life. Those of us who follow Christ would gain life; we must then "deny ourselves". What, in practical terms and from the Gospel perspective, might this mean? This is Benedict's question, and what follows is the fruit of his reflection and his integrated tradition.

He begins with the great Jewish triad, so much a part of Jesus' own life: prayer, fasting, and almsgiving. Prayer, because that is how we come truly to know and be nourished by Christ. Fasting and other such bodily disciplines to train our bodies as servants and fellow-workers, rather than instruments so delicate as to lack the capacity to serve wholly. Almsgiving and service to the sick or afflicted in order to discipline our spirits toward generosity and habitual self-giving.

Reflection: I reflect on these principles of the ascetical life, wondering how they apply to me. What do I think these fundamental disciplines mean for me?

Prayer: openness to communication with God, sometimes in words and sometimes in silence; nourishment;

Fasting: "breaking the cycle between hunger and satisfaction long enough to receive whatever it is I desire."[18]

Almsgiving: teaching myself the freedom to share the best of my life; generosity.

I do remember how central these three were in Jesus' life, and I can sense how important they are to life under Benedict's Rule. I have not thought very much about how they can be integrated into my own life in a practical way, and I see that is necessary. Preliminarily, I notice that prayer becomes more and more important to me. The more I do it, the more I need it! It also seems that as my prayer grows, a natural generosity opens up in me, so that "almsgiving" seems naturally to follow prayer. I have less need to cling to any possessions; I am more free to give away what I know to be gift. However, as yet I do not feel a natural disposition to fasting. Perhaps I am unnecessarily anxious about getting enough; in any case, there is unfreedom in me in that connection at present. Here is room to grow.

In all these spiritual disciplines, Benedict seems to me to offer a balanced approach. Above all, he looks at spiritual disciplines insofar as they show up in our daily activities. He seems to have awareness that daily habits are important things. What I actually practice, over the long haul, day in and day out, is profoundly forming of my spiritual capacity. I never know when I will be called upon to undertake some important task. So often the key issues in the spiritual life are those moments calling forth a spontaneous and immediate response. The way I have trained myself through my daily habits will make a great deal of difference in my capacity to receive the grace God would give me in such moments.

I feel that Benedict advises me that any temporary or extreme behavior is less helpful for my spiritual, as well as physical well-being, than a simple, steady, day-by-day response.[19] I want my spiritual disciplines to be based on this observation.

Prayer/Response:

To keep aloof from wordly actions; to prefer nothing to the love of Christ.

Comment: This book is titled "Preferring Christ" because that phrase captures the essence of the Benedictine spirit. This phrase -- to prefer Christ, to let the love of Christ come first -- occurs both here and in the penultimate Chapter (72:11), almost as bookends framing all that is carried within these pages.[20] The preference for Christ in the Rule is much deeper than simply those verses which specifically use this phrase; throughout the whole Rule, preference for Christ is implicit in everything.

We might begin to explore this preference by asking, who is Christ? How does Benedict understand the nature of Christ? Perhaps strangely to our thinking, Benedict seldom refers to Christ as "friend", though there is clearly an intimate relationship. Yet for him, Christ is primarily one to be respected -- Lord, Father, King: one who carries authority over us.[21] Christ is also one who can be trusted. Benedict often thinks of Christ as the Good Shepherd, or the tender and loving pastor, the one who lays down his life for us. And Christ is also Rock, the steady one who has power over all the powers of darkness and light, showing us the right way.

Very importantly, it is fundamental to the Rule that this Christ (our Lord, Shepherd, Rock) is embodied in the many whom we greet each day. That is especially true of those we serve--strangers and the sick--but also of those to whom we owe obedience--the abbot. The nearness of Christ in the word of God as well as in the very pots and pans (31:10) means that all things may reveal Christ as we learn reverence and gratitude for the world God has given.

If this is who Christ is for Benedict, what does it mean to prefer this One? To prefer someone or something is to wish to be with them, to choose them over all other options. It is to give them top priority, to put them ahead of everything else. It is, in fact, to find them desirable. As always, Benedict is less interested in theory than in practice. Throughout the Rule, he gives hundreds of examples of what preferring Christ means in a practical way: it is no more complex than that every encounter presented to us each day is an opportunity to give and receive the love of Christ. And it is every bit that demanding.

Because Christ is who he is, the demand is matched by a gift. For it is the love of Christ which we are to prefer. And fortunately, that phrase carries a double meaning, in English as well as Latin: the love of Christ means both Christ's love for us as well as our love for him! The burden of preferring Christ does not rest solely on our shoulders. In everything we do Christ's love has first moved toward us, helping us prefer him. Let our whole life be centered in the awesome fact of this love. This is the preference toward which the Rule's guidance is intended.

Reflection: Almost every time I think about it, I feel that I don't know Christ nearly well enough. Yet I also have a deep hunger to know more about him. Perhaps it is like any love relationship: the more I know of someone, the more I feel there is yet to know! A person is a great and wonderful mystery, the more so when they are deeply loved. And this person, Christ, is the best mystery of all.

I do like the idea that it is a matter of desirability, a matter of almost erotic loving. Because then the part of me that draws me forward, that attracts and pulls me so strongly toward another, that part of me causes me to run in eagerness to be with my beloved. It is quite a different feeling that the heavy "I ought to" kind of feeling, in which I am primarily conscious of how unworthy I am. And, I do think there is room in erotic longing for great respect and regard, a deep awe and reverence for the wonder of another.

Preferring Christ....might I actually live each day in such a way that I look with eagerness to discover my beloved Christ greeting me within each ordinary moment of it? I'm reminded of that silly song fragment: "It's a lovely day today, and whatever you've got to do, I'd be so happy to be doing it with you!"

Prayer/Response:

ot to gratify anger: **not to harbor a desire of revenge, not to foster guile in your heart, not to make a feigned peace, not to forsake charity. Not to swear, lest perchance you perjure yourself; to utter truth from your heart and your mouth.**

Comment: If Christ is the center, that has practical applications in the way we live each day. In the modern world, so concerned with motives and with concepts, there is often almost a contempt for these practical lists of good works, such as those we find in the latter part of Paul's letters, or the Sermon on the Mount. Such New Testament sources are Benedict's favorites, and his mind turns toward them far more often than to such passages as the poetic first chapter of the Gospel of John.

Partly this is because of his practical nature. Largely it is because he truly believes that our sanctification is realized in our daily choices and habits.

As humans, we often feel strong passions such as lust, anger or profound impulses for ego-protection that cause us to puff ourselves up. A large part of standard Christian ascetical practice is devoted to the rooting out of such vices as these, and strengthening the corresponding virtues in oneself.

Notice the simplicity of Benedict's ascetical pattern: let it go. It is a sort of mundane meditation-on-the-spot: be attentive to impulses within yourself and when you notice their presence, release them at once. Simply live the day, being attentive to yourself, to God, to your family; and trust that if you are aware and attentive --and prayerful!-- the Spirit will be free to move powerfully within you and your setting. It is an asceticism whose dynamics are rooted in the practice of humility and trust.

Reflection: Recently I have become aware what a demanding spiritual discipline is this simple practice of attention to the present moment! At times of stress, I find myself enmeshed in a complex pattern of self-denunciation, guilt, frustration and weariness which effectively blocks me from being aware of what is actually going on.

Basic simplicity of the heart, rooted in the truth about what really is, turns out to be the disposition of profound spiritual maturity. I find myself having to begin over and over, needing to start yet again in humility as a novice. And yet oddly, there is often a greater gentleness and self-care in such simplicity in this moment, than there is in complex psychological assessment. Both are needed, of course, but what a liberation it is to be able to imagine and hope for the possibility of simplicity as the truest reality of my being!

I think the key here is keeping my focus on Christ. If I forget that focus in an exclusive attention on my own impulses, it is easy to get buried in the quicksand of my own fears and imaginings, losing my capacity to be authentic, spontaneous, indeed present to the here and now, where Christ is.

Prayer/Response:

Do not render ***evil for evil*** **(I Thess 5:15, I Pet 3:9). Do no wrong to anyone; rather, bear patiently the wrong done to yourself.** ***Love your enemies*** **(Matt 5:44; Luke 6:27). Do not render cursing for cursing, but rather blessing.** ***Bear persecution for justice's sake*** **(Matt 5:10).**

Comment: *Love your enemies.* Why is this theme so frequent in the New Testament, and emphasized here by Benedict as direct guidance for our lives? We have heard it often, but find it very difficult to practice. Not only is it hard work, it often seems quite foolish. Why then does it reappear again and again, as something fundamental to Christian life? Its advocates seem to imply some sort of conviction about the way things really are, as distinguished from the way things seem to be. Benedict suggests not simply an expression of a moral duty, but rather an awareness of the way goodness comes into being in a situation that needs reconciliation.

His awareness seems to hint at something like this: if evil is brought into a situation, it appears to have great power to provoke and evoke evil response from others in the situation. But if even one person resists that instinctive reaction, and gently but firmly offers a response of goodness (that fragile flower of tenderness and well-wishing); if even one continues to look for and find Christ in an evil situation or person, then in some mysterious way goodness is not only released there but also does prevail!

Such an awareness must be present in I Peter 3: "Instead pay back with a blessing. That is what you are called to do." Such an awareness of co-operation with a fundamentally powerful force of goodness in the world, must be what Benedict is here affirming.

Reflection: I have often thought recently about the "entitlement ethic"--the idea that each one is entitled to (has by right of birth) things like a comfortable home, a good job, several cars and TV sets, rich food, good health, dutiful children, etc. At first encounter, the entitlement ethic seemed to me a shocking point of view, but gradually I have come to realize how very pervasive it is, even in myself. When I don't get what I want or expect, when people aren't nice to me, when I feel I have done my part and others aren't co-operating (on my scheme), I am often resentful and inclined to "hit back".

I especially notice such resentment when I feel I am not liked or appreciated, or when someone seems very different from me, or when another "gets in my way" when I'm doing something "important". There are hundreds of situations in a week that cause me to feel unjustly put upon, and I want to "give back" to others the baloney I feel has been given to me.

And I think Benedict is here saying to me that each one of these impulses is a golden opportunity for my sanctification. Each time I am tempted to strike back, I have the choice instead to bless. And if I do bless, I am helping to bring about not only my own sanctification, but infinitely more importantly, the Kingdom on earth -- whether or not I can see it!

Prayer/Response:

Do not be proud, ***nor given to wine*** **(Titus 1:7, I Tim 3:3). Do not be a glutton, nor given to much sleeping,** ***nor slothful*** **(Rom 12:11).**

Comment: What is the relationship between serious commitment to God and physical or bodily disciplines? In our time, we might well ask, is there any relationship?! Throughout the ages, Christian practice has involved some physical austerity, but its nature has varied widely. Benedict's response to this question, as to so much else, is moderation.

At first, we might wonder at the combination in this listing of pride, alcoholism, gluttony, and sloth, until we realize that they are alike in taking a good thing too far. In themselves, self-regard, pleasures of food and drink, and rest are all gifts of God and to be enjoyed. But when they become excessive and addictive (controlling us instead of our controlling them), then they are severe barriers to the consecrated life.

One of the most difficult issues we have to face in living out the consecrated life is the right balance between enjoyment of the good things of earth, and the longing for possession of them which results in our very souls being possessed by them. There are more serious and evil barriers to the spiritual life than these physical excesses, but few more widespread or persistent. Perhaps the key to balance here rests in the discovery that exaggerated involvement with the physical is often a frantic effort to hide from ourselves or others the realization of our basic incompleteness. By physical excess we are frequently ignoring or refusing the interdependence of relationship with God. Benedict's citation from Romans reminds us of the importance of such a relationship: Never flag in zeal (not slothful); but on the contrary, allow the Spirit to fill you, realizing that you are engaged in service with/for the Lord. (paraphrased Romans 12:12) In daily life, the material and the spiritual are interpenetrated, because the whole created world expresses its Creator.

Reflection: The spread of material excesses and addictive behavior in our society today is awesome. Indeed, I find myself struggling from time to time with compulsive consumption. The more I try to "kick the habit" (cigarettes, alcohol, food), the more strenuous is the resistance I encounter. Or, I find myself developing an addiction to some disciplinary practice as a substitute for another addiction. (There is some evidence that persons who use biofeedback machines to reduce stress-addiction become substitute-"addicted" to the machine's feedback!)

What is at issue here? I don't know for sure, but gradually my experience moves me in the direction of Benedict's thought. At the bottom of all this compulsive consuming is a painful awareness that I am incomplete, like one-half of a clamshell, or a couple of notes apart from a musical phrase. My addictions help me drug myself away from this awareness. If instead I choose to live with my incompleteness, entering it fully, I discover in the heart of my longings the truth that I am made for relationship with God. The key to any spiritual discipline for me is this willingness to experience the pain of my present partialness, allowing myself to know it as a reminder of my true home.

Prayer/Response:

o not murmur or speak evil of others.

Comment: Benedict is here concluding a section on personal behavior, begun at verse 10 "To deny oneself in order to follow Christ". What has followed is a group of key issues in learning to place God first minute by minute each day:

1. fasting and almsgiving
2. preferring Christ
3. dealing with strong emotions
4. confidence in God
5. dealing with excesses of every type

and now, 6. basic disposition.

We notice the interaction between practical issues and attitude toward God. We notice too that "disposition" sums up both, with its focus on the prevailing quality of one's actions and character. Personal disposition is revealed in murmuring, a term often used by Benedict in the Rule.

What is it to be a murmurer or a grumbler? Fundamentally, it is a refusal of the present moment, a refusal of what has been given in this time and place as adequate for me and/or worthy of God. There are many ways to refuse the present moment. One mode is always to be seeing the Kingdom of God "out there" or "elsewhere". Another equally effective mode is always to be dissatisfied with what is here. One may ignore God equally well by keeping one's vision on the far horizons, or by rejecting what is given in the present vicinity.

Implicit in murmuring is the idea that things "should be" different: "should" because I deserve or need better, "should" because God deserves or needs better, or whatever. But to impose on the present my idea of some different possibility is to miss the full offering that is given in this present moment. C.S. Lewis captures this problem so well in *Perelandra*, where he refers to the clinging of the memory to something past, thus refusing the pleasure of the given present.[22]

In a sense, to speak ill of another involves the same kind of dynamic -- to lay upon another some sort of expectation of what they "should" be like, and to judge them against that, instead of being fully present to who they actually are, in their uniqueness before God, and in their similarities to me and their differences from me. If I am really present to another person, I cannot fully penetrate their uniqueness, so they remain mysterious and attractively unknowable/unfolding to me. If I am really present to another person, I cannot separate myself from them, that is, set myself up as "objective" judge, for I have entered into their experience in such a way that I share their essence.

Obviously, there is a place for "envisioning" possibilities, but murmuring and detracting are ways of saying "no" to what is, and thus of closing off rather than opening up God's emerging Kingdom. They are ways of refusing what God offers abundantly in this sanctified place and time. Sanctified because Godself is revealed in it, if only we are open to receive.

Reflection: Last week I found myself half listening to the dinner-table conversation of the person across the table from me, completely neglecting what he was actually saying, so that I could place him in a neat category in my mind. ("Oh, ho! He is such-and-such a type, and I always can expect certain behavior from that sort. I am of course in a more distinguished category than he, so nothing of value can occur here....etc ad nauseum") And I realized with a start just how much I was closing myself off from any possibility of meeting God -- or even my dinner companion -- in that moment.

And grumbling is like that, too: when I am busy complaining about how hard this work is or how tired I am, I am gaining "control" of the situation -- fitting it into my "known" categories -- at the expense of seeing any newness breaking through. A hundred times a day I catch myself dreaming of the past or planning the future, and effectively closed to the mystery of the present. I think Benedict hopes I will learn to see this, and in the moment, practice making the shift. For my desire to have order and to be in control is to confine the present into an unnecessarily restricted channel, which cannot contain the extravagant abundance of the daily gifts of God. When I can shift to full presence in the here and now, so often do I find my heart full and my spirit high and lifted up. How much more God longs to give than I to receive!

Prayer/Response:

**ut your hope in God. Attribute any good that you see in yourself to God and not to yourself; but recognize and always impute to yourself the evil that you do.**

Comment: The metaphor that comes to mind is that of an accounting ledger. On one side is God's account, with its debits and credits. On another side is the Christian's account, with its debits and credits. Benedict is saying that every time something good happens, even if it seems one has achieved it on one's own, credit it to God's account. And every time evil or sin occurs, debit it to your own account. Thus, all the credits go to God and all the debits go to the person. It is a very out-of-balance ledger.

At first, it seems grossly unfair. But as one enters more deeply into the reflective life, this begins to seem more and more the true situation. For if the essence of goodness lies in one's predisposition, one's first impulse, then self-honesty forces acknowledgment of the poverty of one's own intentions. Over and over we realize how weak is our will to goodness, how greatly we are dependent upon the grace of God in even the most minor matters.

If the first response to the unbalanced ledger is anger at its unfairness, the second response is often that of great fear or utter despair. For we are quite simply nothing, on the only measures that count. It is this realization that is the first essential movement toward salvation, for we must know how profoundly we need God. It is this realization that prompts the whole of Chapter 7 and the Rule's continuing emphasis on humility.

But there is another parallel movement, also essential to salvation, and that is the willingness to give up, to hand over, our fear and despair as well as our pride. For God has come to us in Christ and is now one of us; for God gives us God's own Spirit as inner resource, assuring us of God's desire that we share fully in the reconciliation and wholeness of the world. Hope has only one ground; and it is warranted!

Reflection: To know how best to be God's co-partner in daily life is one of the most difficult tasks I have. Perhaps someday it will be easier, but at this moment I find it confusing and awkward. I keep falling off the path in one direction or another. Some days I feel so important, so good, so righteous, so effective for God; I can do it all myself! Some days I feel unable even to love my family, so utterly remote from love, and sunk in despair, do I feel. My sense is that I do best when I give up thinking primarily about how I'm doing, and focus my attention instead on God's overwhelming generosity. Then indeed does my heart overflow with gratitude, tears, and responsive love which seems to bring all things into harmonious relationship quite naturally.

Prayer/Response:

ear the Day of Judgment: **be in dread of hell. Ardently desire everlasting life with deep spiritual longing. Keep death daily before your eyes.**

Comment: Benedict is shifting to another section of this chapter. Until now, he has given a variety of instructions about the daily conduct of life. Now he begins to probe more deeply: he is exploring directly the reasons why our daily conduct matters, and the spiritual dimensions of daily action.

At first glance, we would tend to slide quickly over these verses because the language feels "out of date". Most of us moderns do not often think of the "four last things",[23] and when we do, there is a curious mixture of discomfort and puzzlement. And yet, as we reflect upon Benedict's words here, it occurs to us that there must be some content relevant for us, underneath these seemingly obsolete concepts.

The underlying point here is that what we do with our lives really **does matter**; in some way far beyond our conscious understanding, each action of each day does cumulatively draw us either closer to God or further away. Each of us is invited to ponder more deeply for ourselves how we understand the nature of that motion. The pondering helps us discover the reality. And then we need to keep the awareness of this reality foremost as a guide for our every action. "Stay awake" is also the word of Jesus in Matt 24:42-25:13: "Stay awake, because you do not know either the day or the hour."

Reflection: Many times have I tried to imagine what heaven or hell might be like, in some terms that might make sense to me, and I always have to give up, because it is beyond my imagination even. But what I can begin to glimpse is what Benedict suggests in his intense phrases: "dread" and "deep spiritual longing". As I grow in faith, I realize that more and more do I exist in fullness only because God is near. And my longing for the nearness of God deepens and my dread of being without God grows. I think heaven and hell must be somewhere along that continuum.

How odd that one small act of kindness or indifference has anything to do with eternal life! And yet, once I begin to see it that way, how comforting the sense that there is some continuity between the fact of charity here and whatever life is like there. My hunch grows that it is by these daily acts that I begin to build habits or dispositions which draw me closer to God or take me further away, till one day I shall realize that the Kingdom has already come and I did not know it.

Prayer/Response:

Keep guard at all times over the actions of your life, knowing for certain that God sees you everywhere.

Comment: These verses certainly suggest one of the key principles of the Rule: the trained awareness that one is always in God's presence.[24] This foundational element of the consecrated life has been called "habitual recollection"--the habit of being collected (brought together) into the truth about oneself and about God. Such a habit is not "natural", in the sense that it is not the normal state of consciousness for most human beings. But it is natural, in the sense that it is the fullest and most accurate awareness of what it is to be human. It is that state of being in which one's heart overflows with the unspeakable sweetness of love (Prologue 49).

The next few verses of the Rule go on to describe how this constant presence can be a source of strength in times of temptation, but it is well to dwell here for a moment to allow these verses in their fullness to enlarge our hearts. For God's constant gaze is profoundly an expression of God's unutterable love, tenderness and care for us, against all expectation. The Holy One of Israel is our Shepherd, and we are his people! (Ps. 95: RB 9:3)

In this sense, keeping guard at all times may mean not only living in faithfulness to those disciplines which curb excesses and guide intentions, but also watching with eager expectancy for the ways in which God will love us this day. One of the best ways to develop the habit of the practice of the presence of God is to reflect afterwards upon the events of one's day, with eyes open to see and ears open to hear God's presence and voice within those events. Discovering how God has loved us by reflection upon the last hour, gives us greater longing to watch for God's presence in the next one!

Reflection: I have for some time developed a rhythmic pattern of reflection on and expectancy for the Spirit's presence in my life. But I confess myself periodically to be utterly overwhelmed by the power and purposiveness with which I seem to be carried significantly deeper into the Divine Life. I begin to suspect that as I reflect upon past experiences, God uses that process to enlarge my heart so that I am able to receive even greater "doses of love" in future experiences. As I reflectively appreciate the work of God which has been done in me and for me, the value and the capacity are made greater in me as God "appreciates" me. My attention is the method God uses to help me become a more effective channel of God's presence within the ordinary. So "watch" means to me not only "watch out", but also "watch for" and celebrate!

Prayer/Response:

Chapter 4, verses 50

ash down at the feet of Christ your evil thoughts, the instant that they come into your heart; and lay them open to your spiritual father.

Comment: Again Benedict refers to Psalm 137, as in the Prologue (see *lectio* on verse 28): at the first instant, dash temptation against the feet of Christ! It has a kind of quaint ring about it, and yet what a simple and practical device for so much that is made so complicated in so many forms of Christianity (and psychology).

At once give it to Christ. Do not let it take root.

This particular foundational element flies in the face of much that many modern "twice-born's"[25] seem to experience. Such sensitive spirits seem burdened by pain and sin, haunted by continuous temptations, drawn back again and again into the whirlpool of pain and suffering from which there often seems no relief. And it only makes it more frustrating when the "once-born" brothers and sisters blithely speak of "thinking positively" or to "letting go and letting God". And yet, without superficiality, even such ones can sense the rich beauty in Benedict's assurance that all are God's children, constantly in God's care, with Christ's protection at every moment.

The sense of this attitude is so well captured in one of the stories told of Benedict.[26] Apparently a young novice was one day assigned to hold a light while Benedict dined. It is said that the novice found himself thinking angry and resentful thoughts about why a person as important and valuable as he should be required to undertake such a menial task. He had not yet quite realized the thoughts to be an unbidden and powerful temptation to pride, when Benedict looked up gently, and admonished firmly, "Brother, cross yourself at once!" Gentle but firm; loving while realistic; insistently pressing the call to every person to share God's own life: such is the Rule.

Reflection: I have lately been so moved by the idea that all the many fears that beset me need to be set into context by the greatest fear of all: the fear of God! I've seen the possibility of letting the other fears assume their proper proportion in relation to that one. The fear of God contains within it the deepest charity; indeed, it is the "negative face of charity".[27] Perhaps this is an odd way to understand the meaning of the phrase, "perfect love casts out fear", but it is one that has more power for me than the sentimental sort of love I previously envisioned. I need a strong and powerful antidote to the strong and powerful fears and temptations that beset me. It is a slow learning for me that these negative pulls are puny things compared to God's great love. But what a great practice to keep setting the two side by side in my own experience, and so to learn their relative value!

I long to let everything in my life find its natural order in relation to the one thing necessary. To remember that Christ has won the final victory, and that victory is actually available for me in this moment, because God never ceases to watch over me. I am hungry not just to believe in, but also to live in, the true Reality of that.

Prayer/Response:

**eep your mouth from evil and wicked words. Do not be excessively talkative. Do not speak vain words or such as move to laughter. Do not love much or excessive laughter.**

Comment: How little we today know about silence! We think of it as the absence of noise, rather than as a fertile soil for the development of wisdom. Compared to other rules of this time, Benedict's Rule is relatively moderate about silence. Yet Benedict firmly insists on the importance of an harmonious relationship between words and silence. Benedict seems to be suggesting that there is an economy of words and laughter, that the fewer they are, the more apt to contain wisdom.[28] Indeed, there is a suggestion that we can become captive to excess with words and laughter, as with other good things.

Everything in the Rule is oriented toward the Word, and the obedient hearing of the Word. When language contributes to that, it is honored, even in the humble routines of the workshop.[29] When language claims our attention for its own sake, drawing us away from Christ, then it is to be quickly curtailed.

It is for this reason that silence finds its place along with these other foundational elements of the consecrated life: it provides a rich fertilizer facilitating the growth of the fragile bud of the soul toward God. It contributes greatly to our capacity to hear the daily Word of God addressed to us.

Reflection: I am aware that often so-called humor carries a considerable weight of anger and prejudice. I have tried to teach myself neither to offer nor to encourage such humor, but occasionally I find myself caught up again by the realization that I have been cruel, when I thought all I wanted was to be entertaining.

"To be entertaining"....maybe that is the crux of it for me. One of my truly painful childhood memories involves such an incident. I had become friends with a neighbor girl, a shy and kind but not very popular person, who was also the niece of our classroom teacher. On several occasions when I visited her, he was also at her home. One day on the playground, I found myself the center of a group of the "popular kids" and I was "entertaining" them by exaggerating stories about our teacher's behavior at her home. Suddenly I saw her striken face on the edge of the crowd, and I called out boldly, "Isn't that so, Carol?" I think the teacher himself might have taken the ribbing in stride, but I knew then and now that I was "buying" the interest of the others at the cost of her dignity and affection.

So it is not so much a matter of eliminating humor from my life, as it is to allow Christ to take away those tendencies of my ego to puff itself up at the expense of others. It is not so much a matter of not-speaking, as it is allowing myself to enter the school of silence, in such a way as to encounter true self-knowledge. It is to learn my true value, not at the expense of others, but in loving relationship to my Source.

Prayer/Response:

isten willingly to holy *lectio*; apply yourself frequently to prayer. Daily confess to God in prayer your past sins with tears and sighs, and amend them for the future.

Comment: For Benedict, there is no separating the response from the listening. There is here implied an attitude and a behavior somewhat foreign to our modern and analytical way of doing things. This is not a series of separate and discrete steps: read Scripture (*lectio*), pray, weep, and change; rather it is all one fluid motion. Benedict takes it for granted that we come to our reading of Scripture eagerly, convinced that here is a word of life for us now; that we listen with expectancy that our lives will be changed by what we hear. Quite naturally then do we move from such listening to praying: "Lord, what is it you are saying to me here?" And our prayer naturally turns then to examen of conscience: "how far short I fall from what I would be! How deeply I yearn to be closer to God, yet I seem always to be falling away from the life/love/relationship to which I am drawn! Oh, Lord, forgive me and help me!" And so from tears and sighs to repentance. "By God's grace, may I this day be more faithful to God and to the self I know God longs for me to be and indeed is already drawing me toward."

Reflection: I am acquainted with the procedure described above, but what a remote acquaintance it is! I know it as a thing separate from my being; not often enough as a lived knowledge, true of me and in me. I ponder, how does repentance and transformation actually happen?

Sometimes I play with the idea that what God longs for me to be already exists somehow and somewhere, and is actually a force that has a drawing power, attracting me now by the fullness of its reality. Possibly the force of that existence is as compelling, as influential in shaping the person I am today, as is any past action or memory or parental influence. Perhaps my unknown future is as important for me this day as my all-too-well known past. Perhaps the effectiveness of this simple scheme of *lectio* is that it accesses such a reality in me and for me.

I always sense in myself some resistance to such an idea, perhaps because I want to "stay in control" of my life. Such a power for good (in me!) seems somewhat like a roller-coaster: once I got on, it might take me places and ways I did not "intend"!

And yet, the resistance is balanced by desire. I want that abundant life that is mine. God has given me a glimpse of what it is like, to belong to my Lord in mind and body and heart and spirit and strength, and I like it. It's better than anything I know. I pray today to say "yes" with all my being.

Prayer/Response:

Chapter 4, verses 59-61

Do not fulfill *the desires of the flesh* (Gal. 5:16): hate your self-will. Obey in all things the commands of the Abbot, even though he himself (which God forbid!) should act otherwise, being mindful of that precept of the Lord: *Do what they say, but not what they do* (Matt 23:3).

Comment: Here Benedict places a finger on what is in many ways the key to his whole asceticism: pride or self-will is the great danger of the spiritual life; it is wanting to "play God" rather than adore God. But it is subtle and pervasive in human experience. How to combat it?

In a sense, the whole Rule consists of guidelines to harness and channel the ego for God. Benedict offers many ways to discipline pride: including attention to the daily interactions in community, and even-handed assignment of humble tasks to all persons, and the limitation of bodily austerities to moderate actions shared by everyone. But the fundamental method to combat pride, undergirding everything else, is simple obedience. Obedience in the scandalous, incarnational way of the Cross: obedience to a flawed human being who has been given as the superior. Obedience for each person in the form of cheerful submission in daily routines to the limited persons who have been given as family and community. These are hard words, for a 20th Century American individualist!

Reflection: For several years now I have deeply pondered this "odd" vow: that of obedience. Benedict insists on it, usually quite literally, again and again. Of course, he acknowledges the need for checks and balances: there must be change, there must be opportunity for all gifts to flower; and leaders do "run amok" in many ways. But obedience is the rule, and civil disobedience the exception. Whereas, for us --for me--it is usually the other way around: I protest/disobey first, and only later wonder about what obedience might have brought.

So what does obedience teach me? My hunch is that, as I learn to be obedient to the people given me, I will discover a much deeper trust in God's Will, in God's own plan working itself out as God intends it. In some contexts, my addiction to what I think of as a rational process of equity and fairness is probably a misleading illusion, masking my own pride and need for control. I suspect that I severely discount the possibility of the work of the Spirit in the real arenas of my life, by my refusal of obedience.

As I have explored obedience in my own life, my discoveries are interesting. First, I find that my initial desire is to assess and evaluate the rightness or wrongness of those in authority over me. Second, I prefer my judgment to theirs, and it is a long, hard struggle interiorly before I am willing to submit to their authority. Third, I discover that as I do submit, in some way I don't understand, God uses that gentle and cheerful co-operation to bring out of the situation as a whole that which needs to happen. It mystifies me and runs counter to my instincts. I have begun to suspect that the interior work I must do in order humbly and honestly to be obedient, is exactly what God needs me to do at this moment, almost in a way that seems entirely independent of the external circumstances....And yet, it also seems to affect those circumstances positively....

Prayer/Response:

Chapter 4, verses 62-73

Do not wish to be called holy before you are so; but first be holy, that you may be truly called so. Daily fulfil by your deeds the commandments of God: love chastity; hate no-one; do not be jealous, nor give way to envy. Do not love strife. Flee from vainglory. Reverence your seniors; love your juniors. Pray for your enemies in the love of Christ. Make peace with your adversary before the setting of the sun.

Comment: These verses conclude Benedict's guidance on the tools of the spiritual craft. In the first part of this chapter, he has emphasized daily actions; in the latter part, he has turned more explicitly to the spiritual foundations of those actions. The image with which he is working is that of the artisan, using the tools of the craft for the slow forming of a work of art, which is the soul in God. This slow formation is concerned with the simple routines of the ordinary day, with the ongoing conversion of our life into the things Christ has given us. Just like any good tools, the instruments enumerated in this chapter make easier that difficult work of discovering God in our dailiness, in our duties, in our doldrums.

The maxims in these verses highlight the performance of daily actions in relation to their spiritual dimensions. Key to all is the first verse here, and the one that follows (in the next section):

(1) "not to wish to be called holy before you are so" -- implies that each one is indeed on the path to holiness and can look forward with expectancy to the growth of holiness;

(2) "Never despair of God's mercy" -- reminds us that the essential meaning of holiness is nearness to God/consecration for and by God. So holiness is not primarily a matter of our own virtue (for who can hope to love one's enemies except in Christ's love!), but primarily a matter of God's everpresent love and power. We may depend upon this nearness, and live within it.

Reflection: Today I feel very far from holiness indeed, and far from God, too, for I allow my own cares and fears to preoccupy me and take up the spaces in my mind and heart.

And I am acutely aware of the value of carrying on in faith that God is here and Christ is forming me, even when I least feel it, even when my experience does not confirm what my head and heart know.

So I go on with my day, trying to be recollected. I find that I am seeking to practice presence to whatever is in front of me. I look for ways to choose to be gentle rather than to be confrontational with myself and others. Even so, I have to remake those choices every five minutes because I keep forgetting! Yet throughout the moments of my day, I am seeking to trust in the mercy of God. In all this, I am thankful for the wisdom of Benedict, who sounds to me as if he also had been in this "place" of yearning and falling short.

Prayer/Response:

nd never despair of God's mercy.

Comment: Benedict invites every person to take seriously the call God makes to each to be holy. He asks for a lifelong commitment, lived out daily, in the context of community life, governed by an abbot and a Rule. He spells out a list of fundamental attitudes and behaviors which the committed one is to strive to express in every moment of life. And he draws all together in this reminder that we must never despair of God's mercy.

Why is such a reminder necessary and appropriate?

As a generalization, there seem to be two main temptations which beset the committed Christian: self-righteousness and despair. The former is the temptation of the mind, and the latter of the heart. As one begins to enter seriously upon the life with God, discovering how much fruitfulness is possible, it is easy at first to be self-satisfied with our "progress" and our perfection. The quality of life is vastly improved, and self-congratulation comes naturally. One may find oneself judging others unfavorably by comparison.

But the organic rhythm of the spiritual life is such that this first phase tends to be followed by a period of discouragement. Perhaps the discouragement comes when one encounters an obstinate refusal in another to accept the glorious liberty of the children of God. Perhaps it comes when some daily incident forces an uncomfortable admission that one's ego is still quite a healthy "monster". Perhaps it comes when inner voices assault with a reminder of just how unworthy one is. These are temptations of the heart; in them there is a realization that, even though one has come so far and worked so hard, there remains even so an inner basic refusal of the divine life. This may deflate one's spirits, and remorse may lead to self-pity and despair.

That is why the fundamental and final tool of the spiritual craft must be: never despair of God's mercy. For indeed, this is the truest expression of the first tool -- to love God with the whole heart -- even and especially when one knows oneself to be nothing.

Reflection: There are days when hope in God's mercy seems impossible to me. I am quite accustomed to having my mind "play tricks" on me, and so long as I am attentive, it is not terribly difficult to tell myself there is another perspective than the one which seems so persuasive at this moment. But it is much harder for me to cope with the fact that my heart (or rather, my feelings) lead me astray. It is very difficult for me to weave the fine emotional line between self-pity and true repentance, between an overwhelming sense of sadness and willingness simply to offer my whole life (again!) to God, knowing it is never as much as I wish it were.

Prayer/Response:

Chapter 4, verses 75-78 (end)

Behold, these are the tools of the spiritual craft, which, if they are constantly employed day and night, and duly given back on the Day of Judgment, will gain for us from the Lord that reward which he himself has promised: "what eye has not seen nor ear heard, God has prepared for them that love him."

And the workshop where we are to labor diligently at all these things is the cloister of the monastery, and stability in the community.

Comment: So much richness in a few sentences! Highlights are:

Everything we have is given to us, even those basic tools by which we do our part to participate in the formation of our souls. For these tools, as for our life itself, we will be held accountable on judgment day. Thus we are responsible to be good stewards, even of such things as governance of our tongue, release of anger constructively, and reverence for those with whom we live. (Luke 19:12-28)

•We shall be rewarded for these efforts: indeed Matthew too speaks of "reward" in heaven (Matt 6:2-4f). What a good insight Benedict has that our reward shall be more even than we can imagine - more than even our heart can conceive. So we are not to waste time worrying about what heaven will be like; just to go on living each day as faithfully as we can.

•The work of this life in Christ is an art, not a science. Certain tasks are basic, but their application day by day in a specific setting must vary, and it takes a keen eye (fixed on Christ) and a generous heart (finding Christ in the midst) to make that application. But Benedict is clear that the work place is simply right here and now. We need not constantly be seeking elsewhere: God is here, and if not here, then nowhere else. So we are to make the commitment to what we are given, and stay with it until death, as the best place to exercise the spiritual craft: just here and just now.

Reflection: It almost seems that my "instincts" run counter to Benedict's guidance in every case:

•I often want my spiritual tools to remain shiny and bright, looking pretty on the wall; but I don't use them nearly as often as I have occasion to!

•To give all this effort for some reward completely unknown--how unfair! Wouldn't it be more reasonable of God to let us know ahead of time what the reward is (so I could have more control over it)?! I want to be a participant (manager), not a recipient (subject)!

•As much as I have thought about stability, I still can't believe it. God here? In the midst of this sinful, unreconciled, bitter, and manic place? Here?!

Prayer/Response:

Interlude II:

a note to the reader...

Is your *lectio* beginning to bear fruit for you?

Perhaps there are times when you find a word or phrase at once, but also times when nothing seems to come at all. Even more troubling, perhaps there are days when repugnance or anger at some verse is so strong that you can't get past that to anything else.

It is just as helpful, if not more so, to "go with" something that repels or angers you as to go with a positive attraction. The strong negative response may be a signal about a major area in your spiritual life, and may open up something until now quite hidden from you.

Several years ago my husband joined a spiritual reading group. He and the others in the group read passages from one of the Christian "classics", and then came together to discuss their insights. (They discovered that they were able to tap the riches of the older texts much more effectively, when they combined their individual reactions.) At one point Doug mentioned that he was marking his text in the margins with pluses and minuses: a plus when he liked and agreed with the point, and a minus when he disagreed with it.

One of his colleagues pointed out that the pluses probably were unimportant markings, because they merely recorded his acknowledgment of what he already knew. In contrast, the minus marks were extremely useful to him, because they noted areas in which new growth was already under way. The point is not that we are necessarily going to make a 180 degree turn-about in our opinions. Rather it is that wherever there is strong emotional energy, some personal engagement is signaled, which is worthy of attention and care.

The Rule abounds with examples of things we are likely to find repugnant: obeying the abbot, always giving credit to God, every day confessing sins, forbidden to do our own Will, avoiding even good speech and laughter, physical punishment, and so on. While there are good reasons to oppose some of the Rule's provisions, there are always also good reasons to include them. Are we free to consider both sides, and if not, what does our unfreedom tell us about areas of blindness or pain we are carrying?

Our *lectio* is a graceful opportunity to explore our energy and emotions in these areas, gently and with care, in light of God's call to each one of us to become more whole. The insight opened by our dislike is an invitation to release unnecessary baggage in ourselves. As you explore these negative attractions, remember this: the Christian life is intended to lead us through death to resurrection. And death--even of unnecessary baggage or strong ego identifications--feels like death; it is costly. But it is not the last word.

Monastic Virtues

Chapter 5: Obedience, verses 1-9

The first step of humility is obedience without delay. This becomes those who hold nothing dearer to them than Christ, And who on account of the holy servitude which they have taken upon them, and for fear of hell, and for the glory of everlasting life, as soon as anything is ordered by the superior, just as if it had been commanded by God himself, are unable to bear delay in doing it. It is of these that the Lord says: *upon hearing me with his ear he has obeyed me* (Ps 18:44). And again, to teachers he says: *he who hears you hears me* (Luke 10:16).

Such as these, therefore, leaving immediately all that is their concern, and forsaking their own will, with their hands disengaged and leaving unfinished what they were about, with the ready step of obedience, follow by their deeds the voice of him who commands. And so, as it were at the same instant, the bidding of the master and the perfect work of the disciple are together more perfectly fulfilled in the swiftness of the fear of God.

Comment: The subjects of Chapters 5, 6, and 7 of the Rule (obedience, silence, and humility) have often been called the monastic virtues, so central are they to the spirit of the consecrated life for which Benedict legislates. Here we turn to obedience, already encountered in the Rule several times as a major element of Benedict's thought; and we note that obedience is also one of the three primary monastic vows. (See Chapter 58, verse 17.)

Earlier we observed that Benedict's concept of obedience is rooted in the ancient notion of listening.[30] The Latin root words upon which obedience is based mean hearing in a way that involves meeting/encounter. The foundation of true obedience is a deep attention in order to receive more fully that which is being spoken/given. The whole point of the Benedictine life is to train the heart to listen for the Word that matters, and when it is heard, to respond with all one's being, so that life springs forth. And indeed, in his reference here to those who "leave immediately all that is their concern", Benedict clearly is thinking of the disciples, who put aside their nets immediately in order to follow Christ when he called them.[31] The point is that each of us receives similar opportunities to follow Christ within the context of our own daily interactions. To be obedient is to listen to our life contexts, in such a way as to develop sensitivity to this call.

It is essential to the Rule that obedience is rooted within the specific, limited, and incarnational setting given to each life.[32] We practice obedience by giving ourselves humbly not just to the uncreated God, but also to the specific superiors and teachers God gives us.

Sometimes the simplicity of the Rule lulls us into forgetting just how counter-cultural it is. The modern American temper not only celebrates individualism, but also a rationalistic spirit in which each person is at all times responsible solely for himself or herself. It is considered a fundamental human right to think through things and decide for oneself. Obviously, obedience can be taken too far, and individual reason is a gift to be exercised by each.[33] But in our time, we attribute little or no value to obedience, and Benedict assigns it primary importance. How does he ground such importance?

Note first that here as elsewhere, the key is holding nothing dearer than Christ. So it is Christ and our love for him that motivates our obedience. Second, we see that as a practical matter, one's superior (just as the poor and the stranger) is seen as Christ and must be obeyed with a ready heart. Third, the objective of obedience is an attunement of Wills in relationship, such that the command and the obedient deed have almost the aspect of a single movement. In other words, there is a profound union which is being created in the eager obedience, a relationship integral to both parties.

Reflection: What a long way I am from a spirit of obedience! It is very difficult for me to set aside my own concerns and tasks, when my husband asks me for something, for example -- at all, much less at once. I remember a time when I was a teenager, and my father asked me to do something, and I stopped and asked him "why?" He was outraged, and I shouted back, "Why are you paying all that money to send me to college, if you don't want me to ask why?!" I felt fully in the right.

Apart from the normal teenage issues of asserting a separate identity from one's parents, it occurs to me that there is also an issue here that touches the core of obedience. There is a goal of harmonious union of mind, heart, and spirit which is utterly smashed by an insistence that each request/instruction be evaluated to determine if it is reasonable and appropriate. It is a form of insisting on separation which is poor training indeed for life in Christ. There must, at some point, be a simple willingness to do what the other asks out of love for the other -- simply because s/he asked. And, painfully, that willingness must be expressed with a real live person, one whose frailities I see all too well!

Prayer/Response:

Chapter 5, verses 10-13

These therefore choose the narrow way, upon whom presses the desire to attain eternal life, of whom the Lord says: *Narrow is the way which leads to life* (Matt 7:14). So that living not by their will, nor obeying their own desires and pleasures, they walk according to the judgment and command of another: thus they live in community, and desire to have an Abbot over them. Such as these without doubt fulfil that saying of the Lord: *I came not to do my own will, but the will of him who sent me* (John 6:38).

Comment: What is Benedict doing here? What he is **not** doing is advocating "fancy" or extreme physical austerities like those undertaken by many in the desert. Instead, he actively discourages such ascetical feats. In contrast, Benedict's essential ascetical discipline is summed up in the two deceptively simple words, "obedience" and "humility". It is clear to Benedict that the great and eternal enemy of the spiritual life is pride; and the best antidote to pride is a genuine submission to another human being. The humiliations likely to come from such a submission are great -- one's own "Will" again and again is put second place.

We all like to think highly of our own opinions and judgments, but Benedict makes clear that often such judgments are mere whims and appetites for self-promotion. He is not, of course, talking about overthrowing our deepest Will --that movement of strong passion in our hearts which draws us ever more closely to our true center in God.

What is our model of the human psyche, and how do we understand the various movements of our thought and emotion? It is important for us to begin to ask ourselves what we know, not only of obedience, but also of humiliation, opinion, appetite. Are those the same or different from passion and Will? How are they connected and interrelated?

Benedict is working from a model largely developed by Cassian,[34] which in turn was a synthesis of much Christian thought of the time. It is less important for us to understand the details of that model, than to consider the assumptions of our own culture, in light of what we are discovering in our spiritual journey. Do the standard formulations of our culture square with what we are beginning to experience, as we ponder Benedict's meanings in light of our own spiritual journey?

Most of all, it is important for us to begin to uncover what is the capacity with which we most fully respond to the call of Christ to us, and how we train that. These are the questions which the Rule encourages us to ask ourselves, and to shape our behavior accordingly.

Reflection: How is my life touched by these considerations? My first response to these questions is to be perplexed. It has not occurred to me that the model of the human person current in our time might not be the only workable model. How do I even start to consider another?

Well, let's see. So far in these reflections, I have observed that sometimes my thoughts are illusions, and even that sometimes my feelings are merely superficial in relation to my deepest self. I have noticed that sometimes what I want is on the level of what might be called "appetite", and that does not feel the same to me as the great hunger I have for God. I know that sometimes my Will is self-centered (protective, anxious, clutching, even greedy or lazy); and sometimes my Will is a thing like a song, when I am deeply in harmony with Something-I-can't-Name. It seems an odd thing, but maybe obedience ("walking according to another's decisions and directions") might help me learn to do God's Will.[35]

Prayer/Response:

But this very obedience will be acceptable to God and sweet to men only if what is commanded is done, not fearfully, tardily, nor lukewarmly, nor with murmuring, nor with an answer showing unwillingness: for the obedience which is given to superiors is given to God, since He Himself has said: *He who hears you hears me* (Luke 10:16). And this obedience ought to be given with a good will, because *God loves a cheerful giver* (II Cor 9:7).

For if the disciple obeys with ill will, murmuring not only with his lips but also in his heart, even though he fulfill the command he will not be acceptable to God. For God sees the heart of the murmurer. And for such action he will gain no reward; rather he will incur the punishment due to murmurers, unless he amends and makes satisfaction.

Comment: Benedict never fully tells us his mind, since he favors succinctness. But here he suggests a very important distinction--almost lost in our time--between compliance and obedience. Compliance is a cringing and sluggish response to a command which reacts to it as though the command and the master were alien things, unrelated to oneself. Obedience is something different, a response given freely and gladly, a response involving love and thus deeply embedded in a relationship of care. Do we today have a concept of obedience that means more than compliance? --that allows a command to come into our heart and be welcomed there?

In some respects, it seems almost foolish for Benedict to contrast something so important as obedience with something so paltry as grumbling. We have already considered that grumbling is fundamentally a refusal of what is given, a refusal to be present here and now.[36] And we see here further into Benedict's insight about grumbling: that it gives us a little "safe place" where our ego can blossom, so that all the other pruning turns out to be ineffective, with that runaway vine in the corner. Grumbling cherishes the "bottom line" conviction that I really know best...even better than God.

Reflection: There is a part of me that is most uncomfortable with the way these issues are framed. Is there no third alternative to the evil of compliance/grumbling on the one hand, and the good of obedience to a human superior on the other? I am enough of an individualist American to feel that as a real pinch.

To whom anyway must I be obedient? Not living in a monastery, I don't have an official "superior" in the sense of an abbot. Not working in an office, I don't have a "boss". Who is given to me for obedience in the specifics of my life?

Well, there is my husband....but we have a "modern" marriage, and obedience is not an issue here. Or is it? I often find myself unwilling to accept the simplest possible action on his part without an explanation. He must justify to me leaving the mail in an odd place or taking a different route home or hundreds of other actions in which I find I am not simply and cheerfully present to him, trusting in his good will and sound judgment without knowing specifics. True, some of my questions are based on a desire to share his life, but it's a fine line between that and wanting to "improve/fix" him.

And what of the Chairperson of that voluntary association to which I belong? She is a wonderful person, but she has a very different style than mine, and I'm always itching to change her, rather than to allow myself to be obedient to her leadership. And often I grumble that meetings didn't go the way the great "I" thinks they should have. True, there is a place for collaboration between two different viewpoints, but it's a fine line between that and refusal of an authentic relationship with another.

Perhaps if I watch for my grumbling, I shall discover new areas in which I need to learn obedience?

Prayer/Response:

Chapter 6: Restraint of Speech, (entire)

Let us do as the prophet says: *I said, I will take heed to my ways that I not sin with my tongue: I have placed a watch over my mouth; I became dumb, and was silent, and held my peace even from good things* (Ps 39:1-3). Here the prophet shows that if we ought to refrain even from good words for the sake of silence, how much more ought we to abstain from evil words, on account of the punishment due to sin! Therefore, on account of the importance of silence let permission to speak be seldom granted even to perfect disciples, even when their conversation is good and holy and tending to edification, because it is written: *In much speaking you shall not avoid sin* (Prov 10:19); and elsewhere *Death and life are in the power of the tongue* (Prov 18:21).

For it is appropriate for the master to speak and to teach; but the disciple is to be silent and listen. And therefore, if anything is to be asked of a superior, let it be done with all humility and deferential reverence, lest more be said than is proper. But as for buffonery or silly words, such as move to laughter, we utterly condemn them in every place, nor do we allow the disciple to open his mouth in such discourse.

Comment: In Chapter Four, verses 51-54, we considered silence previously, but here we encounter it as a statement of one of the three key monastic virtues. A key commentator on silence in the Rule[37] makes clear that silence, obedience, and humility are inseparable in Benedict's thought. These three characteristics are considered central monastic virtues. Perhaps we can readily understand obedience and humility as virtues. But why is silence so important?

Silence is so foreign to our lives that it makes many of us jumpy. Occasionally on silent retreats, a person will compulsively burst out talking, and periodically in a public setting we will see an otherwise quite normal person talking non-stop to herself. Most of us know people who turn on the radio or television the moment they walk into the house, simply to have the "noise". Even in churches, after a full minute of silence during the service, people begin to cough and shift nervously. Many of us have never had the opportunity to experience an hour of silence. So it is difficult indeed for us to imagine why and how silence might be a major virtue.

Benedict knows silence as the fundamental state of things: full, rich, nourishing, and creative; and words are interruptions to this underlying rich texture. Perhaps the key is in Proverbs 18:20-1, where the clear suggestion is made that one who loves words will tend to let herself be satisfied by them, thus stopping short of the true satisfaction. Note especially that Benedict emphasizes the word "disciple" in this chapter. It is the disciple's task (the one who follows Christ) not to make words, but to let her hunger for the Word lead her creatively into daily silence. Human words distract and deflect from this relationship, unless and until they are born out of the silence.

Reflection: Just yesterday I became aware of myself rattling on and on, and I was suddenly ashamed and embarrassed. I think my need to talk came from two sources: one, that I had just before shared some very deep things with my friend, and I was a little anxious about so much intimacy, so I tried to cover it up with a flood of words (deny it?). And the other was that I had also drunk too much caffeine and was unconsciously "wired". I wonder how direct is the relationship between caffeine, noise, sugar, and frantic rushing around so typical of the environment in which I find myself daily? Am I aware of the Lord in all that?

Prayer/Response:

Chapter 7: Humility, verses 1-8

The Holy Scripture cries out to us, brothers, saying: *Everyone who exalts himself shall be humbled, and he who humbles himself shall be exalted* (Luke 14:11; 18:14). In saying this, it teaches us that all exaltation is a kind of pride, against which the prophet shows himself to be on his guard when he says: *Lord, my heart is not exalted nor my eyes lifted up; nor have I walked in great things, nor in wonders above me* (Ps 131:1). And why? *If I did not think humbly, but exalted my soul; then like a child that is weaned from its mother - so you would treat my soul* (Ps 131:2).

Therefore, brothers, if we wish to arrive at the highest point of humility, and speedily reach that heavenly exaltation to which we can only ascend by the humility of this present life, we must by our ever-ascending actions erect a ladder like the one which Jacob beheld in his dream, by which the angels appeared to him descending and ascending. This descent and ascent signifies nothing else than that we descend by exaltation and ascend by humility. And the ladder thus erected is our life in the world, which, if the heart is humbled, is lifted up by the Lord to heaven.

Comment: Benedict's method of introducing any major subject is to turn to Scripture, known by most of the monks "by heart." In a sense, it is a confusing method for the modern reader for Benedict seems to pile image upon image without really explicating any of them. A helpful--perhaps essential--way to understand this is ourselves to turn to the referenced Scriptures and ponder them in our hearts for what meaning they may reveal.

At minimum, Benedict has a simple and straightforward point: the problem of the spiritual life is pride (or self-exaltation); the remedy is humility. Before he goes into the steps of humility, he wants us to think about this point, comparing what we notice in our lives with the words of Scripture about this.

The Scripture he has selected elaborates this point. We notice that the Gospel of Luke uses the same quotation twice in five chapters--a rare occurrence and an important emphasis ("Everyone who exalts himself..."). We notice too that in both these Lukan citations, Jesus is talking to Pharisees, those spiritually "adept" persons who tend to be comfortable in their conformance to external religious requirements, i.e. self-righteous. And we realize at once that for those of us who seriously commit our lives to God, self-righteousness may be a major trap. So, whatever humility is and however it may be gained, we probably need it more than we know!

Reflection: Self-righteousness is a very comfortable bed, and I find myself slumbering in it far more often than I would like to admit. At the moment, I feel it as a dis-ease in one particular way. I have been noticing that the more I pray and the deeper I come into God's heart, the more I am acutely aware of the terrible gluttony, dishonesty, and self-centeredness of our culture. Perhaps in itself that is not bad, but I fear I am developing a very critical spirit, because I am feeling as if "they" were alienated from God, while "I" am superior to them. I am tending to see myself as somehow exempt from these cultural forms of isolation from God, and therefore to see others as inferior to me. It troubles me, but I don't know quite how to take hold of it. I sense that compassion may be an important key, and probably humility as well. I look forward to what Benedict will say about humility.

Prayer/Response:

Chapter 7, verses 9-13

The sides of the same ladder we understand to be our body and soul, in which the call of God has placed various steps of humility or discipline, which we must ascend. The first step of humility, then, is that one always keeps the *fear of God before his eyes,* (Ps 36:2) avoiding all forgetfulness: that he is ever mindful of all that God has commanded; that those who despise God will be consumed in hell for their sins; and that he always considers that life everlasting is prepared for those who fear Him. And keeping himself at all times from sin and vice, whether of thoughts, tongue, eyes, hands, feet, or his own will, let him thus hasten to cast away the desires of the flesh. Let him consider that he is always beheld from heaven by God, and that his actions are everywhere seen by the eye of the Divine Majesty, and are every hour reported to Him by His angels.

Comment: Various commentators trace elements of this ladder of humility to Cassian and the Rule of the Master, or compare it with the elaborated versions of Bernard or Aquinas.[38] Several points may help illumine for us these introductory verses of Benedict's. First, the monastic tradition seems to trace the progressions in the ladder from the internal cultivation of humility to its external manifestations. Thus it may appear to us that the list moves from the harder step to the easier one. Benedict no doubt would insist that outer action be congruent with internal motive, so he begins with work in the heart, even knowing that progress there takes time.

Second, there is an apparent conflict between this verse "the first step of humility is...the fear of God" and the first verse of Chapter 5: "The first step of humility is obedience without delay". Obviously there is a close connection between obedience and the fear of God; obviously they are not the same.

We can imagine that as Benedict turned to think about humility as a whole, his thought at once turned to the fear of God as its fundament. This foundation grounds humility in the recognition that ultimately it is not our work that builds the ladder, but God's work in us. Humility is oriented toward wisdom, and that can come only as gift, not as due wage. However, it is interesting that Benedict does not choose to cite Proverbs 9:10, where this point about wisdom is made, but instead uses the Psalm (36), where the emphasis is negative:

"The wicked (one)'s oracle (conscience) is Sin in the depths of his heart; there is *no fear* of God before his eyes." (verse 1, my italics)

The choice of this Psalm to introduce humility makes clear not only that humility is God's gift, but also that humility is fundamentally motivated by a recognition of who God is:

"Yes, *with you* (O God) is the fountain of life, by your light we see light." (verse 9, my italics)

Reflection: What a good reminder Benedict always is to me! I cannot say the number of times I have undertaken or practiced a discipline, only to become aware that I am preoccupied with what I am doing, losing sight of to Whom I am going.

Partly, of course, that's because I wish I could do it myself (could become perfect myself!), rather than love and praise the One who is truly perfect. Humility is a long time coming, but I can at least see that it begins with the breath-taking recognition of who God is. It is astonishing to me to consider the utter contrast between God and me, while at the same time realizing that God wants a relationship with me. It's hard even to hold that in my mind, much less to learn it by heart.

Prayer/Response:

Chapter 7, verses 14-22

This the prophet **tells us, when he shows how God is ever present to our thoughts, saying:** ***God searches the heart and the mind*** **(Ps 7:10). And again:** ***The Lord knows the thoughts of men, that they are empty*** **(Ps 94:11). And he also says:** ***You have understood my thoughts from afar*** **(Ps 139:3); and** ***The thought of man shall confess to you*** **(Ps 76:11). In order, therefore, that he may be on his guard against evil thoughts, let the humbler brother always say in his heart:** ***Then shall I be without stain before him, if I have kept myself from my sin*** **(Ps 18:24).**

We are, **indeed, forbidden to do our own will by Scripture, which says to us:** ***Turn away from your own will*** **(Sir 18:30). And so too we beg of God in prayer that His will may be done in us. Rightly therefore are we taught not to do our own will, if we listen to the warning of Scripture:** ***There are ways which to men seem right, but the results of them lead to the depths of hell*** **(Prov 16:25); or again, when we tremble at what is said of the careless:** ***They are corrupt and have become abominable in their pleasures*** **(Ps 14:1).**

Comment: Still Benedict searches his memory of Scripture, endeavoring to form and clarify his thinking on this topic. If we follow this content carefully, it contains a tightly-woven theological argument, which invites us prayerfully to enter more reflectively into awareness of who God is and who we are. For true fear of God is motivated not solely by a sense of who God is, but also by a sense of who we are. Self-knowledge is needed; self-knowledge that we are created beings, with motives that often lead us awry.

In these last two quotations, Benedict points toward an understanding of human Will as exceedingly limited. We cannot choose rightly because our knowledge is vague, and our desires pull us in all directions. The only ultimately freeing choice is to choose God, over and over each day, as Lord of our Will. Interestingly, St. Paul chose this same passage from Psalm 14 to make a very similar point: all we can do is throw ourselves upon the mercy of God (Romans 3:10-11).[39]

Reflection: Can I really know the truth of this argument in my heart? One way to learn it, of course, is to find myself embroiled in some disaster which forces me to look clearly at my motives. But short of that, can I really know it as my own reality? I suppose part of its truth is revealed in my very resistance to seeing my own Will as being truly limited. What a cherished dream I carry that one day I shall be all-knowing, all-good, etc. etc.!

And yet, in a positive sense, I do often find myself in situations in which I have an acute sense that alone, I have no business doing what I'm doing, for I haven't the capacity. When I seek to comfort a bereaved friend... When I offer to confront and challenge one who needs to break through to her own true beauty out of the mess in which she is embedded... When I try deeply to forgive a dear friend who has wounded me greatly... When I sense just how contentedly I am caught in the greedy, self-satisfied narcissism of my culture... In all these and other moments, I can only throw myself on the mercy of God.

Prayer/Response:

Chapter 7, verses 23-30

And in regard to the desires of the flesh, we must believe that God is always present to us, as the prophet says to the Lord: *O Lord, all my desire is before you* (Ps 38:10). Let us be on our guard then against evil desires, since death has its seat close to the entrance of delight; thus the Scripture commands us, saying: *Do not go after your desires* (Sir 18:30). Since, therefore, *the eyes of the Lord behold good and evil* (Prov 15:3); and the *Lord is ever looking down from heaven upon the children of men, to see who has understanding or is seeking God* (Ps 14:2); and since the works of our hands are reported to Him, our Maker and Creator, night and day by the angels appointed to watch over us; we must be always on the watch, brothers, lest, as the prophet says in the psalm, God should see us at any time *declining* to evil and *become unprofitable* (Ps 14:3); and lest, though He spare us now because He is merciful and expects our conversion, He should say to us hereafter: *These things you did and I remained silent* (Ps 49[50]:21).

Comment: Here Benedict seems to be describing the "pull" or attraction that is opposed to the fear of God. Our own desires and appetites, if freely pursued, lead toward death and away from God. But notice that the fear of God is likewise an attraction or a desire. What Benedict seems to be suggesting here is that the love of God--that sturdy and virile love which is known in Scripture as fear--is the most effective antidote to our base desires. What keeps our desires pure is the continuous recollection that God sees us and longs for our response toward him in each moment of every day. What keeps us from succumbing to the "desires of the body" is the stronger desire for the only One capable of truly satisfying us.

Reflection: Generally I think of peacefulness as the "right" attitude to have when I am at ease with God. So it has been difficult for me to consider the possibility that sometimes I might feel passionate in God's presence and with God's grace. Gradually, however, I have begun to realize that often my appetites or desires were merely diluted and misdirected longings for "the Real Thing", or God's own self. As a result, I have begun to experiment in exploring my own desires: I ask myself, "What do I really want here?", letting the longing deepen in me. And I have been graced with some moments in which I felt my heart pounding and my whole soul engaged in such a way that I could not mistake the work of the Holy Spirit. I have come to know that God doesn't always want me to be calm and bordering on the passive; there are indeed moments when God actually calls forth my strong passion. One essential here is remembering God, staying recollected to the truth of God's ongoing presence, at all times. So both my passion and my calm can be offered in love to the One who is my creator.

Prayer/Response:

The second step of humility is that one does not love his own will, nor delights in gratifying his own desires; but carries out in his deeds that saying of the Lord: *I came not to my own will, but the will of him who sent me* (John 6:38). And again it is written: "Self-will deserves punishment, but necessity wins a crown."

Comment: The issue is not doing away with one's own Will for its own sake, but in relation to doing that Will for which we were created. We are to imitate Christ in this. As we look at Christ described by John in his sixth chapter, we see a man of great "personal" power. He has done mighty healings; he has walked on the sea; he has fed the 5000. And the people have asked him, "What must we do, to be doing the works of God?" This, indeed, is the question Benedict poses to us this day: what must we do, to be doing God's Will? And Benedict points us to the answer Jesus gives:

(1) let me nourish you: believe in me and feed on me;

(2) and (here Benedict focuses us), imitate me as you see me do not my own Will, but the Will of the One who sent me and who loves abundantly.

How deeply can we make this Scripture our own?, Benedict asks us to ponder and pray.

Interestingly, he supplements the Gospel with a quotation which refers to the martyr Irene (AD 304).[40] The meaning intended is that there is a punishment for self-Will, but a crown for pursuit of what might be called obligation/duty or "inner necessity". We are like kings and queens when we are acting in harmony with our own deepest willing, an "inner necessity." How might we understand the content of such inner necessity, as intended by Benedict? There is some promise of reward, so the willing is motivated by a longing for something known to be valuable. How might we moderns understand the content of this "eternal reward" which invites our passionate response? Such reward must involve a sense of ultimate fulfillment or completion. Might that completion come as a result of deep intimacy or union with One who loves us and is the source and goal of our desire? If such intimacy or union is the reward promised us, then we might begin to sense that to be alone, or separate, or without such intimacy is unbearable. Even this day we would do what we could to move toward that relationship of deep love, and eternity without it would be merely gall and ashes. We are made for love, for completion in union with our God, and the longing movement toward that union is the truest movement of our inner self. Thus, the "necessity" of deepest Will and desire is to allow ourselves to respond to this heart-felt longing to be who we truly are, to belong to the One whose truly we are.[41] This is truly to imitate our Lord, in the power of the nourishment he provides us.

Reflection: Already do I find myself caught up in a song of praise, drawn beyond comment and reflection to prayer! Surely doing God's Will must be something like that: to find oneself caught up in a mighty movement in which one is an integral part, but which is much fuller than simply the result of one's singular contribution.

It is perplexing and difficult and often downright impossible to make these subtle distinctions in my own life between self-Will and God's Will, between unworthy desire and the desire that leads to Life. I know I need to struggle with it, for that is one of the main ways in which I discover a workable response. But also I find that the more I struggle with it in my head alone, the more I find myself in quicksand: stuck and getting more stuck. When I finally allow my heart to lead, and myself to live in the present (with my eyes on Jesus), almost without realizing it, I find myself responding as I would, to God.

Prayer/Response:

**he third step of humility is that for the love of God one submits himself to his superior in all obedience; imitating the Lord, of whom the apostle says: *He was made obedient even to death* (Phil 2:8).**

Comment: What depth in a few words! We have observed previously that Benedict regards obedience to God as operating on the incarnational principle, that is, it is practiced best in relation to other human-and-flawed beings just like ourselves.[42] True obedience is not the same thing as a reasoned judgment that a request is sound and then following it. On the contrary, it is a willingness to follow/respond to what is asked of one, particularly when one does not see the sense of it; so one acts in faith that God is working out what needs to be, even in the obscurity or seeming wrongness of the present situation.

Perhaps we often think of Jesus' obedience as being given to God, who is good, and therefore it made sense. But in practice Jesus' obedience to God caused him to submit humanly to things that didn't make sense--often, even to things that seemed wrong or evil--always in faith that God's power was present and effective, in part because of Jesus' faithful obedience. Surely Gethsemane must have been something like that: it must have looked to Jesus the man as if the devil were triumphing, and every bit of his reason must have urged him to fight the Pharisees and the other petty and vicious human forces arrayed against him. But instead he consented--"in the dark," so to speak, in his human knowing--trusting that God was working in ways he could not guess, to bring about God's purpose precisely in this thing that seemed so wrong.

Both Benedict and St. Paul (in Philippians Chapter 2) make the connection between Jesus' obedience on the cross, and our obedience to each other in community. Often it must seem to us that a great wrong is being done, but always we can also be acutely aware of God's power fully present in the situation, as "in (our) minds we must be the same as Christ Jesus". (Phil 2:5)

Reflection: I can say those words, and realize that I don't have any idea what they might mean in my life. I must look for them: keep open to the opportunities God presents to show me what such obedience can do.

I have been thinking a great deal recently about the "unimaginable.". Sometimes I have a sense that when I freely invite God into a situation or a relationship (even if I do so because I'm at the end of my rope), it blossoms into something so precious I could not have even imagined it. And if I couldn't imagine it, I certainly couldn't create it. So when I insist on staying in control -- or insist that my judgment always be favorable before I proceed --, then I limit the possibilities to those I can envision. I close myself from God's gracious surprises.

What deep trust it requires to consent "in the dark", though!

Prayer/Response:

Chapter 7, verses 35-38

The fourth step of humility is that if in this very obedience hard and contrary things, even injuries, are done to him, he embraces them patiently with silent acceptance, and does not grow weary or give in, as the Scripture says: *He who perseveres to the end shall be saved* (Matt 10:22). And again: *Let your heart take courage, and wait for the Lord* (Ps 27:14). And showing how the faithful ought to bear all things, however contradictory, for the Lord, [the Scripture] says in the person of the afflicted: *For you we suffer death all day long; we are counted as sheep for the slaughter* (Rom 8:36; Ps 44:22).

Comment: Benedict is a realist regarding human nature and social interactions, and while elsewhere he makes stringent demands upon the abbot and other monastic officials to take their stewardship earnestly and in the name of Christ, here he emphasizes to each monk that it will often be the case that the decisions made by our superior (those decisions over which we have no control, which nonetheless form the circumstances in which we must live) may often have harsh or difficult effect upon us.

He is suggesting, in short, that the committed Christian must not expect external circumstances generally to be cheerful, prosperous, and aptly suited to our fondest desires, skills and temperaments. We may suffer, and greatly, even -- and perhaps especially -- when our commitment to Christ is deepest.

But the point, which Benedict emphasizes here by his careful selection of Scripture, is not our suffering (or even our happiness), but only our love of Christ. No one is to suffer for the sake of suffering. One is simply to live -- as fully and as deeply in love with Christ as one can be this day -- and accept whatever comes for His sake. The passage from Matthew emphasizes allegiance to Christ, the lovely Psalm 27 emphasizes the goodness of the Lord, and the final passage emphasizes the key: "for you."

Reflection: Perseverence ... endurance ... I think often of such qualities, realizing afresh how little developed they are in me. I am so little practiced in waiting in trust that Christ is already present. I was reflecting just this morning on our three cats: how well they get along now, but how much bitter violence there was among them when the stray and aggressive kitten first came. For a long period (or so it seemed to me: it was about 15 months), the violence continued, and then one day it seemed to have passed. I had by then seriously considered killing the stray ("putting him to sleep") in order to restore peace.

So it is in my life in many respects. When there is a hard patch, I want to "do something" to fix it or change it. The last thing I think of is to endure through it, for Christ's sake, and in trust that his goodness is already victorious.

Prayer/Response:

And secure in their hope of the divine reward, they go forward with joy, saying: *But in all these things we overcome, through Him who has loved us* (Rom 8:37). And so in another place Scripture says: *You have tested us, O God; you have tried us as silver is tried by fire; you have led us into the snare and laid tribulation on our backs* (Ps 66:10-11). And in order to show that we ought to be under a superior, it goes on to say: *You have placed men over our heads* (Ps 66:12).

Moreover, fulfilling the precept of the Lord by patience in adversities and injuries, they who *are struck on one cheek offer the other; to him who takes away their coat they leave also their cloak; and being forced to walk one mile, they go two* (Matt 5:39-41). With Paul the Apostle they bear with *false brothers,* and *bless those who curse them* (2 Cor 11:26; I Cor 4:12).

Comment: What is Benedict saying in this tapestry he weaves of Scripture? One is reminded of the "prayer" attributed to Teresa of Avila: "if this is how you treat your friends, Lord, no wonder you have so few of them!" And truly does that focus the point: this is how God treats friends! How often have we read this, and yet when it comes to our own experience, we really don't believe it or accept it. Surely, we think, it will be different with me. But Benedict gently layers one quotation after another to remind us it is not and will not be different--even for the monk consecrated to God. Especially for the person consecrated to God!

First, St. Paul: "God has put us apostles at the end of his parade, with the men sentenced to death..." (I Cor 4:9) "So many others have been boasting of their worldly achievements, that I will boast myself:" (II Cor 11:18) and he lists tremendous human suffering he has endured.

Then, the image from the Psalms which is such a favorite of saints through the centuries even before Jesus until now: we are being "tried" as silver in a fire. In some way beyond our understanding, these sufferings purify us. They seem--and often are--manifestly unfair, and yet our simple obedience to the hardships and unjust treatment which come to us somehow brings us nearer Christ.

Indeed, Benedict almost makes this explicit in his free paraphrase of the Matthew quotation. He has suggested that our superiors are often given to us precisely to serve as trials. And when he uses the word *angariati* ("pressed into service") to elaborate on how such superiors may treat us, he is choosing it not from this verse of Matthew, but rather from Matthew 27:32 referring to Simon of Cyrene, pressed into the service of carrying the Lord's cross.[43] So in everything, Benedict is suggesting we look with expectancy to meet and serve the Lord.

Reflection: It goes without saying how far I am from living like this. But I have been struggling much with it just lately, when it seems to me that everything the Lord has trained me for and prepared me to do, is so unwelcome and unwanted in the situation in which I find myself. And I am angry and resentful and I want to change things. (...not to change me, but to change things!) And I find instead that I must simply endure the invisibility and sense of worthlessness and helplessness --simply endure. And while I am enduring, I am also to be aware of God's intimate presence both in the situation and in me. For that is the focus Benedict offers me: God in the midst of it all!

Prayer/Response:

Chapter 7, verses 44-48

The fifth step of humility is to hide from one's Abbot none of the evil thoughts that beset one's heart, nor the sins committed in secret, but humbly to confess them. Concerning this the Scripture exhorts us, saying: *Make known your way to the Lord and hope in Him* (Ps 37:5). And again: *Confess to the Lord, for He is good; for His mercy endures forever* (Ps 106:1; Ps 118:1). So also the prophet says: *I have made known to You my offence, and my iniquities I have not hidden. I said, I will confess against myself my iniquities to the Lord; and You have forgiven the wickedness of my heart* (Ps 32:5).

Comment: Private confession has largely fallen into disuse today. Theologians argue about why one should confess, when God already knows everything, and why confess to another person or a priest, when the sin is between oneself and God.

Benedict suggests to us that confession, even of thoughts and temptations, is one of the key steps of humility. Why does he think so? These passages suggest several major points:

(1) "Confess" to God, in Psalms 106 and 118, is translated in our modern prayer-books as "give thanks" to God. This suggests the wonderful ambiguity about the meaning of confession, so well encapsulated in the phrase "the confession of St. Peter": to confess is at once to realize one's own sinfulness, and to realize and appreciate the terrible awesomeness of God. (Matt 16:15-17, Luke 5:8-9) To confess is to acknowledge that God is creator and lord, in charge of the universe and of me.

(2) Such a God, of course, need not also be a good God or a loving God. It is our faith, given in the Judeo-Christian tradition, that although God is indeed awesome, even more so is God trust-worthy, a loving parent. So in Psalm 118, the constant refrain is "His mercy endures forever" So in Psalm 37, confession implies trust in the One who guides and governs all. Confession embodies such trust.

(3) The first Scripture Benedict chooses here asks us to make our way known to God: to let God's light fall upon all that is in our hearts and illumine it. We think of this action as being the whole of confession. But Benedict's third Scripture here suggests the other half of it as well. A few verses later, Psalm 32 speaks in the Lord's voice to the one who has confessed, saying "I will instruct you and teach you the way to go; I will watch over you and be your adviser" (Ps 32:8). Thus we see that in some implicit manner, when we offer our way to God in confession, it is gently conformed to God's own way, and we are ennobled and empowered to move serenely in that way that we should go, and long to go, with Christ.

Reflection: Again and again I am mystified and left in wonder by this conviction of Benedict's, that our tiny movement in the direction of God (a simple obedience "in the dark," so to speak) should be met by such a glorious and transforming impulse of God's love. He is so certain that the process of transformation is real, immediate, and effectively present in the ordinary events of everyday, if we are willing simply to act "as if" something remarkable were possible. I wonder.... Perhaps I might look for places in my life in which I could so act. Perhaps indeed even I might sheepishly take one small step in that direction, and then watch with awe!

Prayer/Response:

Chapter 7, verses 49-50

The sixth step of humility is for a monk to be content with the most common and worst of everything, and in all that is required of him to esteem himself a bad and worthless laborer, saying with the prophet: *I have been brought to nothing, and I did not know it; I have become like a beast before you, yet I am always with you* **(Ps 73:22-23).**

Comment: Often do we forget the connection between humility and humiliation. Benedict's language here is closer to the side of humiliation -- the consciousness that one is totally out-of-place, clothed with tatters in a place of great elegance, an embarrassment even to oneself, utterly without dignity. There is no pride left to hold onto. What images evoke this condition for us? A modern science fiction novel imagines a meeting between earthlings and a superior race thusly:

"...we are too poor ever to go there, even the richest of us. Anyway, we know they don't want us....And now along comes an invitation (for five of us)...to escape our shabby village. And what do you think will happen when we get there?...We will gawk at the big city and they will laugh at us behind their hands. They will exhibit us to the curious....Have pity on their provincials...."[44]

The point is to capture an image of deserved humiliation: that startling, momentary glimpse of the truth that one is profoundly inferior in the most fundamental sense. Occasionally in our lives most of us get a glimpse of this reality for just a second; but we quickly turn away, for it is too painful to live with it. But Benedict does invite us to learn to live in it, accepting contentedly this recognition of what it really means to be created.

But (and this is an important "but") such a recognition is both more painful and ultimately totally eased by the simultaneous realization that we are always immediately in the presence of the One whose glory is so great that our poor greyness is made even more colorless by comparison. Even in our humiliation, God chooses us as friends!

Reflection: This is one of those tasks of the consecrated life which I would just as soon ignore altogether. To allow myself to be stripped of pride, to give up my entitlement to the extent that I release my right even to personal dignity. Oh, what a wound! Is it as hard as losing a loved one? Perhaps it is not so very different, in that both are felt as death.

Oddly enough, this insight of my true condition comes to me most often from my enemies, or from my "friends" when they strike out in neurotic anger. Suddenly a barb will be hurled at me with enough of the truth in it that I really see myself in three dimensions. And I feel both angry and crippled.

It is hard to allow myself to stay close to such a bitter insight of my humble self. But to do that and at the same time be aware that I am deeply, intimately and overwhelmingly loved! It seems impossible. And yet even the human ones who really love me have known all along this awful, newly "discovered" secret about who I am.

Prayer/Response:

The seventh step of humility is that he should not only call himself with his tongue inferior and more common than all, but also believe himself in the depth of his heart to be so, humbling himself, and saying with the prophet: *I am a worm and no man, the shame of men and the outcast of the people* (Ps 22:7). *I have been exalted, and cast down and confounded* (Ps 88:16). And again: *It is good for me that you have humbled me, that I may learn your commandments* (Ps 119:71,73).

Comment: Again, if we trace carefully the Scriptural passages which Benedict has chosen, we are able to draw out a line of thought something like this:

"I am a worm and no man" is a passage from Psalm 22, that heart-wrenching psalm beginning with the phrase Jesus cries out from the cross: "My God, my God, why have you deserted me?", and leads finally to a conviction of God's ultimate triumph. Throughout, the theme of the psalm is that the only true strength, the only true goodness, is God's. If even God's son must consent to depend utterly on God's mercy, then how much more so must we. The wisdom of humility is to teach us where all good truly lies.

The second quotation "I have been exalted, and cast down" points out in context the importance of those moments in the spiritual life now popularly called "the dark night."[45] The point of this psalm is not so much that there are periods in one's life which seem full of darkness and lack of understanding (though that reality is certainly acknowledged), as it is that the human mind and heart do not have the capacity to put boundaries around God by which to harness and possess God. Thus, there will always be some "darkness" of understanding in this life.

Finally, Psalm 119 seems to suggest that it is good for us to be afflicted and humbled, if we are to follow in God's way. This last section of that long psalm directly concerns the subject which is the underlying theme of Benedict's chapter on humility: the dangers of pride. The parallel is extended in the reference to humility in one's heart; Psalm 119 reminds us that the hearts of the proud are "gross as fat", so that they cannot "learn your statutes with delight."

We notice too that humility is not simply in the abstract, but in relation to others in one's daily situation.

Reflection: There is a point at which I simply rebel. Part of me cries out, "oh no, not this humility stuff again! Some humility is okay, but must we root out pride to every last bit?!" Undoubtedly that simply shows how firmly rooted pride is in me, perfectly willing to be dormant for a while if need be, but fully expecting to blossom forth again next spring, like a hardy old weed.

So, in my heart (that deepest place, that center) I am to be humble. How do I do that? I suppose I accept the opportunities life naturally offers me to accept dependence, when I need others. Perhaps I might also consider acknowledging and even welcoming differences in others, recognizing that the Body of Christ needs strengths the "great I" cannot give. In a sense, I can practice my dependence on God, by being aware of my dependence on my brothers and sisters.

If humiliations are opportunities for humility, I imagine the best opportunities I get are the regular reminders of my limitations and my weaknesses. Recently I have several times noticed how angry I become when I discover that I cannot do something. For example, any period of brief sickness is sure to trigger depression in me, because it compels me to acknowlege my limits. Yet Benedict invites me to see these limitations as friends, reminding me who I really am, and putting me back in right relationship with God and my neighbor.

Prayer/Response:

Summary Chapter 7, verses 1-54 (to date)

Paraphrased Text: Let us pause to summarize the first seven steps of humility. The ladder begins with the internal cultivation of humility, the development of that interior purity of heart which is the essence of prayer and the fundamental disposition of the one who seeks Christ above all. These are the components:

(1) Always be aware that I am in the presence of the Holy One. Know that God is doing the work in me, and I participate chiefly by allowing God to purify my desires until my Will becomes more and more congruent with God's Will for me.

(2) Love not my own Will, but day by day release it.

(3) Submit obediently to my human superiors.

(4) Accept obedience even in unjust conditions, trusting that is the surest method for me to share the death and resurrection of Christ.

(5) Confess temptations to a human person, and accept the forgiveness given therein.

(6) Be content with the humiliation of my (true) created condition.

(7) Believe in my heart that I am inferior.

These steps are based on the words of our Lord that whoever is humble shall be exalted, and the implicit corollary that humility in our hearts is the condition for entrance into heaven.

Comment: The above language does not appear in the Rule, but it seems good to take a brief moment in the midst of this important chapter to look for a moment at the territory we have climbed. There is so much richness here that one is almost struck dumb in the face of such power. Perhaps that is why Benedict valued silence so greatly and was himself so laconic.

Obviously, the most effective thing to do with the above list is to pray it, slowly, at length, and over and over. The reason for its power is, of course, that we do not naturally have humility in our hearts. Basically our Wills are governed by our ego and by our self-pride. So this ladder of humility is a concrete and practical way to train one's Will. Its goal is gradually to build the disposition in one's most fundamental orientation to choose God.

Reflection: As I become aware of the disposition of my deepest self, my Will, I am appalled at how petty and self-serving I am. During the day, many moments slip up on me in which my spontaneous response reveals how self-satisfied I am. I find myself "complimenting" someone, in a way that lets them know that I have long experienced what I am pleased to see they are just learning. Or perhaps my tone of voice conveys the opposite of my words, so that effectively I let another know that he is infringing on my precious time. (And then I wonder why my husband gets angry, when "all" I said was something very innocent!) Yet again, I find myself eagerly trying to "manage" the interaction of those around me, so that I will control the outcome, rather than let it be the product of the organic contributions of everyone. And all this in only one day! What a long journey I have yet.

Prayer/Response:

The eighth step of humility is for a monk to do nothing except what is authorized by the common Rule of the monastery, or the example of the seniors.

Comment: Benedict is moving from a discussion of humility as a matter of disposition of the heart, to humility as expressed in daily actions. The very first things he mentions are the rules which govern the life of the faith community. For Benedict, the Christian life is most fruitfully lived in community. We do not have to live in a monastery to benefit from this advice.

Functioning as an integral part of a community of faith is essential for one committed to Christ. Fundamentally, this is a living out of the truth that as a Christian, one is a member of the Body of which Christ is the head. This biblical image often seems obscure or irrelevant, but it must mean something like: there is no such thing as an individual Christian any more than there is a living set of lungs or little finger, apart from the living creature's body.

To be a part of a community of faith means, on the one hand, to share in the liturgical enactment of the redemptive events of Christ's life through regular community worship. On the other hand, it also means to share some daily events of ordinary life with our community.

This insight is foundational to the Rule. But its placement here suggests that Benedict recognizes that resistance to the truth that we are mutually the Body of Christ stems in part from personal pride. It is the work of humility to accept and live out one's place as a member of the Body.

Reflection: Often I ponder how seldom I have actually experienced myself as a member of the Body of Christ. How rare it is for me to be a part of a community (even a small group) where gifts and differences are recognized and celebrated, where each rejoices in the strength of all, where each accepts limitations and is glad to receive the help of a stranger to complete what is needed. Often have I longed for such a place.

And Benedict invites me to consider that maybe I don't long for it quite as much as I think. Maybe my own reluctances to need others, to welcome strangers, to rejoice in another's strength or to enjoy what is different (in short, maybe my own pride) prevent me from receiving what otherwise might have been there for the sharing!

Prayer/Response:

Chapter 7, verses 56-58

The ninth step of humility is that a monk restrain his tongue from speaking, keeping silence until a question is asked him, as the Scripture shows: *In much talking you will not avoid sin* (Prov 10;19); and, *The talkative man goes without direction upon the earth* (Ps 140:12).

Comment: In commending silence here, Benedict is primarily condemning loose, easy talk or speech which is not "watchful." But here and elsewhere, he does actively encourage silence, so we must take him to mean not merely that loose talk is to be avoided, but that silence itself is meritorious. He seems to suggest two principal objections to wordiness:

(1) talking seems inevitably to go along with sinning, and

(2) talking prevents us from discovering our authentic human roots in God.

How can we relate these two concerns to the matter at hand, that of humility?

The passage of Proverbs from which Benedict quotes is concerned with contrasting the behavior of one who is wise from that of one who is foolish. Interchangeably, the contrast is between one who is righteous, and one who is wicked. To be wise is to be righteous; to be foolish is to be wicked. This is not merely a redundancy, but is rather a symbol, intended to point to the truth of a deeper reality. In the context of humility, we see that silence reveals much about our usual motives for speech: to feel important by displaying superior knowledge, to control outcomes as we wish, to distract and entertain others, and generally to express our willfulness and pride. Seldom indeed is the impulse to speak an expression of humility, wisdom, or righteousness. Thus speaking is often not merely foolish, but also wicked.

It is long practice of silence which begins to nurture in us the humble word -- the word of praise or compassion. Without this silence, it is difficult to learn how truly to speak, for without it we hide from ourselves (in noise) the truth of who we really are and what our authentic place is in the universe. In other words, silence roots us. Silence helps us become established in God. Words generally carry us in the other direction, so that we drift like gyrovagues, slaves to our own wills. (RB 1:10-11)

Thus the practice of silence is an essential outward expression of humility.

Reflection: Silence is a gift seldom offered in our present world. Often I feel I must "fight" for it, and then when I do get exterior silence I realize with shock that I have become so habituated to noise that interiorly I create numerous words to overcome the silence.

I am aware, too, of how often I rush into the silence between another and myself, because I am uncomfortable with the intimacy of the silence. Too, I frequently use words to organize the shape of reality, rather than giving myself to the flow of it. Isn't it odd? I would have said that I don't have any sense of silence as a positive element, and yet in these two sentences I reveal to myself that I have indeed experienced the creative power of silence as an invitation. Perhaps that is just how silence works.

Prayer/Response:

The tenth step of humility is that he be not easily moved and prompt to laughter; because it is written: *The fool lifts up his voice in laughter* (Sir 21:23).

Comment: Like the verses from Proverbs cited in the last *lectio*, Sirach and much of the so-called "wisdom literature" of the Bible are devoted to the question of what constitutes the wise life, practically and concretely. In these contexts, wisdom has a deeper meaning than simple knowing, and foolishness a deeper meaning than ignorance or playfulness.

Thus, the question revealed by the quotation, the one on Benedict's mind here, is "how does one live the centered life, the life grounded in the real and the important?" Or we might say, what gives a life richness, quality, full-bodiedness? And the related and immediate issue for us here, is "why is ready laughter not part of such a life?"

First, what provokes or evokes laughter? Certainly, the response to this question must involve a long continuum, for in one important sense, laughter is uniquely human, almost a sign of what it is to be human, an expression of joy and compassion. But in another equally important sense, laughter is an acute method of focusing hostility and embodying separateness. Very frequently we use laughter to criticize superiors (e.g., mothers-in-law no less than abbots), "put down" those deemed inferior (e.g. Polish and Italian jokes), or enjoy the awkward position of another (when someone slips on a banana peel). Laughter can be almost a lightning rod for that kind of pettiness which has as its purpose the nourishment of self-importance and pridefulness.

Second, what does it mean to be "prompt" to laughter? The phrase suggests an awareness of where our attention lies. While it is true that the whole Benedictine spirit is to be present fully to what is given in this time and place, such presence is intended to have a sacramental quality. That is, we are always to be looking within what is given for God's presence. In contrast to this, there is a kind of presence to the material which is all external, which has no vision for the mysterious and wonderful and upsetting inner and spiritual gift of the present. One given to ready laughter is likely to be one whose attention is focused in such a way as to miss the true quality of the present moment. Such a one finds only separation and hierarchy, rather than union in humble community.

Reflection: How is my life touched by the question of fullness of life? What gives my life richness and quality? I'm not sure that I even ask those questions of my life.....And yet I see that in some measure, these questions do lie underneath all my activity. As usual, I begin to see it first on the negative side. In the last few weeks, I have been away from home in a variety of different settings, and I have begun to sense how integrated are all the elements of the Rule. I have been in strange settings with strange rhythms, so I have lost that sense of organic unity of the day which is possible in the habitual routines which I have begun to adopt at home. Here, I am also acutely aware of how little rooted I am in the present. There are so many new stimuli constantly bombarding me that I feel totally disoriented, and unable to give real attention to any of them. I am all lost in the pure materiality of things -- like the one who laughs too much, I feel at the moment that my awareness is locked in the purely physical; I'm not truly present to anything. There never seems to be time or space to be present to anyone or anything long enough to know its truth, and thus discover the way in which I am part of it, and it a part of me.

In this temporary absence of some of the patterns I have been adopting from the Rule, I begin to sense their importance to the overall quality of my life. I sense that humility, presence, silence, daily rhythms, all are integral elements for me of a life recollected in God.

Prayer/Response:

Chapter 7, verses 60-61

The eleventh step of humility is that when a monk speaks he does so gently and without laughter, humbly, gravely, with few and reasonable words, and that he is not noisy in his speech, as it is written: "A wise person is known through his few words."

Comment: In this section of the chapter on external manifestations of humility, Benedict orients three of five steps to matters having to do with speech. Why, we might ask, is speech so important to humility?

Humility, as the fundamental monastic virtue, is intended to correct excessive pride, that human characteristic so destructive of intimacy with God. Pride and humility are also evident qualities in the ordinary interactions of human relations, and speech is the primary vehicle of these interactions. One does not want to minimize the importance of body language, nor of interior motivation (the subject matter of the first seven steps), but even taking these factors into account, speech remains one central means by which we interact with each other. Thus, speech is a remarkably good mechanism by which to practice and assess the growth (or lack of it) of humility in our spirits.

What does Benedict suggest we might look for in the speech of a humble person? First, restraint; not much talk; willingness to conserve and persevere. Second, attention to central or important concerns; seriousness not so much in the sense of gravity as in the sense of being centered in the vital issues of life. Third, reason; let no one claim that the person of prayer must be illogical or otherworldly. Fourth, absence of force; not raising the voice; letting truth "speak for itself". Finally, gentleness; a quality of compassion so great that one will "not break the bruised reed nor quench the wavering flame". (Isa 42:3; RB 64:3)

So often today are we preoccupied with issues of power and authority, what constitutes them and how they can be expressed. And, as so often in our culture, much "hype" surrounds these discussions, whether they focus on the church or the political arena or the family. In contrast, the simplicity of this description Benedict gives of the speech of the humble is truly powerful. Here indeed is a vivid portrait of what authority looks like in the humble person, the person who stands near to God.

Reflection: Often do I long to be able to speak like that -- out of the center of my being, simply and with authority. But recently I have begun to recognize that when doing so, one risks invisibility. For while there are those who will be deeply moved by the power of humble speech, there are many more who will not notice it at all, for it is out of the range of their vision. Our culture gives so much attention to noise, neon, and main force, that many among us have lost sensitivity to certain ranges of human experience, notably the humble and gentle ones. And my ego wants to be noticed.

On the other hand, I'm equally uncomfortable with the awesomeness of this speech for those who do notice, for I don't know quite "how" to be so near God. Humility, it seems to me, stands in the center of these two responses, as a discipline which directly helps me learn intimacy with God.

Prayer/Response:

The twelfth step of humility is that the monk, not only in his heart, but by means of his very body always shows his humility to all who see him: that is, in work, in the oratory, in the monastery, in the garden, on the road, in the field, or wherever he may be, whether sitting, walking, or standing: with head always bent down and eyes fixed on the earth, he always thinks of the guilt of his sins and imagines himself already present before the terrible judgment seat of God, always saying in his heart what the publican in the Gospel said with his eyes fixed on the earth: *Lord, I a sinner am not worthy to raise my eyes to heaven* (Luke 18:13). And again, with the prophet: *I am bowed down and humbled on every side* (Ps 38:7-9; Ps 119:107).

Comment: One of the most wonderful concepts of the Christian saints throughout the ages is that of "recollection", that attitude of concentrated awareness in which one is continuously attuned to the truth about who God is and who oneself is in light of that relationship with God. One is collected again -- not fragmented, scattered, dispersed and partial -- but centered in the truth which makes one whole.

Five minutes given to the practice of recollection is an excellent teacher that it is a learned behavior, one which takes years and years of practice. Part of the reason why it is so difficult to stay recollected is that it combines what seem to us to be paradoxical truths: that we are creatures (in fact created/made by the High and Lofty One who inhabits eternity) and that God loves each one of us utterly. It is hard to hold the truth of both these ideas simultaneously in our consciousness.

And yet that's just what Benedict is asking us to do here. Psalm 119 expresses the human confession that I am deeply troubled (in sin, confusion, and alienation from my true self), but I trust that you (God) will preserve and make unified my life, as you have promised. The quotation from Luke is one which Benedict has freely blended with Matt 8:8, thus deepening our understanding of the publican's humility by including the confession of faith by the Centurion (that one which we now use at the center of our Eucharistic celebration): "Lord, I am not worthy to receive you, but only say the word and I shall be healed."

Reflection: I was vividly impressed by an image of Jim Wallis' that the Christian spirit involves something like this: constantly keeping before our eyes both the image of a child's suffering face in bombed Hiroshima and the image of the deepest love and comfort we have ever known.[46] To hold both at once, as the conviction of the truest reality in which we live, since either one alone is incomplete. As I ponder that, I experience my own helplessness to contain such profound and opposite (?!) passions. Yet, I sense too that this helplessness throws me back into that dependence upon God in which I am silent and waiting.

Prayer/Response:

Chapter 7, verses 67-70 (end)

Having, therefore, ascended all these steps of humility, the monk will soon arrive at that love of God which, being *perfect, casts out fear* (1 John 4:18): whereby he shall begin to keep without effort and as it were naturally and by custom, all those precepts which he had formerly observed not without fear; now no longer through dread of hell, but for the love of Christ, naturally, through a good disposition and delight in virtue. This God will grant to appear by the Holy Spirit in His laborer, now cleansed from vices and sin.

Comment: It is a rich passage in I John which Benedict cites to draw this chapter to a close. God is love; when we love, we abide in God; love is possible thanks to the gift of the Spirit; as this love is perfected in us, we lose fear, for we come to know God as Lover.

Words are inadequate to express the great mystery that is the relationship between our discipline and God's grace, as we come more and more to be the persons we are called to be. Benedict's sentences are one beautiful expression; St. John's are another. The invitation is to find words of our own to express this mystery as we grow to experience it in our lives.

In this chapter Benedict has shown that humility consists of both inner motive and exterior expression. We might say that humility is a growing disposition, as is daily action, and both are formed in prayer. Don't be fooled by the image of the ladder into thinking this is a progressive achievement of human perfection. Above all, humility is growth into a relationship of love.

At the heart of the whole process is a profound sense of inability to undertake any of this work without the help of God. And that is coupled with an eager longing to undertake it for the love of God. Humility encompasses both inability and eager longing. And it does lead us to new life.

Reflection: Do I really believe in the possibility of new life? Is there a way to get from here (fearfulness) to there (perfect love)? Am I allowing the Spirit to work God's love in me? Probably yes and no. Some days yes. Some days no. And what I hope is that gradually there are more yes-days.

If I reflect on the mystery of the work of God's love in my life, however, I do see a growing response in me to Love. I act as best I can, and find my simple and hesitant steps greatly enhanced by love operating inside as well as outside me. And then some moment when I'm not looking, something fundamental shifts inside me, and I look back surprised, realizing I am forever changed. This inner shift does express itself in outer actions. And the whole process repeats itself again and again.

Since each day I'm dealing with today's issues, I don't always notice these shifts, except when I look back reflectively. But I do think that noticing is a form of co-operation with the Spirit. That's one of the main reasons that I do journal, and do annually review my journal. It often astonishes me to see what God has done in me!

Prayer/Response:

Interlude III:

A Note to the Reader...

How is the pace of this *lectio* for you?

Perhaps sometimes it seems as if we are spending too long on one point, which you already have well integrated. Perhaps also it seems as if we rush too quickly through an area of insight that would lend itself well to a more lingering approach.

We do not know exactly how the Rule was crafted, but as we explore it, it seems likely that it is the result of years of pondering both Scripture and daily life in community. Sometimes we encounter perspectives that seem quite new, or suddenly evoke a resonance which we did not previously recognize. As we consider the consequences and implications of such a perspective, it may be that we also feel drawn to take time with it.

Feel free to do just that. If a word or phrase or segment of the Rule is particularly powerful for you, there is nothing at all wrong with spending several days or weeks or even months with that one word or phrase. As long as it holds you, and seems to be working creatively within you, stay with it.

One way to linger with a passage is simply to re-read it each morning, preferably out loud, letting your body become engaged with the passage via your lips and teeth and tongue. Repeat it over and over again several times softly to yourself, letting it sink to the level of your heart, as well as your mind, taking root and setting fire there.

Then quietly ponder the passage over and over in your mind. Review its fundamental meaning and then explore the feelings it evokes in you today. Consider its relation to your life setting, as you understand it at this moment. What might God be asking of you or offering to you today with these words? Bring your needs and longings to God and offer them in response.

Finally, rest in peace. Give all your reflections back over to God, for whatever God wishes to do with them in your life. Physically, even, release all your wonderments back to God with a big sigh. Then sit in silence for a few moments, waiting on God, enjoying God's presence. Receive the gift God offers you, most especially the gift of Godself.

Gently and thankfully return to your day.

Continue this each day with the same passage, until you are ready to go on to the next passage.

The Divine Office

Chapter 8: The Divine Office at Night (entire)

In winter time, that is, from the first of November until Easter, the brothers are to rise at what is reasonably calculated to be the eighth hour of the night, so that having rested until a little past midnight, they may arise with their food fully digested. The time that remains after Vigils should be spent in study by those brethren who still have some part of the psalter or readings to learn.

From Easter to the aforementioned first of November the hour of Vigils should be so arranged that after a very short interval, during which the brethren may go out for the necessities of nature, Lauds (which are to begin at daybreak) may begin without delay.

Comment: Without preface, Benedict has jumped immediately into directions for celebration of the monastic "divine office" (often called today the "daily office" or the "liturgy of the hours"). The next twelve chapters spell out Benedict's explicit instructions about this central feature of cenobitic life. The desert hermits hoped to pray unceasingly, and thus minimized specific periods of prayer as a concession to human weakness. In contrast, the urban cathedral communities of the early centuries had regular daily periods of prayer, roughly corresponding to the ancient Jewish synogogue and temple customs, in which a few select persons daily offered formal prayers on behalf of the whole community of the faithful.

Benedict takes the best of both these traditions, and adds his own insight that the liturgical and corporate prayer of the (whole) people of God leads the people through the cycle of Christ's life, reproducing in their own lives the life and passion of Christ in order that they may become his Body.

The full Benedictine office will be set forth in Chapter 16. As we proceed with the detail of these next chapters, it will be seen what Benedict considers the essence of these times of community prayer. In introduction, however, it is important to note that he places this section as close as possible to the first seven chapters of the Rule on the "spiritual theology" of monastic life, and as the essential bridge to the "practical living" section. It is the divine office more than anything else which informs the quality of the whole monastic Christian life, and which forms the monk in his goal of letting nothing be preferred to Christ.

As a last introductory comment, let us note the way in which Benedict builds even this essential work of God on the human foundations: it is integrated in natural seasonal rhythms of day and night, and natural human rhythms of nourishment, digestion, elimination, and rest. All of life is regarded tenderly and viewed as consecrated for God.

Reflection: Much as I know better, I still find myself separating those things which are worthy and holy, from those things which are unimportant and profane. I do not truly love and cherish my body, for example, and how much Benedict startles me when he sets forth instructions about prayer within a framework of adequate time to rest and go to the bathroom! In contrast, I find myself more within the dualistic tension represented in part by Becker's wry definition of humans as "gods with anuses".[47] My heart experiences with amazement the difference between the weary cynicism and despair implicit in the modern view of the body, and the Rule's consistent tenderness for the ordinary, the weak, and the creaturely (i.e. the person). Benedict unites the holy and the mundane, the body and the Spirit, in an attitude of utter simplicity. More than anything else, that attitude of Benedict's teaches me what God's love must be like.

Prayer/Response:

Chapter 9: How Many Psalms are Sung at the Night Hours (entire)

In winter time Vigils begins with this verse, repeated three times: *O Lord, open my lips; and my mouth shall declare your praise* (Ps 51:16).[48] Then follows Psalm 3 with *Glory be to the Father*; then Psalm 95 with a refrain, or at least chanted. After that comes an Ambrosian hymn, then six psalms with refrains.

These being sung, a versicle is read and the abbot gives the blessing. All being seated in their places, the brothers read in turn three lessons from the book on the lectern; three responsories are sung between the readings - two of them without *Glory be to the Father*, but after the third the cantor is to sing *Glory be to the Father*, all the monks rising from their places out of honor and reverence for the Holy Trinity. The divinely-inspired books of the Old and New Testaments are to be read at Vigils, as well as commentaries upon them by the most renowned and orthodox catholic Fathers.

After these three lessons with their responsories six more psalms follow with a sung "alleluia". Then a lesson from the Apostle is said by heart with a versicle and the petition of the Litany - that is "Lord, have mercy". And thus the Vigils of the night come to an end.

Comment: The office of Vigils begins the day, and Benedict sets it forth as an expression of honor for the mystery and wonder of God. An appropriate ending to the night's deep silence is that the monks' first speech is the prayer: "Lord, open our lips and our mouths shall declare your praise". Repeating this phrase not only sets the monk's mind and heart on God, but also unites the monk with the solemn worship of Jesus' time, when this verse was used to introduce the 18 Benedictions of the synagogue.[49]

Psalm 3 is a reminder that the Lord is our shield and our glory and our deliverer, and a request for the Lord's blessing on his people this day. Psalm 95 emphasizes the central Benedictine theme of listening for God: He is our God and we are his people; this day if each of us hears God's voice, we dare not harden our hearts!

Later we shall notice that Benedict calls for all 150 psalms to be covered during the divine office each week. Since early Jewish times, the psalms have been understood as the prayer of God's people, expressing the full range of human longing, confession, confidence - in short, complete relationship with God.

To join in the corporate prayer of the psalms is to claim our inheritance in a long tradition of faith in God. But it is more. It is to participate in that marvelous ongoing ambiguity of relationship with God concerning how prayer begins. Are the psalms God's word to us through Scripture, or our prayer as humans crying out to God, or both?! Benedict emphasizes this mutuality in the nature of the office, by the regularity of the refrain/response to the prayed and heard Scripture. The refrain is a reminder of the fact of immediate and personal communication between God and each/all of the beloved people. The stipulated responses of praise (alleluia), reverence (Glory be) and petition (Lord, have mercy) span the range of our engagement with God.

This office and all those during the day are a recalling of who God is and who we are, and also a celebration of the conviction that God calls each of us as the beloved. The office forms a way of recollection or repetition which lets these truths enter deeply into our beings and become the whole truth of our hearts.

Reflection: I feel fortunate that the daily office is a gift of the church to me as a laywoman. The Anglican morning and evening prayer services are modeled very closely upon Benedict's formula, so I too may begin the day by opening my lips in praise of God, and being reminded of God's calling out to my heart. It seems to me that the prayers must be offered in community, but on those occasions when I pray them "alone", I am acutely aware of being part of those living and dead, in my "time zone" and elsewhere, who are praying with me.

At first, it is odd to return to the same words each day, and to discover my mind resisting the sometimes blatantly offensive sentiments of the old psalms. The boredom and routine often seem a burden. Distractions are numerous, and the temptation is great to let it go.

Yet, oddly enough, I am growing to realize how much more profound and joyful an experience the office is, after it has been faithfully and foolishly repeated hundreds of times. Some days I realize my heart is singing with the wonder of these great truths that belong not only to me but to all God's people of all time.

Prayer/Response:

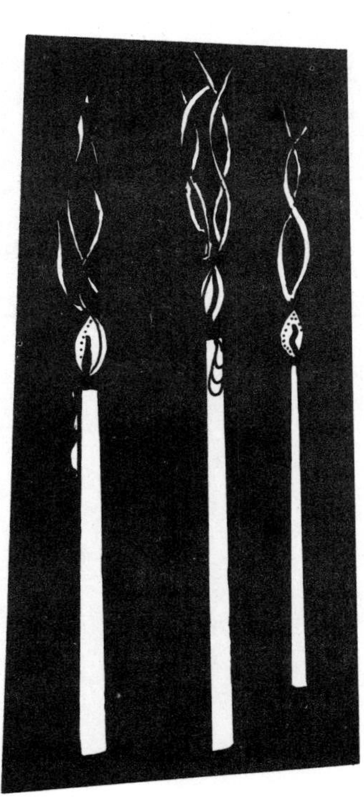

Chapter 10: How the Night Office is to be Sung in Summer (entire)

From Easter to the first of November, the same number of psalms is sung as described above; however no lessons are to be read since the nights are shorter. Instead of those three lessons, one from the Old Testament is said by heart, followed by a short responsory; the rest is as described above. In other words, there are never sung less than twelve psalms at Vigils, not counting Psalms 3 and 95.

Comment: The daily office consecrates and is consecrated by the whole of life. Not only is Benedict sensitive to the needs and rhythms of the human body, as he constructs the format for these times of community worship, but he also weaves the prayer very intimately with the cycle of nature.

In the modern age, we are so accustomed to electricity and standard measurements of time, as well as to a variety of means of insulation from seasons and crops, that it may be difficult for us to imagine the more intimate relationship with nature in Benedict's age. There were then two basic divisions to each day: the period from sunup to sundown ("day") and the period from sundown to sunup ("night"). Each of these periods was divided into twelve segments called *horae* ("hours"). But since sunup and sundown varied throughout the year, so did the length of an hour![50]

Thus Benedict, instead of following the modern tendency to force the natural rhythms to conform to his desire for completion of certain activities, bows generously to the natural rhythms by adjusting the requirements of the Rule. This shift reflects an understanding of the human as steward of nature, co-operating in harmony with it toward an organic sense of wholeness. In this as in many other places, Benedict reverences and praises the work of God in creation, as well as adoring the work of God in redemption.

Reflection: Again and again I am humbled by the realization of how profoundly Benedict loves God in all things. I see how deeply I am separated from natural and organic rhythms, how very inattentive I am to the existing situation and movements, with which I might work harmoniously. Instead, my first question is always more of a "managerial" one: what do I want to accomplish here? and how can I proceed to get it?

For example, in nature there is a far better balance of work and rest than I normally follow in my day. There are seasons of great fruitfulness, and seasons when all lies fallow. I sense that much the same is true indeed in the rhythms of my social and spiritual life and that of others. Several years ago I noticed that, even in my service to others, I normally started with what I thought needed to be done, and often found myself exhausted with very little to show for it. So instead I began first to ask, what is already beginning to bloom that needs nurture in order to continue its growth? Then I would seek to co-operate with what I noticed already underway. Gradually I realized that the latter mode means asking, where is the Holy Spirit already at work? And co-operating there with God.

Prayer/Response:

Chapter 11: How Vigils is Sung on Sunday (entire)

On Sundays the brethren are to arise earlier for Vigils, in which Vigils there must also be be discretion with regard to quantity. When six psalms and a versicle have been sung (as already prescribed), and all are seated on benches in their proper order, four lessons with their responsories are to be read from the book as before: and only to the last responsory is the reader to add a "Glory be to the Father", all reverently rising as soon as he begins it.

After the lessons six more psalms follow, with their refrain and versicles as as as above; then four more lessons with their responsories are read in the same way as described. Next follow three canticles from the prophets, as the abbot appoints, the canticles being sung with an Alleluia. After the versicle and the Abbot's blessing, four lessons from the New Testament are read as above. At the end of the fourth responsory, the abbot begins the hymn "We praise you, O God". After the hymn, he reads from the Gospel while all stand with awe and reverence. The Gospel being ended, all reply "Amen", and the abbot immediately begins the hymn "To you be praise"; after the blessing, Lauds begins.

This order for Vigils should always be followed on Sundays, summer and winter, unless (which God forbid) they arise too late. In this case, the readings or responsories should be somewhat shortened. All care should be taken that this does not happen; but if it does, the one through whose neglect it has come to pass must make fitting satisfaction for it to God in the oratory.

Comment: This office is obviously constructed with great care, for it is, of course, the first community prayer of the week. Yet what personal freedom Benedict expresses in his simple acknowledgement that sometimes the monks might oversleep, and then things would have to be shortened! This is the more particularly remarkable since, at this time, other monastic abbots required an all-night vigil/watch on Saturday night to welcome Sunday morning. Benedict seriously means his admonition to "discretion". Everything is ordered to God, in light of the limits set by human nature. He takes very much to heart the words of our Lord, "What I want is mercy, not sacrifice." (Matt 9:13)

Sunday begins the week, because it is the Day of the Lord, the central Christian feast, the wondrous acknowledgement of God's saving and loving work in Christ's death and resurrection. The monastic cycle of the weekly office begins with Sunday Vigils, always with Psalm 21 (RB 18:6) which rejoices in the strength and blessings of the Lord. Particularly do we see this celebration of the Day of Resurrection in the third segment of Sunday Vigils, which begins with the hymns/canticles, continues with the "alleluias" (since Jewish times, this word has expressed thanks for the saving might of God), the New Testament readings, the Gospel and the hymns of praise. This format is much like that which developed in the Syrian Christian Church in the fourth century, known as the "resurrection vigil".[51]

The whole of the monastic vocation has been summarized in the word "paschalization": reproducing in one's own life the pattern drawn by Christ, so that one becomes like Christ to the glory of God the Father.[52] This first office of the week invites the monastic to take to his/her own heart the present wonder and joy of Christ's resurrection.

Reflection: I think paschalization is a process not limited to monks, but offered to every Christian who is open to the ongoing call of God. In particular, I find my own experience of God in Christ greatly deepened by regular participation in the liturgy. To experience the seasons of the church year and week, as moments of the life and death and resurrection of Christ, is to deepen my apprehension of the ways those mysteries appear in my own life. It is to discover a different and more whole way of interpreting my daily experience; it is to gain peacefulness about whatever happens and to feel great thanksgiving in the midst of ordinary events. The words I have for it are very inadequate, but I know myself to be gradually transformed from the inside out.

Prayer/Response:

Chapter 12: How the Office of Lauds is to be Sung (entire)

At Lauds on Sunday Psalm 67 is first sung straight through without a refrain. After this, Psalm 51 is sung with "Alleluia", and then Psalms 118 and 63 are sung. After this follows the *Blessed are You* [Canticle of the Three Young Men], the *Praises* [Psalms 148-150], a lesson from the Apocalypse said by heart, a responsory, an Ambrosian hymn, a versicle, a canticle from the Gospel, the litany; and thus it is concluded.

Comment: Let us look in detail at the composition of this important office, continuing the Sunday morning praise, which is prayed particularly in thanksgiving for and celebration of the power of God made known especially in the resurrection of our Lord. Every element of this service contributes to the fullness of this praise.[53]

Psalm 67 begins the day with a petition for God's blessing, always followed by the penitential petition of Psalm 51. On Sunday, this is set in the context of the "Alleluia" antiphon/refrain. Psalm 118 is a reminder that "This is Yaweh's doing...a day made memorable by Yahweh" (verse 24) and Psalm 63 is a recentering in one's fundamental longing for God.

The Canticle and Psalms 148-150 are full of praise (indeed, they are sometimes simply known as "Blessed are You" and "the Praises"), and again the "Alleluia" theme recalls us specially to this day of resurrection. The Lesson from the Apocalypse/ Book of Revelation celebrates the victory of the Lamb, shared by the Church. And here as so often, in his gentle way, Benedict reminds us that this shout of triumph is best spoken from the heart, for this passage is not to be read but memorized, ie. "said by heart".

The Ambrosian hymn reflects Benedict's awareness that this fullness of joy may seek expression more exuberantly than allowed by ordinary chant.

The Gospel Canticle is always the Song of Zechariah (Luke 1:68-79)--on every morning at Lauds--and always does it recall the ancient Jewish idea that morning is the time of deliverance: "our God who from on high will bring the rising sun to visit us, to give light to those who live in darkness" (verses 78-9). And the Litany includes prayers for the church and for the world; past, present, and future; living and dead.

Benedict concludes with a phrase often translated "let it come to an end", which might equally well mean "let it be so with me".

Reflection: My desire in response to this hymn of praise as crafted by Benedict is myself to offer up many of those words and phrases which compose it. They are words which belong to us all; I pray they will more and more become my own.

My own God, give me and my family in Christ, your blessing.

Have mercy on me: Create in me a clean heart and renew a right spirit within me. Most of all, do not cast me away from your presence.

Alleluia, for you hear my prayer before I call.

You are good and your mercy endures forever.

You have acted this day, and I rejoice in it!

Eagerly do I seek you. My soul clings to you and your right hand holds me fast.

Blessed are you, Lord God of our ancestors! We will praise you and highly exalt you forever. We rejoice in you our Creator, for you take pleasure in your people.

By right, O Christ, do you have splendor and honor. For not only are you our maker, but also our redeemer. Your deeds surpass our understanding, and we draw near to you to offer you our grateful thanks and praise.

Prayer/Response:

Chapter 13: How Lauds are sung on Ordinary Weekdays, verses 1-11

On ordinary weekdays, Lauds is to be sung as follows: Psalm 67 is sung without a refrain and somewhat slowly as on Sunday in order that all may be in time for Psalm 51, which is to be sung with a refrain. After this two more psalms are sung according to custom, that is: on Monday, Psalms 5 and 36; on Tuesday, Psalms 43 and 57; on Wednesday, Psalms 64 and 65; on Thursday, Psalms 88 and 90; on Friday, Psalms 76 and 92; on Saturday, Psalm 143 and the Canticle from Deuteronomy, which is to be divided with two *Glory be to the Fathers*. But on other days Canticles from the Prophets are sung, according to the practice of the Roman Church. Then should follow the *Praises* [Psalms 148-150], a lesson from the Apostle said by heart, a responsory, an Ambrosian hymn, a versicle, the Canticle from the Gospel; and thus it is concluded.

Comment: The whole practice of the offices is to repeat the words from Scripture, the words of salvation and covenant and promise, not only as God's words to us, but also as our words to God. As we rehearse and remember these holy events, they are to become real, deep within our own personal experience. We are to be drawn more and more into the life of God. Thus, in this first office after daybreak, Benedict selects psalms for each day designed to remind us of the essential ingredients of our primary relationship with God. These ingredients are well summarized in the Canticle from Deuteronomy (Song of Moses, Deut 31:30-32:43), contrasting God's faithfulness with Israel's faithlessness, and celebrating God's love for, and ultimate victory on behalf of God's people.

Again, we note the gentle touch of Benedict's own loving kindness: some will undoubtedly be late for the first psalm, so let it be sung slowly so that all at least will be present for the second one.

And so the day begins with God's praises on our lips and in our hearts.

Reflection: It almost seems like it would be good to take a week, simply beginning each day with the two psalms Benedict recommends, saying them slowly, and letting myself wonder about them during the day following. What, if anything, do these words have to do with me today?

- The one who wishes life must fear God (Psalm 36 - Monday);
- My heart is fixed on God and I find myself singing (Ps 57 - Tuesday);
- and so on...

It feels a little foolish even to think of it, but why not regard it as a sort of experiment? Is there really something different about taking the words of Scripture and praying them as my own? And maybe I could even try it in community, that is, when I knew that a few other Christian friends would also be reading the same psalms that morning in their own homes? It is an idea which "tempts" me greatly.

Prayer/Response:

Chapter 13, verses 12-14 (end), and Chapter 14: How the Office of Vigils is Sung on Saint's Days (entire)

Most certainly, the Offices of Lauds and Vespers should never conclude without the Lord's Prayer being sung aloud by the Superior so that all may hear it, because of the thorns of scandal which are likely to spring up: in this way the brothers are warned by the covenant which they make in that prayer: *Forgive us as we forgive* (Matt 6:12), they may cleanse themselves of this sort of vice. But at the other Offices, only the last part of the prayer is sung aloud, so that all may answer: *But deliver us from evil* (Matt 6:13).

(Chapter 14:) On the feasts of saints, and indeed on all solemnities, the Office should be ordered as on Sundays, except that the psalms, refrains and readings suitable for that day are used. Otherwise the arrangements are the same as described above.

Comment: At the beginning and end of each day, the monks are to remember the words of the Lord's Prayer, the essential prayer of one seeking God. The attention here given to two petitions of this prayer, highlights a purpose underlying all the prayers of the office: the fact that the daily office is intended to influence the daily life of the monks, particularly in their relations to each other. As we pray to be forgiven as we forgive, we are essentially making a commitment to be forgiving with those now praying with us. This doesn't sound like a radical idea, but as we look at the way we live with each other, we see how profound a conversion is involved, each time we pray.

This instruction reflects a clear-eyed recognition that committed Christians are human, and thus we will indeed encounter thorns, contention and evil in each day--not only outside ourselves, but inside as well. Each time we notice this yet again, we are reminded of the centrality of the "spiritual instrument": never despair of God's mercy (RB 4:74).

And then we continue on, to the next item of ordinary life and its shape, dealing as best we can with what is given in each moment. We weave our course between pride and despair, holding to the truth that God's name is hallowed, and God's Will is to be done on earth, as we open ourselves humbly to God's Spirit and God's care.

Reflection: Lately I have been pondering greatly why it is that the Church often seems to be the least holy place I can imagine. There may be many reasons for that, but I am struck by Benedict's approach to the problem. He seems never to be surprised when anyone falls short, which makes me think he was well acquainted with his own shortfalls. But on the other hand, he also always insists that we are daily called to greater intimacy with God.

In contrast, I usually tend either to wallow in my shortfalls or others', depressed and fearful, convinced that I shall never be released from the power of sin and death. Or else, I ignore the possibility of shortfalls, only to be reminded with shame all too soon. How difficult it is to keep a balance between the two: remembering that this world is not yet fully free, and equally remembering that Christ has already won the final victory, and the darkness cannot overcome the Light. I struggle to hold that vision firmly; and to live each day simply, in accord with it.

Prayer/Response:

Chapter 15: At What Times of the Year "Alleluia" is Said (entire)

FROM HOLY EASTER until Pentecost, without interruption, "Alleluia" is said both with the psalms and the responsories. From Pentecost until the beginning of Lent, it is to be said every night at Vigils with the second six psalms only. On every Sunday except during Lent, the canticles, Vigils, Lauds, Prime, Terce, Sext and None are said with "Alleluia"; however a refrain is used at Vespers. The responsories are never to be said with "Alleluia", except from Easter to Pentecost.

Comment: The Jewish practice was to say "Hallel-Yah" (Praise Yahweh/God) at the beginning of the psalms. Christian custom adopted the term early, as a heart-felt expression of joy and gratitude at God's saving action especially in Christ, in the Paschal Mystery of death and resurrection in which each Christian is also born to new life. This paschal theme is at the heart of Benedict's understanding of monastic life, and is symbolized among other things by the term "Alleluia" in the offices.[54]

The whole consecrated life of monasticism is a way of responding to the baptismal covenant of each Christian. In baptism, each dies to the old life and is born to the new; each shares the work of Christ and benefits from its fruits. In baptism, this dying and rising is given as a seal and a first-fruits. The full integration of this promise into one's life is the purpose of the life of consecration to God. Benedict's Rule intends to show how one can be faithful to the promise of baptism in the daily consecration of life.

One of his key ingredients is the centering of the life in the daily office and the liturgical calendar. "Alleluia", that small word of praise and thanksgiving is a simple way to highlight and punctuate the shift of liturgical seasons. During Lent, a time of penitence and preparation for Easter, the Alleluia is suppressed altogether. During Easter season, on the other hand, it is said with all the psalms and responsories. On all Sundays except in Lent, it is said with the psalms. And each night, on arising for the first office and recollecting oneself to the truth of things, the Alleluia is said with the psalms (again excepting Lent).

Here, too, Benedict's simplicity is evident. He is glad to make use of a small word to engage the body (the mouth, the ear) and thus to reach the mind and spirit and heart.

Reflection: One year a friend of mine from a non-liturgical church joined me for mid-week worship during the seasons of Lent and Easter. During Easter week, she told me with tears in her eyes: "Now I see why the Alleluia was suppressed during Lent. On Easter I received it and the gift of the season with much joy!" I was profoundly moved by her words.

As I write now, it is Ash Wednesday, and the season of "darkness" begins. We prepare for the cross, and for those moments when God seems far away, when our minds cannot comprehend God's wisdom. We pray in repentance and in trust in God's mercy. And "Alleluia" is gone for a time.

Prayer/Response:

Chapter 16, How the Work of God is to be Performed During the Day

As the Prophet says: *Seven times a day I have given you praise* (Ps.119:164). We will complete this sacred number of seven if at the times of Lauds, Prime, Terce, Sext, None, Vespers and Compline, we fulfill the duties of our office. For it was of these daytime hours that he said, *Seven times a day have I given you praise* (Ps 119:164); just as the same Prophet said concerning Vigils, *At midnight I arose to give praise to you* (Ps 119:62). At these times, therefore, we should sing the praises of our Creator for his just judgments: Lauds, Prime, Terce, Sext, None, Vespers and Compline; and *at night let us arise to give* him *praise* (Ps 119:164,62).

Comment: Here Benedict sets forth the daily schedule for the divine office, the periods during which the monks come together for prayer.[55] By setting this schedule in the context of Psalm 119, Benedict implies several things about the purpose of the office.

First, it is for praise of God. Prayer may be for many purposes and all are legitimate in the context of communication and communion with God. Yet, is it not the case that at the heart of all the other reasons, praise is the joyful overflow of a heart filled with gratitude and delight?!

Traditionally, the 119th Psalm is the one chosen to be recalled in the midst of ordinary routines, to recollect oneself to the central realities of God's presence and governing power in all created things and movements. It is said at noonday and on Wednesdays in the American Anglican cycle of prayer -- exactly in the midst both of the day and of the week, to recall us to our center. There are those who regard it as a legalistic prayer, since each verse recites some application of God's law. And others interpret God's law as the essence of God's being -- Love. In any case, it is a helpful way of centering one's attention in the sacramental reality of the present moment: God is here! God is now!

And this is the purpose of punctuating the day with the office, to ground oneself in God, to build habitual recollection of the I-Thou relation in one's deepest spirit. Seven is a "sacred number", as it signifies perfection or completion,[56] and we might imagine that both Benedict and the psalmist envision recollection as embodying both the perfection of the person and the glory of God.

Reflection: Is praise a learned response, or a spontaneous emotion, or both? Sometimes when I think about praise, I feel that I know nothing about it. What is praise, and how does one come to experience it? Sometimes too, my heart "naturally" flows over, in what is partly love and gratitude, but partly also something more --nearer awe or wonder, or even respect. I've never thought of respect as a heartfelt emotion, yet I see that it may be....

I do think that in some sense praise is learned, or at least practiced to deepen one's capacity for it. And I see what a good setting the office (the community's prayer) is for the practice of praise. When I am together with others in worship, recalling the promises and actions of God in history as a reminder that God is present today, then I begin to apprehend how mighty and how loving is the God who was and is and will be. I realize how much I am in debt, and how deeply I am integral to an astonishingly rich world of creatures and created matter, and I glimpse how great must be the One in whom we all find our source and goal. All this is something that grows in me as I practice turning myself toward it. Or so it seems to me....

Prayer/Response:

Chapter 17: How Many Psalms are to be Sung at these Hours (entire)

We have already dealt with the order of psalmody for Vigils and Lauds. Let us proceed to arrange for the remaining hours.

At Prime three psalms are to be sung, separately and not under the same "Glory be to the Father". The hymn at this hour is to follow the opening versicle, *O God, come to my assistance* (Ps 70:2), before the psalms are begun. Then, at the end of the three psalms, one lesson is to be recited with a versicle, the *Lord, have mercy*, and the dismissal.

At Terce, Sext, and None prayer is celebrated the same way: that is, the verse, the hymn proper to each hour, three psalms, the lesson and versicle, the *Lord, have mercy* and the dismissal. If the community is somewhat large, the psalms are to be sung with refrains; if smaller, the psalms are sung straight through.

The Vespers Office is to consist of four psalms with refrains: after the psalms a lesson is to be recited; then the responsory, the Ambrosian hymn and versicle, the canticle from the Gospel, the litany, and, immediately before the dismissal, the Lord's Prayer.

Compline consists of the recitation of three psalms, to be said straight through without refrains; then the hymn for that hour, one lesson, the versicle, the *Lord, have mercy*, the blessing, and the concluding prayer.

Comment: Benedict is not, of course, creating this schedule of offices "from scratch"; he is calling upon many sources, and integrating them as seems best for his purposes. In the whole Rule, Benedict never seeks to be original, but rather to draw upon the wisdom of the tradition in light of the Gospel and his community's needs. His goal is deeply to penetrate the truth of the Gospel as it is best lived in the concrete setting he faces. Paradoxically, his attentiveness to the limitations of his setting resulted in guidance profoundly relevant to our own situatedness.

The quality in this overall structure of the offices is reminiscent of the Prologue's promise that there shall be "nothing harsh or burdensome" (verse 46). Each office during the day is concise and succinct, a gathering briefly to praise and to recollect oneself to God, but none is elaborate, lengthy or strenuous.

The distinction made for practice between large and small communities suggests a desire that the office be participative, not entertainment for the many by the few, but every person joining in the worship of God.

Two ingredients in particular seem to tie all the offices together in continuity and unity. One is the hymn at each hour (is this because the hymn is a glorious natural way to express the fullness of praise?!), and one is the versicles ("O God, come to my assistance"; and "Lord, have mercy"). These two short prayers were firmly established in the Christian community as key means of recollection, even by Benedict's time. They were understood to be prayers to be taken into all the moments of one's day, in one's mind and heart, in order to pray constantly, to deepen one's habitual awareness of the relationship with God.[57]

Reflection: I do not often leave worship or prayer, taking with me what Francis de Sales calls a little "bouquet"[58]--a verse or phrase of prayer to sustain me during the hours of the day and night that follow. It seems a lovely idea; it gives me comfort just to think of it, and yet I seldom do it. Perhaps I might try it for a week or two and discover what effect, if any, it has in my life and my attitudes.

Prayer/Response:

Chapter 18: In What Order the Psalms are to be Sung (entire)

At the beginning of the day hours this verse is always to be said: *O God, come to my assistance; O Lord, make haste to help me* (Ps 70:2) with the *Glory be to the Father*, followed by the hymn proper to each hour. At Prime on Sunday, four parts of Psalm 119 are said. At the other hours, that is, Terce, Sext and None, three parts of this psalm are said. At Prime on Monday three psalms are said: Psalms 1, 2, and 6; and so in the same way every day until Sunday, three psalms are said at Prime in consecutive order up to Psalm 20. Psalms 9 and 17 are each divided into two *Glorias*. And thus it shall be that that Vigils on Sunday always begins with Psalm 21.

At Terce, Sext and None on Monday, the nine remaining parts of Psalm 119 are said, three parts at each hour. This psalm having thus been completed in two days - Sunday and Monday - the nine psalms from 120 through 128 are said on Tuesday at each of the hours of Terce, Sext and None, three psalms per hour. These psalms are repeated at the same hours every day until Sunday. The arrangement of hymns, lessons and versicles remains the same for these days. Thus Psalm 119 is always to begin on Sunday.

Vespers is to be sung each day with four psalms, begining with Psalm 110 and ending with Psalm 147, omitting those of their number already set apart for other hours, namely, Psalms 118 to 128, Psalm 134 and Psalm 143. All the rest are to be said at Vespers. And as this leaves three psalms too few, the aforementioned somewhat longer ones should be divided: namely, Psalms 139, 144, and 145. But because Psalm 117 is short, it should be joined to Psalm 116. The order of psalms for Vespers having been dealt with, the rest - that is the lesson, responsory, hymn, versicle and canticle - are arranged as above.

At Compline the same psalms, that is 4, 91, and 134, are said each day.

The order for psalmody at the day hours now being arranged, all the remaining psalms are to be equally distributed among the seven nocturnal Vigils by dividing the longer psalms into two, and assigning twelve to each night.

Above all we recommend that if this arrangement of the psalms is displeasing to anyone, he should, if he thinks fit, arrange it otherwise; taking care especially that the whole psalter of 150 psalms is recited every week and always begins anew at Vigils of Sunday. For those monks show themselves lacking in devotion for their service who say less than the entire psalter in the course of a week with the usual canticles. For we read that our holy Fathers resolutely performed in a single day what we, lukewarm as we are, may achieve in a whole week.

Comment: Is there a theological reason for the distribution of the psalms, with certain themes recurring on certain days and hours? Some commentators think so, and perhaps indeed, Benedict had such in mind. In any case, he has clearly given careful thought to the distribution of the psalms among the offices, obviously taking into account those usual matters of his concern, such as length and uniformity and ease in the daily offices.

A question that perhaps occurs to the reader is, why the psalter at all? Many have wondered what the devotional significance of the psalms is, for Christians. As indicated previously in this segment of reflections, the richness of the psalter as a devotional framework seems to emerge over time spent praying it. The psalms are a precis of the Old Testament: they give Christian faith its roots in the history of God's covenant relationship with the beloved people. And they are written in utterly human and personal terms, revealing the intense range of emotion involved in this intimate relationship. When prayed, they draw the worshipper into God's own life of loving communion. Regular prayer in the psalms is one main source of that humility which can allow Benedict to say of his careful crafting here: let one who sees a better way freely choose that option!

The psalms are both God's word to the people and the people's prayer to God. And notice, Benedict here calls the psalms the monk's zealous service to the Holy One. This is the work of God, to which nothing is to be preferred (RB 43:3).

Reflection: I am aware that this detailed instruction is not obsolete advice, merely of academic interest, for my own prayer book lists the daily evening psalms for Compline as 4, 91, and 134! It often occurs to me that not only we Christians daily pray in the psalms, but so did Jesus in his life at Nazareth, and his Jewish disciples their whole lives long. The psalms were so deeply ingrained in Jesus' own human consciousness that he found in them the language of his own temptations in the desert (Luke 4:10-11, Psalm 91) and the language of his own despair/comfort on the cross (Matt 27:46, Psalm 22). How connected to God and God's people do these prayers make me feel!

Prayer/Response:

Chapter 19: The Discipline of Singing Psalms (entire)

e believe that the Divine Presence is everywhere, and *that the eyes of the Lord behold the good and the evil in every place* (Prov 15:3). Especially do we believe this, without any doubt, when we are assisting at the Divine Office.

Let us, then, ever remember what the prophet says: *Serve the Lord in fear* (Ps 2:11), and again, *Sing wisely* (Ps 47:8); and, *In the presence of the angels I will sing praise to you* (Ps 138:1. Therefore let us consider how we ought to behave in the presence of God and of His angels, and so assist at the Divine Office that mind and voice be in harmony.

Comment: This simple chapter may well be the most important one in the Rule: certainly it is a keystone to all the rest, for here Benedict deals explicitly with the key disposition of the Christian life, which monastic practice is designed to develop and deepen. "God's omnipresence is not just an idea: it is a habit that calls for cultivation."[59] The habitual awareness of and responsiveness to God's presence is a very deep attitude of mind and heart, a disposition, which might be described as a vivid, integrated knowing of who God is and who we are in relation to God in this moment. The word "discipline" in the title of the chapter is a clear call to cultivate this particular habit or disposition.[60]

Very likely this chapter and the next are meant to be read in tandem as a supplement or summary to the ordering of offices presented in the preceeding chapters. "Singing Psalms" (Chapter 19) is about listening to the word of God in Scripture and the psalms; "Prayer" (Chapter 20) is about the subsequent silence in which the word percolates into the heart. All this liturgical code intends that each office contain the rhythm of psalmody and prayer, of listening and silent response. Of course, such an inherent rhythm is typical not only of the ancient monastic office, but also of the entire art of *lectio*, which we are imitating in our process with this text.

In this chapter, it is no accident that the flow of ideas are directly parallel to those in the first degree of humility (RB Chapter 7, verses 10f).[61] The Christian's essential awareness begins with the fear of God, an awed silence in the face of power and mystery utterly beyond comprehension. Gradually this awareness permeates into every segment of one's being--and astonishingly enough, bears fruit in praise. This is fundamental not only to the divine office, but also to the whole of the Christian life.

Reflection: The phrase that touches me is "let us consider how we ought to behave in the presence of God". What an astonishing idea. I hardly even know how to begin.

To start with, I believe that in fact God is with me here and now. Certainly I believe that when I pray, or I wouldn't be praying. But the question is, does it make any difference to my behavior that I think God is here? Well, yes; but on the other hand, no. The truth is, I guess, that I forget. I forget that God is here. But even more, I forget who God is. Occasionally, I am overwhelmed by an acute sense of who God is -- when I take time to breathe in a sunset, or when I ponder the astonishing world of the stars or the microbes. And even less occasionally, I think about who I am in relation to One who could be Creator of all that. It is sometimes humiliating and sometimes comforting; in comparison to That One, I might as well be an ant. Yet everything in the tradition invites me to be aware that I am a beloved ant!

The psalms are wonderful grist for this mill of reflection. They emphasize over and over (in the language of their times) who God is and what the human is by comparison. And they never forget that there is an essential relation between us. The daily morning psalm (95) is one of the best for a reminder of all that.

Generally, I only glimpse this mystery, and then I back away, for it is well beyond my ability to conceive in its fullness. Yet as I pray the prayers of God's people, over and over in daily sequence, my heart begins to understand and rejoice in the truth of that relationship, that loving, which comes against all probability to the "odd couple" of God and me.

Prayer/Response:

Chapter 20, On Reverence in Prayer (entire)

If, when we wish to make any request to those in power, we presume not to do so except with humility and reverence; how much more ought we with all humility and purity of devotion to offer our supplications to the Lord God of all things? And let us remember that we shall be heard, not for our much speaking, but for our purity of heart and tears of compunction. Therefore prayer ought to be short and pure, except when it is occasionally prolonged by the inspiration of divine grace. But let prayer made in common always be short: and at the signal given by the superior, let all rise together.

Comment: This is one of two whole chapters in the Rule explicitly devoted to the subject of personal prayer (Chapter 52 is the other), and these two provide the only direct comments Benedict makes on the matter. As might be expected, there have arisen elaborate discussions on the meaning of these few short verses. One common argument is that Benedict does not really "approve" of personal prayer apart from the office, since this chapter is clearly connected with the liturgical code. Others argue about whether these comments are simply appeals to common sense, or instead are specific technical terminology based in Cassian's work.[62]

Several points seem central. The desire to make distinctions (like those raised here) is a modern Western phenomenon which would have seemed quite foreign to Benedict's thought. Of course, there exist both corporate and personal prayer in the monastic community; how could one exist without the supplement of the other?! Of course, this language is both technical, as used in Cassian et al, and common sense; after all, is not the deepest wisdom of the truly prayerful grounded in common sense?!

The fear of presumption is also an idea which eludes the modern mind. In ordinary 20th Century America, "our basic rights" are so fundamentally engrained that we tend to ask favors assertively, as if we deserved them, and had been robbed of them by cruel and unjust oppressors. This is, no doubt, one of the main reasons why our prayer is seldom accompanied by tears; tears suggest not only that we do not deserve that for which we long, but that it has been given abundantly even so!

Purity of heart is the essential characteristic of prayer, as Benedict understands it. Of course, no human heart is truly pure, but that is the goal for which we aim. A good synonym for purity of heart is singleness of eye, that is, focus on the one thing necessary. Pure prayer is directed toward God, undistracted by competing claims. Indeed, such prayer belongs to God, for it is made possible by the inspiration of divine grace. This brief, pure moment of prayer is what the long hours of waiting, preparation and listening (which we call prayer) are attuned toward--the moment of exchange from God's heart to ours, comforting, inspiring, and enabling.[63]

Reflection: More and more do I feel myself drawn to prayer, and yet less and less do I have any idea what prayer is. How well I know the dangers of self-righteousness, simply because my need for prayer grows stronger! How well I know the dangers of presumption, simply because God's nearness to me sometimes blurs my awareness of what Utter Being is! But--praise God--beyond and through all that do, I know primarily the song of my soul: that God claims me, and teaches me who I am.

Prayer/Response:

Interlude IV:

A Note to the Reader....

Are you feeling more at ease with your pattern of daily *lectio*?

Perhaps it goes in fits and starts, some days easily, some days with great difficulty, if at all. Perhaps it goes fine when you can get to it, but you're finding it hard to get the time. Perhaps even when you do sit down, your mind races and you are unable to release the many things you are trying to juggle.

There are a few practical tips that are a great help to effective *lectio*. They have to do with "stopping". Let me start with an analogy. Here in Southern California, we are very much oriented toward the freeways. When we come on to the freeway from an on-ramp, we are gaining speed on the on-ramp, so that we can merge into the stream of freeway traffic at its full speed of 55 mph. It was quite a revelation to me to try driving the expressways in our East Coast, where the pattern is to come to a full stop at the entrances, look carefully for traffic, and only then pull out slowly onto the expressway lane.

That image provides a helpful analogy to any process of meditation, reflection, or prayer. Often we busy moderns think that we can enter a time of meditation just like Southern Californians enter the freeway--at full speed, without any real period of transition. The truth is that in meditation such nonstop momentum is counterproductive.

Because what we are hoping for in *lectio* is true dialogue with the Word, an essential component is relaxed waiting for the Other. There must be a transition from busyness, a fundamental shift in the mode of our presence. That's why the simple instructions we all know are so important to follow.

Find a quiet place and time, when you won't be interrupted for 15 minutes to an hour, depending on your preference. Sit comfortably but alert, and shake out any tension or discomfort in your body. Breathe deeply about three times. Give yourself permission to release any preoccupations or worries for this few minutes, coming back to them later if you need to, but giving them up for now. Be aware consciously if you can that you are not alone, but in the presence of the living God. Then turn to your *lectio*. And when you are finished, take some time to make the transition back.

As Christians, we inherit the astonishing tradition of the sabbath: a time to withdraw, to rest, to marvel and to praise. At the heart of sabbath is the concept that we can leave our important work to God, at least for a few moments, in order simply to be with God for worship and refreshment. This is, of course, what the Benedictines are doing in the daily office. This is, of course, what we are doing in our *lectio*.

Disciplines of Community

Chapter 21: The Deans of the Monastery (entire)

If the community is large, let there be chosen from it certain brethren of good repute and holy life to be appointed deans. Let them carefully direct their deaneries in all things according to the commandments of God and the orders of their Abbot. And let such men be chosen deans as the Abbot may safely trust to share his burdens: let them not be chosen according to order, but for the merit of their lives, for their learning and wisdom.

And should any one of them, being puffed up with pride, be found worthy of blame, and after being thrice corrected, refuse to amend, let him be deposed and one put in his place who is worthy. And we order the same to be done in the case of the Prior.

Comment: A strategy for small groups in the time of Benedict! Should that surprise us really? For one concerned as Benedict was with deep integration of the life of faith, and one as sensitive to actual human development, it must have been clear that individual monks were far more likely to develop fruitfully if they had a keen sense of belonging, and a fellowship in which they were specially valued.

The word "dean" literally means one in charge of a group of ten (*decanus*=dean/*decania*=group of ten). The idea is rooted in Moses' decision to establish the smallest units of ten persons for the Israelites wandering in the desert (Exodus 18:13-17; Deut 1:9-18), as well as the early Christian church's decision to have special servants of the people (Acts 6:3). This deanery group was a common practice in early monasteries.[64] As the Scriptural sources suggest, the deans are both responsible for the care of those in their group, and for obedience to the abbot, as God's representative.

The dean's own life must be an example of the monastic ideal: the language Benedict uses for "holy life" is *sanctae conversationis*. "Conversatione" is the third monastic vow, which we can approximately translate "ongoing conversion of heart", or the monastic life in capsule. The reason why pride is such a grave failing in a dean is that it reveals him to be centered in his ego rather than Christ. And yet Benedict is well aware that promotion is a frequent stimulus of pride.

Why is this chapter here? The section on the daily office was offered as a bridge between the theological framework and the concrete realities of daily life in the monastery. This unit begins the daily life section with discussions about the discipline of living together with others. Living together, community life, is for Benedict a fundamental aspect of Christian formation. It is both rigorous and fruitful for our spiritual maturation, if we allow it to be so. For the asceticism of community is a marvelous harness on pride. Community speaks of membership in one another; pride speaks of being separate. Community speaks of the importance of participation; pride of the importance of self-sufficiency. Community speaks of the way in which our weaknesses can be remedied by the strengths of others, even as we offer our strengths toward others' care; pride speaks of "flying" alone. We shall see that the principal punishment of the Rule is to subject a monk to the absence of community: excommunication.

Reflection: How do we move from longing to be faithful to God, through prayer, to living a virtuous life? My own experience certainly confirms what I believe to be Benedict's hunch: I more readily make that transition as I belong to and have the support and accountability of a few other Christians who really care about me. The last few years I have been meeting regularly with a very small group of friends, and we are helping each other to clarify concretely: what is Christ asking me to do in my life circumstances today? We love each other and pray for each other, and we also are risking to help each other think about and respond to the opportunities our life holds for us to be more faithful Christians. I have found blind spots in my own perceptions revealed. I am called to account for my own life in a way never before experienced. Occasionally I am willing to take a step toward Christ in a specific situation, that I don't think I would have had wisdom or courage to do, without them. And remarkable fruits blossom.

Prayer/Response:

Chapter 22: How the Monks are to Sleep

Let them sleep each one in a separate bed, receiving bedding suitable to their manner of life, as the Abbot shall appoint. If it is possible, let all sleep in one place; but if their number does not permit this, let them sleep by tens or twenties with the seniors who have charge of them. Let a candle burn constantly in the room until morning.

Let them sleep clothed, and girded with belts or cords (but not with knives at their sides, lest perchance they wound themselves in their sleep) and thus be always ready; so that when the signal is given they rise without delay, and compete with each to the other in hastening to the Work of God, yet with all gravity and modesty. The younger brethren should not have their beds by themselves, but among those of the seniors. And when they rise for the Work of God let them gently encourage one another, on account of the excuses which the drowsy tend to make.

Comment: This subject matter seems more suited to "domestic arrangements" than community disciplines. In fact, this chapter is a kind of disciplinary measure, although Benedict treats it with great tenderness, in part by juxtaposing it to a reminder of the great vocation to which we are called by our liturgical prayer. Indeed, the office is explicitly mentioned here twice, for the monks arise from sleep about 2am to go directly to the office.

What is the discipline here imposed? For the 4th Century Egyptian monks, the private cell was the principal place of prayer, a sort of private oratory. And by the 12th Century, the monastic cell had been re-introduced. However, in the beginning of the sixth century, the private cell was abolished in favor of the dormitory as the norm, as a move to remedy the abuses of the private cell. Benedict adopted the practice current in his time, that of the dormitory. The discipline of the dormitory is designed to forestall occasional temptations to abuse of a private space. No doubt the special practices Benedict introduces, such as the watch of the seniors and the burning candle, are also instituted to insure "elementary good morals".[65]

Yet there is a wonderful integration of motives in these disciplinary measures. It is clear from the tone that even here Benedict has the greatest tenderness toward his monks. His tenderness reminds us that the night is the time of great danger, for which we yet pray daily for deliverance from the "shadow of death".[66] Night carries with it many temptations and the power of the evil one; night is the symbol of death, and daybreak always brings the renewed joy of resurrection. All these arrangements of discipline are thus also arrangements of care-giving, just as with God. The living power of the paschal mystery becomes nightly present to each monk, as the community together embarks upon the trust of sleep.

Reflection: Tenderness is so difficult for me to accept and live out, especially when it is juxtaposed to danger and to fear, not to mention when it is juxtaposed to "backsliding"! What a model Benedict is for me in his constant, loving care for souls. He is so "at home" with human weakness, just as he is with the call to each one to share the divine life. He really does never lose hope in God's mercy, or God's power to transform.

So often I have considered people who always see the good, the redemptive, as innocent and unrealistic. Yet Benedict helps me see that is a "put-down" not only of them, but also of myself. Benedict has a profound realism (in many ways, he is "unshockable"); yet that only deepens his faith and conviction in the living and active power of God.

Prayer/Response:

Chapter 23: Excommunication for Faults (entire)

If any brother shall be found obstinate, or disobedient, or proud, or a murmurer, or in any way despises the Holy Rule and the orders of his seniors, let him, according to Our Lord's commandment, be once or twice privately admonished by his seniors (Matt 18:15-16). If he does not amend, let him be rebuked in public before all. But if even then he does not correct himself, let him be subjected to excommunication, provided that he understand the nature of the punishment. Should he, however, prove unable to understand it, let him undergo corporal chastisement.

Comment: The so-called "Penal Code" of Benedict comprises Chapters 23-30 and 43-46 of the Rule, and there is some controversy in modern scholarly circles about whether it has much "spiritual profit" for the contemporary reader, particularly as it does specify corporal punishment.[67] So, we must give careful attention to these chapters to inquire what they offer us.

The organization here is to place these chapters within the category of "Disciplines of Community", because as previously suggested, the fundamental punishment is exclusion from the community. This chapter emphasizes three elements of the discipline of community, of which we shall see more as we continue. First, the title. Second, a listing of behavior viewed as "faults". And third, a graded series of punishments.

The title of the chapter calls our attention to excommunication, that is separation from the community, as the key to the Rule's punishments. The motives for this seem to include both the practical and the spiritual. Practically there must be enforced some order and common behavior if the monastic community is to preserve itself from dissolution.[68] Spiritually, the model of Christian life which undergirds the monastery is the community of the Acts of the Apostles.[69]

Benedict's community is rooted in the conviction that we learn to be Christians precisely in the normal daily interactions which constitute the community. Thus, his list of faults which includes utterly ordinary behaviors--obstinacy, murmuring, and pride--suggests that a fault is not simply an offense against others, but also a serious impediment to one's own spiritual growth. The two aspects are merely different sides of the same issue. And the penalty of excommunication is simply an enforcement of the separation which the monk has already asserted by his behavior.

The range of punishments is provided to enable the monk to understand and take responsibility for his actions, repent, and return to health. Benedict realizes both that it takes maturity to recognize the seriousness of these faults against the community, and also that we do not always act on what we know. Thus, various punishments are to be applied depending on appropriateness and need, and centered in the Matthean Gospel warning of wrath and promise of forgiveness. (Chapter 18: 7-9, 21-2).

Reflection: During Lent this year, I asked my pastor to help me forgive the wound administered by a "friend" about which I felt only anger. Fortunately, he is a wise and compassionate man who helped me look at why I needed to hold onto my anger. Thus began a somewhat painful but gradually liberating journey. For I discovered that beneath the anger, indeed beneath the wound, was the truth that I was insisting on being "my own person". My pride was a way of hiding from myself no less than others my active need to be held in another's caring love. What I could not do for myself, I refused to admit I needed. And the natural consequence of that pride was to exclude me from experiences of deep friendship. Pride does prevent me from being open to love. Thus indirectly the wound was the gift of a merciful God who aches for me to know more fully how much I am loved -- a reality obscured by my preference for self-sufficiency.

Prayer/Response:

Chapter 24, On the Degrees of Excommunication (entire)

The measure of excommunication or chastisement should correspond to the gravity of the offence, the estimation of which shall be left to the judgment of the Abbot. If any brother be found guilty of lighter faults let him be excluded only from the common table.

And this shall be the rule for one deprived of the fellowship of the table: he shall intone neither psalm nor antiphon in the oratory, nor shall he read a lesson, until he has made satisfaction. Let him take his meals alone, after those of the brethren, in the measure and at the time that the Abbot shall think best for him. Thus, for example, if the brethren eat at the sixth hour, let him eat at the ninth; if they eat at the ninth, let him eat in the evening, until by proper satisfaction he obtains pardon.

Comment: It is evident that Benedict has carefully sought to let the punishment correspond to the fault -- not only in amount, but also in kind. As noted before, the offender who has in essence rejected the community life by violating its rules is propelled further in the direction of his own willfulness, that he might see its natural consequences; that is, he is excluded from the community life even more.

Perhaps at first we are suprised that Benedict speaks of faults in prayer in the same breath as faults at meals. Obviously, Benedict highly values the shared mealtime. The physical meal that the monks share is a common symbol of the life of Christ, shared mystically in the Eucharist and ordinarily in all the common events of the day. Thus it is natural that one who does not participate fully in the mealtime, likewise does not participate fully in the prayer time. Notice carefully: it is the community life from which the offender is removed, not the food. He does eat and is not required to fast from physical nourishment. It is the human warmth from which he is removed, the nourishment given in the koinonia (community).

Reflection: How seldom am I attentive to the nourishment I actually receive from being with those with whom I am obliged to interact each day. I may enjoy or not any specific interaction -- feel it as pleasurable or useful or not. But rarely do I acknowledge that I am fed by it, made whole and given vitality by it.

How often does my self-will see others as feeding me insofar as they co-operate with or at least do not interfere with my plans and hopes. Insofar as I can possess or manage others, I see them as contributors to my self-enhancement.

But to appreciate and be grateful for their gift to my being simply because they are -- when they are complete strangers, or opponents, or indifferent -- simply because they exist and have been given to me and I to them! To recognize that they are ear and I am nose; both of us essential to the Body of Christ! To see that I am complete and whole only in the presence of the fullness of their being! To allow myself to be changed by others in ways I do not expect!

What a challenge. And what an awesome possibility!

Prayer/Response:

Chapter 25: Serious Faults (entire)
And Chapter 26: Those Who, Without Permission, Associate with the Excommunicated (entire)

Let that brother who is found guilty of a more grievous offence be excluded both from the table and from the oratory. Let none of the brethren associate with him or speak to him. Let him be alone at the work enjoined him, and continue in sorrow of penance, remembering that dreadful sentence of the Apostle: *That such a one is delivered over to Satan for the destruction of the flesh, that his spirit may be saved in the day of the Lord* (1 Cor 5:5). Let him take his portion of food alone, in the measure and at the time that the Abbot shall think best for him. Let none of those who pass by bless him, nor let the food that is given him be blessed.

(Chapter 26) If any brother presumes without the Abbot's permission to associate with an excommunicated brother, or to speak with him, or to send him a message, let him incur the same punishment of excommunication.

Comment: The one who defaults on his or her commitment to the community is reduced to being alone. He or she is allowed fully to enter this separation, to endure it and to drink it to the full. Perhaps Benedict is here echoing Psalm 129, which also presents a refusal even to be blessed by those who pass by, set in the context of the ascent to Jerusalem and the folly of refusal to fear God.

If we ponder deeply the quotation from Corinthians and other such statements of St. Paul, as Benedict clearly has done,[70] what do we make of it? There is a profound concern for lack of faithfulness in the context of God's proffered covenant of love. It is not lack of "belief"; rather it is behavior inconsistent with belief: an assertion of self-will as against that of God and God's community. Such behavior by its nature keeps one away from salvation. There are clear echoes here from the Sermon on the Mount: better to tear out and throw away the offending part, be it the person's body, or the person from the body, if it comes to that. (Matt 5:29-30)

Benedict believes that the choice for or against salvation is real, and that it is made in the context of behaviors for and against membership in the community of faith. The danger of choosing "against" is very great; it is like a viral attack that is very infectious. The offending and diseased part must be burned and cast out. But all this is for the sake of healing and ultimate wholeness.[71]

Reflection: It is hard to take this seriously. So much of my cultural upbringing not only finds self-will a fairly innocent disease; it actually often applauds it. A deadly virus that will keep me dead for all eternity? It's difficult to believe.

And that is true not only for myself but for others. When someone is suffering the consequences of self-will, instead of letting them taste them in full, I am always tempted to intervene and offer "comfort". Tough love is a hard learning, as all of us who have lived with alcoholics and other compulsives have discovered.

But, there is a part of me that experiences the truth of this conviction of Benedict's. Just yesterday I was talking with a friend about those moments when I see clearly that God is calling out to me with love, and I am deliberately slamming doors in God's face, so to speak. I can feel it in myself, when I am resisting the divine invitation with all my aggressive energy. Who knows why I do it? For fear I will lose control or be asked to do something I don't like? For fear of becoming too close to that "refining fire" that is God's love, and having to give up some identity I feel is essential to me? Whatever it is, it is an assertion of self-will, and there are moments when I weep for my own hardness of heart.

Prayer/Response:

Chapter 27: The Abbot's Care for the Excommunicated (entire)

Let the Abbot with all tenderness take care of offending brethren, for *those who are healthy do not need a physician, but those who are sick* (Matt 9:12). To this end he ought to behave in every way as a wise physician, sending *senpectae* to sympathize with him. That is to say, some brethren of mature years and wisdom may, as it were secretly, console the wavering brother, induce him to make humble satisfaction, and *comfort* him, *that he not be overwhelmed by excessive sorrow* (2 Cor 2:7); rather, as the Apostle says, *Let love be strengthened towards him* (2 Cor 2:8), and let all pray for him

For the Abbot is bound to use the greatest care with erring brethren, and to strive with all possible prudence and zeal not to lose any one of the sheep committed to him. He must know that he has undertaken responsibility for weak souls, not tyranny over the strong; and let him fear the warning of the prophet, where God says: *What you saw to be fat you took youselves, and what was diseased you cast away* (Ezek 34:3-4). Let him imitate the loving example of the Good Shepherd, who, leaving the ninety-nine sheep on the mountains, went to seek one which had gone astray; on whose weakness He had such compassion that *He* chose to *lay it on His* own sacred *shoulders* and thus bring it back to the flock (Luke 15:5).

Comment: Physician and shepherd! Here as in Chapter 2, Benedict uses these key metaphors to describe the quality of governance essential for Christian community.

It is important to consider the tone of this chapter in relation to the concerns of the previous two chapters. There Benedict turns our attention to the virulent disease of sin and the attacks of Satan which confront Christians as they live out their journey. Even in this chapter that reality appears as a factor in the abbot's life (Ezekiel quotation).

But Benedict does not use this awareness as an excuse to become hysterical or rigid. Indeed, he sees it as the sure sign of the necessity for even greater loving kindness, openness, and humble dependence upon God's Spirit. We noted previously the twin temptations of the consecrated life as being both pride and despair.[72] In this chapter Benedict assures that the abbot will be sensitive to both sorts of temptations, as well as discerning in his application of remedies. The attitude of the abbot is always to be that of "a good shepherd or physician, who is not shocked or dismayed by sickness, but challenged by it".[73]

The terms care, compassion, love infuse this chapter. It suggests a whole way of being which involves gentle firmness and health-giving care. In the Latin, the prose here has the rhythmic and beautiful cadences typical of the liturgical formulas of the Roman office.[74] In this chapter as in Chapter 20, Benedict's deep prayer informs and infuses the word as well as spirit of the Rule, for the task of disciplinary health-giving is one above all in which the abbot is dependent upon co-creative grace. Therefore, let all pray.

Reflection: I believe this model of care could fruitfully be applied to my peer relationships with others, and also to my attitude to my own "sickness". I suspect I am least gentle to myself of all, least accepting of my own limitations and sinfulness. Yet to accept them in a way which involves hope and wholeness is the "trick"!

One of the regular matters I ponder is how reconciliation comes about in our world. Our catechism states that it is the baptized Christian's main ministry to join Christ's work of reconciliation in the world, and I remember being utterly dumbfounded when I once heard someone say that reconciliation is needed only where there is brokenness. I always thought of reconciliation as the "after" state, rather than as the "potential" state. So brokenness, weakness, and sin are actually boundless opportunities for reconciliation. I think this is how Benedict sees "waywardness"--as a moment of special opportunity for wholeness.

Sometimes I try to remind myself in moments or circumstances of brokenness that Christ is present, longing to be released by a cry for help. One time in the frantic setting at the Los Angeles airport, when my husband Doug and I were both very anxious and angry, it suddenly occurred to me that this was a place badly in need of reconciliation. So I slipped over to Doug and whispered, "Breathe!" He looked at me and we both laughed and the next half hour was easier to bear!

Prayer/Response:

Chapter 28: Those Who Do Not Amend after Frequent Correction (entire)

If any brother who has been frequently corrected for some fault, or even excommunicated, does not amend, let a more severe chastisement be applied: that is, let the punishment of the rod be administered to him. But if even then he does not correct himself, or perchance (which God forbid!), puffed up with pride, he even wishes to defend his deeds, then let the Abbot act like a wise physician. If he has applied bandages and the ointment of his admonitions, the medicine of the Holy Scriptures, and at last the cautery of excommunication or corporal chastisement, and if he see that his labors are of no avail, let him add what is still more powerful - his own prayers and those of all the brethren for him, that God who is can do all things may accomplish the cure of the sick brother. But if he is not healed even by this means, then the Abbot may ultimately use the sword of separation, as the Apostle says: *Put away the evil one from you* (1 Cor 5:13). And again: *If the faithless one depart, let him depart* (1 Cor 7:15), lest one diseased sheep should infect the whole flock.

Comment: One is reminded here of John 6:60: "This is intolerable language. How could anyone accept it?" It is one of Benedict's strengths that he can look intently at the Day of Judgment, and speak gently but firmly of its requirements. Here again, he joins St. Paul in asking difficult questions about the relationship of faith and behavior: how real is our faith when tested against how we actually live?

In Latin, the close relationship of the words health (salus) and salvation (salutare) is more evident than in English. Benedict's "Penal Code" is utterly oriented toward salvation; it has none of the vindictiveness and formalism often found in other Rules of the period.[75] His foremost concern is for measures which will draw the offender into repentance and thus into health and salvation. He is not interested in measures which induce defensiveness, pride, or a spirit of rebellion.

This is why his penultimate remedy is simply the power of prayer. The phrase in verse 5, "God who can do all things," is probably a reference to Matt 18:26, where the servant who cannot pay is forgiven his debt[76]. Again and again, Benedict relies on his keen awareness that salvation is not possible to anyone, save for the fact that we may always trust in the mercy of God (RB 4:74).

But, finally, it is the choice of each one whether he or she will accept to be indebted to this mercy. And the one who persistently refuses must at last be separated, as they continue to insist they already are.

Reflection: Refusal of the divine invitation... At first it seems totally improbable that anyone would choose to do so. Yet upon deeper reflection, which Benedict invites in this whole section, I realize the many ways in which I do so refuse each day. I feel that Benedict has invited me to ponder on those specifics and offer them up to God as fully as I can. But I am also aware of another underlying dimension of refusal which is implicit here: I can refuse God by refusing my sisters and brothers. That is, it is not just a question of allowing my life to be interpenetrated by God's life. It is also a matter of allowing my life to belong to the community of persons I am given. I learn about, and receive, God in the here and now.

Both are so hard for me. How deeply ingrained in me is the desire to "be my own person", to work out my own salvation! I also deeply desire to belong, but it takes training and practice for me to learn how to live that out. I see that at least one of the things the community is, is a place to be trained and to practice this way of belonging. The community provides rules and boundaries against which I can break off some of my sharp edges (or they are broken off!). And it provides authentic models, which is one of the best gifts Benedict gives me. It's hard work, but I think good work. I feel better, more whole, when I give myself to it.

Prayer/Response:

Chapter 29: Whether Brothers who Leave the Monastery May be Readmitted

If any brother, who through his own fault departs or is cast out of the monastery, is willing to return, let him first promise complete amendment of the fault for which he left. Then let him be received back into the lowest place, so that his humility may thus be tried. Should he again depart, let him be taken back up to the third time. But let him know that after this all way of return is denied him.

Comment: There is a quality to this paragraph much like that of Jesus' instruction about how many times one must forgive another (Matt 18:21-2). Again and again the community is to welcome back the one who has rejected them by turning away. (This is also characteristic of a family, is it not?) True, the one returning must make amends and show willingness to grow in humility, but these are prudent safeguards of the authentic repentance of the returnee. The essential matter is that the monk is to be forgiven and welcomed home in all charity.

This requirement is surely a practical consequence of Benedict's conviction about the nature of the Kingdom of God. It suggests that (1) God is a wildly extravagant lover; (2) our response to that love is the matter of eternal salvation, the essential matter of our lives; and (3) individual response is most fully lived out in the context of Christian community. True community exists always and only within this matrix of salvation and forgiveness/mercy.

Reflection: Today my emotional response to this passage is centered in the costliness for the community of the required openness. (On other days, it might be more along the lines of the grief and joy of the one who finds oneself blessedly re-united.) When I live with someone, whether I "like" her or not, part of me inevitably grows in intimacy with her. Thus, when and if she is pulled away from me, it is an enormous, wrenching pain. That is especially true if it is because she deliberately turned her back on my values and chose a different path. Even when I can accept this intellectually, the hurt in my heart throbs. To welcome such a one home willingly and fully involves opening myself in vulnerability to her, risking restoration of the lost intimacy. I may be able to do that once, but again and again?! I do not have the necessary resources.

It is an issue that occurs with acting-out children, stubborn parents, and unfaithful spouses. Again and again in every life, we are given the opportunity to risk this restoration. And, as one who has been hurt in this way, I am aware that the risk is involved not only in the same relationship, but also in the next one. Will I ever trust anyone again with my most tender feelings? It also occurs over and over again even in a good relationship: dare I trust/love this person one bit more?!

As I understand it, Benedict's insistence on this welcome (this openness where there has been a wound, this risk where there is vulnerability) is a profound affirmation of the power of love. I may not have the necessary resources, but God does, offering them to me generously for my use and in my need.

Prayer/Response:

Chapter 30: The Manner of Reproving Boys (entire)

Every age and understanding should receive what is appropriate to it. As often, therefore, as boys, or those under age, or those who cannot fully understand the greatness of the penalty of excommunication, commit faults, let them be punished by severe fasting or sharp strokes, in order that they may be cured.

Comment: The 59th Chapter of the Rule (below) makes clear that boys may be offered "to God in the monastery" by their parents, and that this was a binding way of entering monastic life in Benedict's time.

In this chapter, Benedict is concerned about how to discipline these and other members of the monastic community whose maturity is insufficient for reasoned communication to bring their souls to repentance. As always, the goal is health and salvation. Reproof in the Christian community is always to lead to that goal. Thus, it is to be "appropriate", that is, specially designed to produce positive response in the one receiving it (not simply the habitual temperamental preference of the one administering it).

Benedict acknowledges that the developmental stage of some persons is such that physical punishment is the most effective remedy.[77] Even so, he stops short of actions called for by other rules in his time, such as whipping and severe beating.[78] And his whole goal in this entire section is the gradual drawing of every member of the community into that keen awareness of deepest regard for this ordinary Christian gathering as Christ's Body.

Reflection: Some time ago a professor of mine asked the members of a class whether we would prefer to be physically ill or mentally ill, if we had to choose. By far the majority of us, myself included, chose physical illness. And yet, both he and we understood at once that most of us moderns "go overboard" to care for our physical health, but are very lazy, independent, and undisciplined about our mental health. And, of course, if we add our soul's health to the comparison, it probably would come in last in terms of actual disciplined care and attention.

What am I prepared to do for a healthy soul in this life and the next? How seriously am I willing to discipline my body, mind, and spirit when I know that would be helpful for my maturity in Christ? How fully do I understand such concerns to be lived out in the traditions and daily practices of my community of faith? And how can I help those around me to learn to appreciate these life-giving practices? Benedict's guidance on community discipline forces me to wonder about all this, as I live into it day by day.

Prayer/Response:

Interlude V:

a note to the reader...

Are you feeling sometimes "stuck", during your *lectio*?

Perhaps occasionally your experience is like a dog chasing its tail: you seem to go around and around the same issues, not getting anywhere. Perhaps you wonder once in a while if you're not walking through quicksand: you've raised a lot of sticky stuff, but you're not sure whether it's got you, or you've got it. Or perhaps you just wonder if you're on the right track, and would like some feedback.

You have undertaken a regular process of reflection on your life experience in light of the Gospel (via the Rule). It is a powerful process and it's not unusual to feel the need to share it with someone else. There is a need for some feedback and new insight: Am I being honest with myself? Am I dwelling on one issue too long or not taking enough time with something else? Am I really being faithful to God in all this? How can I know?

A spiritual director is a friend who is committed to help you listen carefully for God's voice in your experience. Usually, the director is a person acquainted with the Christian traditions of prayer and discernment, who has some feel for the normal patterns in an evolving relationship with God, and who thus can help you assess your present situation in that context.

We often think that what a director will help us with primarily is the matter of accountability. It seems so easy to delude ourselves about our motives and our behavior, that we seek a director to "keep us honest". But my experience is that far more often the director's role is to remind me of how greatly I am loved. I am far more likely to forget my value than my sins.

How do we find a director? We may neglect the obvious first step: be a part of a Christian community, a place where like-minded people come together in worship, praise, and thanksgiving. Many cities have special spiritual centers or retreat houses you might contact. Having taken such steps, then keep your eyes open. Let God know you desire a guide, and watch with expectancy. Keep praying. When you discover someone whom you respect, tell them what you seek, and ask if they will join you in listening for the Spirit in your life.

What do we say to a director? We talk about our life, our experiences, our reflections, our longings. We talk about who God is for us, and who we are for God, much as we are doing in these daily *lectio* meditations. And then we listen together. When two are gathered in Christ's name, the Spirit is in their midst.

Domestic Arrangements

Chapter 31: The Qualities of the Monastery Cellarer

verses 1-9

Let there be chosen from the community as Cellarer of the monastery, one who is wise and of mature character, temperate, not a great eater, not haughty, nor headstrong, nor offensive, not dilatory, nor wasteful, but God-fearing; one who may be like a father to the whole community. Let him have charge of everything, but do nothing without permission of the Abbot. Let him take heed to what is commanded him.

Let him not sadden his brethren. If a brother ask him for anything unreasonably, let (the Cellerar) not treat him with contempt and so grieve him, but reasonably and with all humility refuse what he unreasonably asks for. Let him be watchful over his own soul, remembering always that saying of the Apostle: *he who has ministered well purchases for himself a good standing* (1 Tim 3:13).

Let him have particular concern for the sick, for children, for guests, and for the poor, knowing without doubt that he will have to render an account of all these on the Day of Judgment.

Comment: Now begins that section of the Rule here termed "Domestic Arrangements", and elsewhere called "offices of service to the community".[79] "Cellarer" is a specifically monastic term, referring to the one responsible for the storeroom (*cellarium*). The job of cellarer includes a wide range of responsibilities we might call business management, meaning both the accounting and treasury functions as well as the management and distribution of needed goods.

The overall tone of this chapter is one of care, or stewardship. In a sense, Benedict here guides all those who deal with things, especially when they are in a position of authority. Such ones are to be God-fearing, above all, remembering that all goods are God's gifts. In the interactions by which goods are shared (again!) lies the matter of salvation. Especially is the cellarer to care tenderly for the weak and vulnerable, whenever possible seeing Christ in those who come needy to him, and treating them as if they themselves--the supplicants--were precious gifts of God, even when their requests are unreasonable.

All those in the monastic community who carry authority of any kind are to be persons of the most profound humility and devotion. This is indeed the mark of true authority. Good service, charity, and tender loving care: these are the signs that we are Jesus' disciples. (Matt 20:25-28) In Benedict's usual practical way, he shows that the best opportunity to practice these virtues is with an irate customer.

Reflection: I am struck by the interchangeability of the terms "domestic tasks", "business management", and "good service". One of the qualities of Benedict which often hits me like a bucket of cold water is the simple insistence on the opportunity to serve God right in the midst of my daily annoyances and interruptions. Sometimes it seems like it would be ever so much simpler to give my life as a martyr than to be sweet-tempered when my cat gets under my feet (again!) at just the moment everything on the stove is ready to be served up! On the other hand, as I begin seriously to consider the possibility that salvation can be fulfilled in such ordinary service, there arises a glimpse for harmony and wholeness in the context of my very situation which is breath-taking.

Prayer/Response:

Chapter 31, verses 10-19 (end)

He should look upon all the vessels and goods of the Monastery as though they were the consecrated vessels of the altar. Let him not think that he may neglect anything: let him not be given to greed, nor wastefulness, nor be a squanderer of the goods of the monastery; but let him do all things in proper measure, and according to the bidding of his Abbot. Let him above all things have humility; and to him on whom he has nothing else to bestow, let him give at least a kind explanation, as it is written: *A kind word is above the best gift* (Sir 18:17).

Let him have under his care all that the Abbot has entrusted to him, and not presume to meddle with what is forbidden him. Let him distribute to the brethren their appointed allowance of food, without arrogance or delay, that they may not be scandalized: mindful of what the Word of God declares he deserves who *scandalizes one of these little ones* (Matt 18:6).

If the community is large, let helpers be given to him, by whose aid he may with peace of mind discharge the office committed to him. Let necessary things be given and asked for at appropriate times, that no one may be troubled or grieved in the house of God.

Comment: Benedict is concerned here with stewardship, or how to serve God in caring for the material goods entrusted to us. Key phrases for this lesson are presented in the first and last sentences of this *lectio*: "consecrated vessels" and "house of God". Essentially, Benedict views these material goods as gifts given from God which have the potential for revealing God's glory. Like Zechariah, he proclaims that even the "horsebells will be inscribed with the words 'sacred to Yahweh'." (Zech 14:20-1) For one who learns to see the created order in this way, there arises naturally a humility, tenderness and wonder which informs all interactions.

And this vision is intended not only for inanimate objects, but also for humans. Even the brothers are sacraments of God, to be treated tenderly and with respect, as "little ones" precious to God and somehow revealing of God's nature. Notice that not only is each monk accountable for his own deepening humility, but also each is responsible not to stimulate or arouse the pride of one's brother or sister. For the life together is God's household, where all are to support and encourage the deepening holiness of each.

One thought especially valuable for us is that enough persons are to be assigned to do the necessary work that no one need be frantic or manic. Good stewardship calls for care of one's own body and spirit, and habitual recollection toward God's presence in the ordinary seeks a peaceful and spacious setting in which to flourish.

Reflection: I am touched by the contrast between Benedict's spirit and the spirit of the environment in which I normally find myself. In my environment, there is not much authentic mutual support and not much peace. But I wonder if that is always due to forces I cannot control. It is within my power to begin to behave in those ways myself, wherever I am placed, and to pray for the Spirit's strength and guidance as I do so. There is a possibility that such action would positively influence the environment I now have, which is after all God's gift to me.

It is also within my power to be more realistic about what actually does need to be done today, and to value more the contributions of whatever sort that come from my colleagues. These seem almost stupidly simple things to try, but why not?

Prayer/Response:

Chapter 32, The Tools and Possessions of the Monastery (entire)

The Abbot should appoint brethren on whose manner of life and character he can rely to responsibility for the tools, clothes, and other possessions of the monastery; and let him consign the various things to their care as he shall think fit, to be kept and to be collected after use. Of these let the Abbot keep a list, so that as the brethren are reassigned to different tasks, he may know what he gives out and what he receives back.

If anyone treats the possessions of the monastery in a slovenly or negligent manner, let him be corrected; and if he does not amend, let him be subjected to the discipline of the Rule.

Comment: One of the most remarkable qualities of the Rule is the ease with which Benedict shifts from the sacred to the mundane, which for him clearly form an integrated unity. In the previous chapter we noticed the obvious perspective that all material things are sacraments, transparent to the divine. Here there is no weakening of that theme (i.e., verse 2: "to be kept"; verse 4: "[not to] treat the possessions in a slovenly or negligent manner"), but it is juxtaposed firmly with the awareness of the temptation to greed which "things" often present. Here Benedict requires the keeping of careful records and appropriate locks, in much the same way we might say "Don't leave money clearly visible in a vacant car, lest you unnecessarily contribute to someone's downfall".

Probably Benedict is drawing on Sirach Chapter 42, which has a very similar juxtaposition of prudent calculation and wonder at the glory of creation. Yet again, this suggests the resonance of his own spirit to the capacity not to be shocked or dismayed by human sinfulness, while also not allowing it to be a diversion from divine goodness, eternally offered even and especially to the sinner.

Let us note in this context that the last two sentences are an indication of one of the "faults" for which monks become subject to the Rule's discipline. Such faults give insight into a fundamental basis for the disciplines of the Rule: to provide a salutary framework in which one can so practice the presence of the sacred that eventually it becomes deep inner disposition.

Reflection: Learning this disposition to respond to the sacramental in all things is not easy. I tend to alternate abruptly between carelessness and excessive care, forgetfulness and pride. The difficulty and the challenge is to practice a calm and patient willingness simultaneously to see both responses in myself, set within the context of God's constant presence. It is never easy for me to see that all (given exactly its condition and its limits) belongs to God.

I think it helps me greatly to have models. And isn't it interesting that when I notice someone treating something especially gently or lovingly, it is as if they abruptly brought me back "into myself". I mean that suddenly I am awakened to the presence of the sacred in that moment and in everything I see. And for a short time, I too live in the pleasure of that.

Prayer/Response:

Chapter 33: Whether Monks Ought to Own Anything (entire)

Above all let the vice of private ownership be cut out of the monastery by the roots. Let no one presume to give or receive anything without leave of the Abbot, or to keep anything as their own, either book or writing-tablet or pen, or anything at all; since they are permitted to have neither body nor will in their own power. Rather, let them trust that they will receive all that is necessary from the father of the monastery. Nor are they allowed to keep anything which the Abbot has not given or permitted. *Let all things be common* to all, as it is written, *nor let anyone say* or assume *that anything is his own* (Acts 4:32).

But if anyone is found who indulges in this most corrupt vice, and after one or two admonitions does not amend, let him be subjected to correction.

Comment: In a world as acquisition-oriented as ours, the language of this chapter seems very strong. Nowhere else is Benedict as adamant. Our guide who is ordinarily flexible and "realistic" is here uncompromising: private ownership is to be pulled out at the roots in the Christian community.

It is fascinating to compare this with the two prior chapters concerning the importance of care for material goods. It is considered a truism in the real estate business today that where there is no ownership, there is no care. It is "common knowledge" in the city planning profession that housing development areas designated for "common use" are the trashiest, since no one takes responsibility for them. If it "belongs" to everyone, it belongs to no one. Or so we believe.

And yet Benedict insists that no one can own what actually belongs to all. (Not even a pencil!) He insists that true care--human stewardship of God's gifts--comes only when we recognize that we do not possess anything. And this is perhaps the key: sacramental awareness is to involve not only awareness and appreciation but also stewardship or co-participation with God in the ongoing creation of the world. When we see the world in this light, we recognize at once that we cannot do it alone. Even and especially stewardship must involve the integration of gifts brought by many loving hands.

Note too that the model Benedict is using is the Christ-empowered post-Pentecost community of Acts (of which Benedict and we will have more to say later), and that the "punishment" here as elsewhere is separation from the community.

Reflection: I can't imagine it! Not even a pencil to call my own! Quite apart from things I buy, there are several key things I think are "mine" because of use. For example, there is my favorite chair in the living room which whenever anyone else uses it, I feel slightly violated .

I've been reflecting recently on the situations or events that stimulate me to use the word "my" or "mine". One acute example is how often as parents speaking of our children, we use "my" language. The odd thing about that is not only that it leaves out our spouse (the other parent), nor even that it suggests perhaps the children belong to us more than to themselves. The truly odd thing is that a child above all things is clearly a gift from God, for which we have stewardship only for a time. How can I learn mentally not to "possess" that to which I am giving such a deep and loving part of my own caring energy? (Note: *my* energy!)

Prayer/Response:

Chapter 34: Distribution of Necessities According to Need (entire)

It is written: *Distribution was made to each, according to his need* (Acts 4:35). By this we do not mean that there should be partiality concerning individuals (God forbid!) but rather consideration for infirmities. Let the one, therefore, who needs less thank God and be not distressed; and let him who requires more be humbled because of his infirmity and not puffed up by the kindness that is shown to him: thus all the members shall be in peace. Above all, the scourge of murmuring must not be manifested, for any reason or by any word or sign. If anyone is found guilty of this let him be subjected to the most severe punishment.

Comment: This chapter is almost a culmination of the several preceeding ones, a rising to a peak of what feels like praise. Read thoughtfully, it illumines a concept of the monastic community that is a celebration of God's goodness and glory. Each member is special, unique and precious. Each has been gifted with needs and with a capacity to give, all of which taken together in harmony unfolds in the most glorious symphony. The passage here cited from Acts is a very crucial one in Benedict's own prayerful reflection, for he cites it not only here and the preceeding chapter, but also in Chapter 55:20.[80] Clearly, he has pondered at length the shape and experience of that first Spirit-filled Christian community, and it is his model for the monastic family.[81] Here he expresses his joy at the wonder of an empowered human gathering in which there is kindness. (In English, kindness is a pun on the meaning "belonging to one kind"; and in Latin it clearly expresses an imitation of God's mercy.) Indeed, such a community contains the fullness of peace.

Again, realism is always a part of Benedict's vision of peace. Benedict recognizes that participation in such a community is learned, and the seniors must guide and discipline and model for the juniors. The goal is mutual uncovering of ways not to block the experience of God's wondrous gifts. Grumbling, that assertion of ego, is a serious refusal of this vision of uniqueness-within-community which Benedict is building. Thus it is to be immediately curbed when it appears.

Reflection: I flatly dislike my limitations. Very little else can so quickly stimulate my grumbling behavior. Indeed, I strenuously seek to avoid any experience of my own inadequacy, my fatigue, or my failure. As a result, I would very much rather give than receive.

So, I have a hard time being a real participant in a giving community. It is difficult for me simply to receive help with thanks. I know others gladly give what is necessary to strengthen and support me, but I hate to need it. Recently someone promised to pray for me, and for a moment I was actually alarmed, wondering if I had somehow signaled that I needed prayers. And then I laughed at myself.

Prayer/Response:

Chapter 35: Weekly Servers in the Kitchen, verses 1-9

Let the brothers serve each other in turn, so that no one is excused from the work of the kitchen except on account of health or because he is engaged in some matter of great importance. For in this way greater reward is obtained and love is acquired. Let the weaker brethren, however, be helped so that they do not work in sadness: and let all generally have assistance according to the size of the community and the circumstances of the place. If the community is large the cellarer should be excused from kitchen service, as well as any others who are engaged (as we have said) in matters of greater importance. But let the rest serve one another in love.

Let him who is ending his week's service clean up everything on Saturday. He must wash the towels with which the brethren wipe their hands and feet; and both the one who is finishing his service and the one who is beginning it are to wash the feet of all.

Comment: The discussions of the sacramental quality of things, and of the Spirit-filled life of gathered Christians, serve as prelude to what now becomes a review of the mundane matters of monastery life. Many have regarded these details not only as being of no interest to the spiritual life, but also as only of passing relevance to contemporary monastic communities. They are seen somewhat like quaint corsets, as simple reminders of the now-antiquated usages of former times. One does not need to argue that each detail must be adhered to precisely, in order to observe that there is much here of profound contemporary interest, even for those of us who have no vocation to the specifically monastic life.

At issue in this chapter is the matter of what it means to be a creature. Our bodies are nourished by food, which we intake, assimilate, and excrete. Our bodies interact with the natural environment in such a way that they become dirty, smelly, and calloused. Engaged in our "god-project", we like to pretend that we can and do "rise above" these natural phenomena. Preparation of food and removal and cleansing of waste are ordinarily considered menial tasks, to be assigned to those who "cannot do anything of value".[82] Soaps, deodorants, perfumes, and fancy clothing are among a few of the responses we over-emphasize in order to hide our creatureliness even from ourselves.

So the shared service of one another described here is yet another example of Benedict's intention to practice a crucial shift in disposition. Instead of disdaining the creaturely, we learn to honor it and treat it with reverence, as appropriate to God's good creation. This service is a way of accepting our own true place in the scheme of things: being willing to be creatures of God. This acceptance, this willingness, is the first step in learning to notice God sacramentally present even in the frailest and "dirtiest" of our beings.

Reflection: There is so much to be reflected upon here! Today, I think of the necessary relation between charity and the creaturely. Is it perhaps the case that I can only fully experience charity in and through acceptance of my body? When I consider St. Francis kissing the leper, or Mother Teresa cradling a broken and maimed begger, it occurs to me that their outpouring love must involve such acceptance of the creaturely. What is required not to be repelled by such disfigurement? Among other things, it must be an ease with one's own bodily functions, a profound sense of one's place in creation.

Recently my grandmother anticipated a severe worsening of her health. Many years ago she had a colostomy, which she personally has cared for and cleansed each day. Anticipating her decline, she described to me the necessary procedures, willing to turn them over to me, should circumstances require. There was a profound intimacy in the conversation, and I was humbled and uplifted. I became aware that I was praying, both to be able to serve her in openhearted and easy grace, and in deep thanksgiving for her trust.

Prayer/Response:

Chapter 35, verses 10-18 (end)

Let the server hand over to the cellarer the vessels used in his work, clean and in sound condition; and let the cellarer hand them to the one beginning his service, so that he may know what he gives out and what he receives back. An hour before the meal these weekly servers shall receive, over and above the appointed allowance, a drink and a piece of bread, so that they may serve the brethren at meal time without murmuring or excessive fatigue. On solemn days, however, let them wait until after Mass.

On Sunday, as soon as Lauds has ended, both the incoming and outgoing servers for the week shall bow deeply in the presence of all and ask their prayers. Let the one who is ending his week say this verse: *Blessed are you, O Lord God, who have helped and consoled me* (Dan 3:52; Ps 86:17); and when this has been said three times let him receive the blessing. He who is beginning his service shall then follow and say: *O God, come to my assistance; O Lord, make haste to help me* (Ps 70:2). Let this also be repeated three times; and having received the blessing let him begin his service.

Comment: Every action is undertaken in the sight of God: this is a fundamental precept of the Christian life for Benedict. Again, it doesn't sound radical, but actually to practice it is a remarkable idea. The kitchen service is officially to be set within the framework of prayer. Benedict does this in two ways. The servers are to receive a little extra food after mass in order to keep up their strength as they prepare and serve the one meal, in late afternoon. The physical nourishment of bread and wine is a prayerful action.

And second, the actual service in the kitchen itself is set within the context of the daily office, with time taken each week in Sunday Lauds to give thanks for help received and to ask for grace to come. The phrase from Psalm 70 is also the one used to begin each of the midday offices, and the unceasing prayer of the desert fathers.[83]

Reflection: It occurs to me that this routine on the one hand ritualizes and thus provides opportunity for sacramental integration of the truth that God assists all work. But it also carries the danger of any ritual--that is, it might become "routinized", a rote performance carried out automatically, without inner meaning. Our modern world has discarded most rituals because of that danger, but what have we lost?

At Eucharist, for example, I am aware that repetitive actions do sometimes become routine, not carried in my heart nor felt with any personal engagement. But even so, there is a sense in which the participation of my body and my Will allow me to carry around some possibilities that any moment may bear fruit in the new consciousness of God's presence. And, particularly when the routines are shared ones, sometimes I am sustained by the engagement of others, even when my own engagement is weak.

Prayer/Response:

Chapter 36: The Sick Brethren (entire)

Before all things and above all things, care must be taken of the sick, so that they may be truly served as Christ Himself, for He has said: *I was sick and you visited me* (Matt 25:36) and, *Whatever you did to one of these, my least brethren, you did to me* (Matt 25:40). But let the sick themselves consider that they are served for the honor of God, and not grieve their brethren who serve them by their demands. Yet must they be patiently borne with, because from such as these is gained more abundant reward. Therefore the Abbot shall take the greatest care that they do not suffer neglect.

Let a room be set apart by itself for the sick brethren, and an attendant be appointed who is God-fearing, prompt, and painstaking. Let the use of baths be granted to the sick as often as it is appropriate; but to those who are well, and especially to the young, baths shall be seldom permitted. The use of meat, too, shall be permitted to the sick and to the very weak, that they may recover their strength; but when they are restored to health, let all abstain from meat in the accustomed manner.

The Abbot must take all possible care that the sick are not neglected by the cellarers or their attendants; because he is responsible for whatever is done amiss by his disciples.

Comment: In several locations, Benedict cites this passage from Matthew 25.[84] While he is not minimizing its reference to the Day of Judgment, it is interesting that in his usual affirming way, he uses it primarily to remind us that we can meet Christ within our daily context of simple and mundane service for one another!

In this chapter we also see the careful balancing of separate interests within the one Body, so characteristic of Benedict. The brothers are to care for the sick; the sick are not to distress the brothers by their demands: both are to offer themselves to each other in mutual obedience. The brothers are to serve generously; the abbot is to supervise them wisely: obedience carries obligations on both sides. The weak are to receive special privileges; it is not to be presumed by the healthy that such privileges have established a precedent: life is best lived in the context of sufficiency and frugality.

Finally, Benedict has raised that important concept from the Gospel of Matthew of "reward".[85] Today it is often considered that Christian behavior should be "altruistic", that is, with no expectation of reward. Benedict and Matthew would have been startled by such thinking. For them, our behavior ought to be motivated by desire for God's reward, presented in terms like "Kingdom of Heaven", "children of the Father", and "life in abundance". Benedict invites, indeed encourages, us to reflect deeply upon God's promised rewards (esp. Ch. 4:46,76), so that they may increasingly form our aspirations and our behavior.

Reflection: Benedict insists that I take our Lord seriously in Matthew 25 when he says: "(I)n so far as you as you did this to one of the least of these brothers of mine, you did it to me." In other words, Benedict tells me, the normal encounters of each day provide an opportunity to receive Christ. In relationship with one another, we may receive Christ. Lest I miss the point, he emphasizes that receiving Christ involves things like taking care of a sick and cranky relative!

As he suggests to me when he balances interests off against one another, every relationship has its high and low moments. No matter how glorious, loving, or even "spiritual" the relationship, it does not take me very long to become aware of certain weaknesses and inadequacies in the other. Shall I then withdraw part of me from this all-too-human person? In some respects, it is a great deal easier to take refuge in the "real" thing, Christ unmediated. But the "scandal" of incarnation (now, in my sisters and brothers, as well as once for all in Jesus) has its positive dimensions as well as its negative ones. Recently, I have discovered that if I continue to risk myself to another in the presence of Christ, quite wonderful and unexpected outcomes may occur. In other words, when I try to be fully present to the actual person in front of me, in light of the fact that Christ is here with us, a new quality of relationship becomes possible in which I learn more about love than I ever dreamed existed.

The wedding rings which my husband and I wear have crosses cut out of their centers, so that sunlight daily burns Christ's symbol into our flesh. When we chose the rings I was speechless with the sudden awareness that with Christ so central, we could really risk what otherwise would have been impossible to us. What happens when we believe that another person "embodies" Christ for us? My hunch is that what "happens" is both very ordinary and near miraculous. And my hunch is that Benedict lived that ordinary-miraculous life every day. Can I as well?....

Prayer/Response:

Chapter 37: The Old and Children (entire)

Although human nature of itself is drawn to feel pity and consideration for these two times of life - the elderly and children - yet the authority of the Rule should also provide for them. Let their weakness be always taken into account, and do not allow the full rigor of the Rule as regards food to be maintained in their regard. Rather, let kindly consideration be shown to them, and let them eat before the regular hours.

Comment: This chapter is characteristic of Benedict's constant care for human weakness and limitation. Never is it a matter for shame or disgust, but always an opportunity for stewardship and charity. Concern and love are to be expressed not only by those giving care, but by those receiving it.

How strict is the Rule generally in the matter of food? Soon we shall come to Chapter 39, on "The Proper Amount of Food", but meantime let us note that there were many days of one meal only, late in the afternoon. Other days there were two meals, a heavier one mid-day and a lighter supper in the evening. This is a somewhat meagre regimen by our standards, but generally it was the norm even in the secular world in Benedict's day. As monasteries moved forther north from the equator, adjustments were made to provide heartier fare, in accordance with Benedict's general principle that there was to be sufficiency within frugality,[86] because an alert and responsive body was a needed support in the Christian life of service and love.

Reflection: It occurs to me that monastic practice has not been all that successful in attaining this balance recommended by Benedict -- either in the matter of strictness of diet, nor in the matter of taking lack of strength into account. That gives me some comfort as I realize that neither have I! In food, I alternate between self-indulgence and self-punishment; and in the matter of lack of strength, I generally am embarrassed by it.

As I reflect on the themes that seem to recur in these chapters, I see that there truly is an important connection between humility, stewardship, and sacramental awareness. Both self-indulgence and self-punishment are poor stewardship. Both are undoubtedly rooted in lack of self-acceptance: they are a refusal to acknowledge the way things actually are. I have already confessed my discomfort with my own occasional lack of strength, which is to say, with my creatureliness. Yet here for the first time I realize that by refusing humility (acceptance of my body and my limitations), I am actually closing myself off from the awareness of the presence of God within my situation. I am refusing the opportunity to receive the strength and assistance of those who would give it.

Perhaps "kindly consideration" is the mark of a humble person, of God's person. To give and receive kindliness is a mark that one belongs to a community, the Body of Christ. I need to ponder this further....

Prayer/Response:

Chapter 38: The Weekly Reader (entire)

When the brethren are taking their meals there should always be reading. Yet no one shall spontaneously presume to take up the book and read; rather let the one who is to read throughout the week begin on Sunday. Let this brother, when beginning his service, ask all after Mass and Communion to pray for him, that God may keep from him the spirit of pride. And let this verse be said three times in the oratory by all, he, the reader, first beginning: *O Lord, open my lips, and my mouth shall declare your praise* (Ps 51:17). And so, having received the blessing, let him begin his reading.

The greatest silence should be kept at table, so that no whispering or voice, except the voice of the reader alone, is heard there. Whatever is required for eating and drinking the brethren shall offer to one another so that no one need ask for anything. Should anything be wanted, let it be asked for by an audible sign of some sort rather than in words. Let no one ask any question there about anything else, *lest occasion be given [to the evil one]* (Eph 4:27; 1 Tim 5:4); unless, perhaps, the superior should wish to say something briefly for the edification of the brethren.

The brother who is reader for the week shall receive some mixed wine and water before he begins to read, on account of the Holy Communion, and lest it be too hard for him to fast so long. He shall take his meal afterwards with the weekly cooks and servers.

The brethren, however, are not to read or chant according to their rank, but only as may edify the hearers.

Comment: This chapter is about hearing and receiving the Word of God, but in Benedict's usual way, that idea is stated not in a theological treatise, but within the framework of the ordinary routines of the community; not in terms of the text, but in terms of the responsibility of the human channel for communication of God's word.

Silence at meals was routine in monastic communities of the time, but Benedict's emphasis is quite different from most of his peers. For him, silence is not introduced for the negative purpose of stopping conversation (which might give rise to arguments or bawdiness), but rather for the positive purpose of listening to the Word of God.[87] The silence at meals is because God is speaking in the Scripture and the Fathers, and the monks are to listen eagerly and attentively.

Notice, however, that the written word is not the only source of God's word. The brothers are to be attentive to each others' needs as they eat and drink; and to the superior's words of instruction. And they come to dinner immediately following Holy Communion.[88] This community meal is thus both a highly sacramental and a deeply ordinary moment, to be attended to with all one's heart. The reader must know that this whole communal action of praise and thanksgiving is the one in which his work finds essential part.

Reflection: This moment is both highly sacramental and deeply ordinary. In a sense, that is what Benedict is saying in many different ways in this whole section on Domestic Arrangements. Do I see my domestic setting that way?

Occasionally I do. There are mornings when I look out the window above the sink, while my hands are in the hot, soapy suds, and my heart leaps for joy at the sun and the trees and the birds. There are moments when I look at my husband's funny fingernails on his thumbs, and I'm dizzy with happiness at the tangibleness of him. But they are fleeting moments.

It's odd, though. Moments of that sort do seem to involve a specific attentiveness to something ordinary and concrete, as well as an awareness that it is an opening to something else. If I start out looking for God, I seem to get confused and lost. Whereas, if I start out really attending to what is actually given in this moment, I discover God.

Prayer/Response:

Chapter 39: The Appropriate Amount of Food (entire)

We think it sufficient for the daily meal, whether at the sixth or the ninth hour, that there be at all the tables two dishes of cooked food on account of the variety of weaknesses: so that one who may not be able to eat of the first may make his meal of the other. Therefore let two cooked dishes suffice for the brethren; and if there are any fruit or young vegetables, let a third dish be added. Let a good pound of bread suffice for each day, whether there be only one meal or both lunch and dinner. If they are to have dinner let a third part of the pound be kept back by the cellarer and given to them for dinner.

If however their work has been greater, it shall be according to the will and in the power of the Abbot (if it is desirable) to make some addition [to the meal], provided that excess be avoided above all things, and that no monk suffer from overeating. For nothing is more contrary to any Christian life than overeating, as Our Lord says: *Take heed that your hearts are not heavily laden through overeating* (Luke 21:34). To children of tender years the same quantity should not be allotted; rather they should receive less than their elders, frugality being observed in all things.

But let all abstain from eating the flesh of four-footed animals, except the very weak and the sick.

Comment: In Benedict's time, the general practice among persons consecrated to God was severe abstinence regarding food and drink, often surpassing these "natural austerities" in his Rule. Benedict adopted moderation as his pattern, seeing in severe physical abstinences the danger of spiritual pride, as well as the possibility of a weakened body incapable of being a supportive partner in the life with God.

Benedict's approach to disciplining the body and its appetites is given boundaries by three concepts in this chapter: abstinence (a very limited practice, here only relevant to flesh meat); overindulgence (a sin to be avoided at all costs); and sufficiency (the moderate amount that will suffice for all). Sufficiency is his standard, and one useful for us to consider in many contexts.

Why is overindulgence such a sin? Luke's Chapter 21 reveals the context not only of this quotation, but also of the whole Christian life, so far as Benedict is concerned: preparation for the great day of judgment. In all we do, we are preparing (whether we know it or not) that glorious day when Christ shall come into his own. Overindulgence minimizes our capacity to be alert, to be responsive, to the Christ in our present environment bringing us into that future one.

Reflection: What is sufficiency? How do I know when I have enough? In every arena of my life, this is an important question. Already have I reflected on the issue of enough food, but there are also the issues of enough talent, enough self-esteem, enough love, enough security, enough money, and on and on.

I think our society generally operates on the principle of scarcity, so that each of us feels we must claim and hoard, in order to get our fair share. It is a startling contrast to the principle on which Jesus seems to operate, that of abundance, so that there is always more than is needed. I see this in Jesus not only when he feeds the 5000, but also in his parables, and in such words as "to the one who has will more be given". (Matt 13:12)

Sufficiency must have something to do with Christ's abundance. Can I be satisfied with what is sufficient for now, because I trust in the Lord who clothes the lilies? I wonder if I can begin to experience what I am already receiving not only as sufficient, but also as abundant?

Prayer/Response:

Chapter 40: The Appropriate Amount of Drink (entire)

Everyone has *his proper gift from God: one this, another that* (1 Cor 7:7). And therefore it is with some reluctance that we determine the measure of another's living. Yet, making due allowance for the weakness of some, we think that a *hemina* of wine a day is sufficient for each. But let those to whom God gives the gift of abstinence know that they shall receive their proper reward.

If either local necessity, the work, or the heat of summer require more, it is in the power of the superior to grant it, care being taken in all things that satiety or drunkenness not creep in. Although we read that wine is by no means a drink for monks, yet, since in our days they cannot be persuaded of this, let us at least agree not to drink to satiety, but sparingly: because *wine causes even the wise to fall away* (Sir 19:2).

But where the place is such that not even the aforesaid measure can be supplied, but rather much less or none at all, let those who dwell there bless God and not murmur. This above all we admonish, that they refrain from murmuring.

Comment: Here as we deal with matters of food and drink, we are probing the nature of human desire, its value and its restraint, in the whole of the spiritual life. Benedict is here drawing on many sources,[89] weaving together a moderate approach which honors the human body and its construction, yet keeps the central orientation on God. As we look at the two passages of scripture cited here, and Benedict's use of them, we gather his approach is something like this:

The one dedicated to God must always be thinking of the hour of death and the day of reckoning. Consciousness of that reality helps us remember always that who we are and what we do does matter. An essential element in this regard is to restrain our desires. Unchecked expression of desire for many things dilutes the formative power of our great desire for the One. And yet each person will find that the spirit of wisdom guides him or her differently in the choice of disciplines and expression of vital energies. One needs discernment as one seeks knowledge of those elements in one's makeup which are gift, and those which are indulgences. The orientation which will best guide the whole process is to love God above all.

Benedict summarizes his thought in the last paragraph of this chapter: wherever you are, whatever the conditions in which you find yourself, bless God and be thankful. This is so central that murmuring may be a greater sin than occasional over-indulgence, because murmuring is the opposite of thankfulness.

Reflection: Sirach says: seek wisdom. Paul says: live by the Spirit. Benedict says: bless God. In Benedict's handling, all this advice on spiritual essentials has an earthy quality, a kind of fullness of delight in what actually is. It is far removed from the kind of shriveled-up prudery or harsh penitence that I so often associate with spiritual discipline. How much I would like to live in a community where these constraints-infused-with-glory provided the daily rhythm! And yet, no doubt even in such a place, one would have to learn to recognize what was actually there.

I'm reminded of that song fragment: the joy of the Lord is my strength! What a paradox it is that moderation is the natural outcome of joyous living! I wonder if it's better to start with the joy, or start with the moderation? Maybe a little of both.

Prayer/Response:

Chapter 41: At What Hours the Brothers are to Take their Meals (entire)

FROM THE HOLY FEAST of Easter until Pentecost the brethren should have lunch at the sixth hour and dine in the evening. But from Pentecost throughout the summer, if the monks do not have to work in the field and are not inconvenienced by excessive heat, let them fast on Wednesdays and Fridays until the ninth hour and take their meal on other days at the sixth hour.

Should they have field labor, or should the heat of the summer be very great, let a meal at the sixth hour be the norm, at the discretion of the Abbot. Let him likewise modify and arrange all things so that souls may be saved and that the brethren may fulfil their tasks without any justifiable murmuring.

From September thirteenth until the beginning of Lent let the brethren always take their meal at the ninth hour. During Lent, however, until Easter let them dine in the evening. But let the evening meal be so arranged that they do not need lamps while eating, and that all thing may be finished while there is still daylight. Indeed, at all times of the year let the hour for lunch or dinner be so arranged that everything can be done by daylight.

Comment: Patterns of consumption are to be frugal and yet moderate. Although monks are encouraged to stretch themselves by fasting until a later meal, this is to be offset not only by the reasonable needs of the body (relating to hard labor and heat) but also by a concern not to be wasteful of candles as well as food.

We notice the term "justifiable murmuring". On several occasions, Benedict has referred to murmuring as a severe disobedience to the spirit--if not the letter--of the Rule. And yet here he mentions that there might be occasions which justify such grumbling. Again, as always, responsibility is mutual: monks are not to grumble; superiors are to arrange external circumstances so as to minimize unnecessary distress.

But unquestionably the most important point about spiritual disciplines here occurs in the first verse: fasting must be in relation to feasting, for the Christian. The joy of the resurrection is to be celebrated; the banquet table is prepared by Christ's victory; all are to partake in the feast! Everything in Christian life, including discipline, must take its place in relation to this joy.

"The mystery of Easter is the crux on which (everything) hangs....Everything is done in relation to the resurrection; even the midday meal becomes a way of celebrating it."[90]

Reflection: In what ways do I integrate intentional feasting with intentional fasting? How do I know myself served and loved by the Lord, as well as loving and serving him? A friend of mine starts each day by asking: how will God love me today? And then at the end of the day, she asks again: how has God loved me today? Having reviewed that, she gives thanks.

I suggested that pattern to another friend who was utterly startled by it. She had often pondered how she was loving God, but had never thought of how God was loving her. It seems almost "sinful" at first. Yet I think there is good evidence to suggest that the human Jesus was empowered by God's ongoing word to him: "I love you!" In a sense, that was the word both at Jesus' baptism and transfiguration. And we are certainly invited to participate in both, as we are drawn into Christ's life. What more wonderful feast than that!

Prayer/Response:

Chapter 42: That No One may Speak after Compline (entire)

At all times silence should be cultivated by monks, but most especially during the hours of the night. And this shall always be the case, whether on fast days or ordinary days. If it is not a fast day, as soon as they have risen from supper all are to sit down together and one is to read the *Conferences* or *Lives of the Fathers*, or at least something else which may edfy the hearers; but not the Heptateuch, nor the Books of Kings: for it will not profit those of weak understanding to hear those parts of Scripture at that hour; they are to be read at other times.

If it is a fast-day, then shortly after Vespers they should assemble for the reading as we have said; four or five pages being read, or as much as time allows, so that during the interval provided by this reading all may come together, even those occupied in some assigned project. When all are gathered together let them say Compline; and when they come out from Compline no one shall be allowed to speak further to anyone. If any are found evading this rule of silence, let them be punished severely; unless the presence of guests necessitated it or the Abbot needed to give a command to someone. But even this must be done with the greatest seriousness and proper moderation.

Comment: Benedict is often less systematic than organic, using a free-flowing style to address issues as they come to him. This chapter is about silence, as well as about meals, reading, community. In short, it is about listening to and responding to God. In a sense, that has been the theme of all these chapters about domestic arrangements: God is here and now in the routine matters of our day. Let us notice and respond to that presence.

Benedict reminds us in these chapters that material things are sacraments, that is, outer signs of an inward presence. We are to treat things tenderly and attentively, that they may reveal God. If we see only the outer, we may seek to possess rather than care for things. If we see only the inner, we cease to value and tend the lovely created world which God has given into our charge. In all we do, no matter how frail or ordinary it seems, we are seeking to listen and respond to God. This is possible, because God in Christ is giving Godself to us all the time. All the arrangements of the domestic setting are designed to bring one continually into contact with these truths.

Silence is an essential framework, if one is to practice this task of listening for God in all. Silence in the Rule is always ordered toward hearing God's word.[91] Night silence brings rest, and allows the Word to take root in the monk's heart, that he might truly open his lips and pour forth God's praise in the morning. (Chapter 9:1)

Reflection: Benedict's fluidity in his organization of the Rule forces me to encounter it less with my mind (and analysis) than with my heart (and receptivity). If I stay with the Rule, I find myself being opened to the unknown, and I discover that I am transcending myself.

I sense newly that is exactly what the Gospel is and does. It offers a gentle but steady invitation to grow beyond myself and what I can "know" with my mind, in order that I might come to be "known" in the ancient Hebrew way: penetrated intimately by the abundant Love who knows me already better than I know myself. And this wonderful process seems in fact to happen in the ordinary daily round of waking and sleeping, eating and eliminating, sickness and study, weakness and work. Astonishing!

Prayer/Response:

Interlude VI:

A Note to the Reader...

Are you finding that it's hard to keep up your *lectio* when you're doing it alone?

Many people are very interested in keeping a regular routine of meditation, but find it hard to sustain interest without companionship. Such persons often are energized and stimulated by the conversation and ideas of others, and they simply don't have the heart to keep up a discipline absent from that vital exchange. In such a case, it's a good practice to make the *lectio* a group endeavor.

A group *lectio* process might work something like this. Several individuals (anywhere from four to eight is a good number) would commit to each other to do private *lectio* meditations of a certain number between the meeting times. Then when you meet together, you have a free-flowing discussion of individual insights, questions, wonderments. Say you had agreed to complete three *lectio* units during the week. When you gather, you could review all three units systematically, or instead jump right in to a place where one of you got stuck, or had a great insight, or the like. The point is simply that in the process of sharing, you build on one another's wisdom, and gain support for your own process.

For the group meeting times, it's a good idea to begin and end with prayer, either spoken or silent. As you do your sharing, one person might want to bring outside resources explaining the history or context of the Rule in that section. But, in general, the emphasis should be on your own perceptions. That is, the point of the devotional effort is to co-operate with God's work deepening your spirit, so the focus is not on information as such, but on the way it impacts your life. Try to concentrate on "I" statements rather than "they" statements. Stay centered in your own strong attractions and repulsions. Pay attention to places where the text evokes a resonance in you. Listen to one another.

In order for such sharing to be fruitful, it's good to trust one another and commit to confidentiality. Whatever is said in the group should not be mentioned outside without specific permission. Trust grows slowly and should not be forced, but gently permitted to bloom among you. Most of us haven't words to speak of our relationship with God, and we recognize that we experience great vulnerability as we try to do so. A supportive response from others is enormously helpful in claiming our own reality.

If you begin or join such a group, be aware that God is in your midst, and is giving you to one another in love.

Lukewarmness And Its Remedies

Chapter 43, Those Who Arrive Late at the Work of God or at Table, verses 1-9

At the hour of the Divine Office, as soon as the signal is heard, each one is to lay aside whatever he may be engaged on and hasten to [prayer] with all speed; yet with seriousness, so that no occasion be given for levity. Indeed, let nothing be preferred to the Work of God. Should anyone come to Vigils after the *Gloria* of the ninety-fourth psalm (which for this reason we wish to be said very slowly and deliberately), let him not stand in his usual place in the choir, but last of all, or in the place set apart by the Abbot for such negligent ones. There they will remain, visible to all and to himself, until the Work of God being ended, he makes penance by public satisfaction. The reason why we have judged it fitting for them to stand in the last place or apart is that, being seen by all, they may amend out of shame. For if they were to remain outside the oratory, there might be one who would return to his bed and sleep, or else sit outside and give himself to idle tales, and so *give occasion to the Evil One* (Eph 4:27; 1 Tim 5:14). Rather let them come in, that he may not lose the whole and may amend for the future.

Comment: This chapter and the next three are known as the minor penal code of the Rule: Benedict is here concerned about minor offenses; offenses of incomplete observance representing a lukewarmness or slackness in behavioral commitment to the consecrated life.[92]

It is fitting that Benedict should begin these chapters thus with a reminder of what the consecrated Christian life is: response to the call of God. (compare Prologue 9) God calls; we hear; and we respond at once, immediately. This work of response to God is the only work we do, whatever else we are doing. Benedict's language reminds us of the word so characteristic of the Gospel of Mark: immediately! The good news of the Gospel of Christ is given, and the human heart leaps in response.

But the intensity of initial fervor is not often matched by the consistency of persistent response. What Benedict presents in these chapters is a profound view of the nature of the whole spiritual life, a layered view building upon the moral theology not only of St. Paul, but also probably of St. Augustine.[93]

Why does lukewarmness matter? Being late for office is not such a grave matter, after all....Why even address it in this formal document? Because it gives occasion to the Evil One (here and also RB 38:8). The ascetical life is the building up of an habitual response to God, characterized by Paul as "put on the new self that has been created in God's way, in the goodness and holiness of the truth." (Eph 4:24). This is strenuous and challenging work, which requires constant attentiveness. While it is true that the first suggestion of sin is innocent, or even that an occasional tardiness is minor, it is also true that such a slip represents a first step away from God, and there are so many steps toward God, into which we would be growing. Thus, even for these minor matters, satisfaction -- in the sense of an inward turning of heart, expressed in outward behavior -- is a valuable and necessary response.

Reflection: It occurs to me that if I take such a view seriously, it would involve a valuing of every moment of my life in a way vastly beyond my present considerations. Am I really that important -- each action I take, each thought I entertain? And to God am I really that important? That takes some pondering.

It seems also to require a growing attentiveness to what is actually going on, both in me and around me, and a constant re-offering of all that to God for consecration. I want to look further at how that might actually work.

Prayer/Response:

At the Day Hours, anyone who comes to the Work of God after the verse and the *Gloria* of the first psalm which is said after the verse, must stand in the last place, as stated above. Nor should he presume to join the choir in their chanting until he has made satisfaction, unless the Abbot allows him: yet even so he is to make satisfaction for his guilt.

He who does not come to table before the verse, so that all may say it praying together and sit down to table at the same time, must be corrected once or twice if this be through negligence or fault. If after this he does not amend, let him not be allowed to share in the common table, but be separated from the company of all and eat alone. His portion of wine should be withheld from him until he makes satisfaction and amends. Anyone who is not present at the verse which is said after meals is to undergo the same punishment.

No one should presume to take any food or drink before or after the appointed time; but if something is offered to one by the superior and he refuses it, and afterwards wishes to have what he had rejected or something else, let him receive neither this nor anything else until he makes proper satisfaction.

Comment: We note that Benedict includes tardiness at worship and at the dinner table in the same category. Tardiness is then a laziness about or indifference to that which is constituted by the community of faith. In this sense, it is an assertion of pride or self-will above the common and shared aspects of life together. It is in effect saying: "What I was doing is more important than that which we do together." This setting oneself against or apart from the community, even in small things, is a danger less to the community than to one's own salvation. For it is through the common life that we enter salvation; it is as we come to experience our commonality with our family that we claim our true membership in Christ's Body.

Satisfaction is the term used by Benedict to express a concrete and external action designed to effect a deepened humility.[94] It is thus an outward sign completed in co-operation with an inward movement or intention, so like the sacramental reality of the ordinary which we met so frequently in Benedict's "domestic arrangements". Again Benedict points to the sacrament of the present moment, seen even in a common act of sin and repentance.

Reflection: The Christian concept of community (*koinonia*) has always been greatly mysterious and greatly attractive to me. Yet it also has always seemed out of reach. Benedict is helping me see more clearly how great the distance is between aggressive individualism and *koinonia*. He makes me re-think some basic values, for I have always understood that it is good to stress my individuality and to differentiate myself from the common. I think with what disdain I used to say: "But he's so common." And yet "common" is the root meaning of *koinonia*, as well as of community and communion. It is an affirmation of our kinship, in contrast to our distinctions.

It seems to me that so much in my environment supports the impulse to be uncommon. Even much Christian talk encourages me to believe that salvation itself is a singular and solitary experience.

Yet Benedict challenges that. I believe he suggests that salvation itself is a participative experience, a sharing not only in God's life but in one another's. How far out of reach that seems! And yet, today brings many concrete opportunities for me to try it.

Prayer/Response:

Chapter 44: How the Excommunicated are to make Satisfaction (entire)

One who is excommunicated for graver faults from the oratory and the table must lie prostrate in silence before the door of the oratory at the end of the hour at which the Work of God has been celebrated. He should say nothing, lying face down at the feet of all as they leave the oratory: this he should do until the abbot judges that satisfaction has been made. Then, when the abbot bids him, he is to prostrate himself at feet of the abbot, then at the feet of all the brethren, that they may pray for him. And then, if the abbot orders, he may be received back into choir in the rank the abbot assigns: however, he should not presume to lead a psalm, a lesson or anything else in the oratory unless the abbot again commands him. Moreover, at every hour, as the Work of God is ending, he must prostrate himself on the ground in the place where he stands until the abbot again bids him cease from this satisfaction.

But those who are excommunicated for less serious faults from the table only must make satisfaction in the oratory as long as the abbot commands. This they do until he gives his blessing and says: *It is enough.*

Comment: This chapter seems very harsh to a modern reader--unnecessarily humiliating, we might say. But we must consider it in two contexts. The first is in relation to other sources of the time, which emphasized corporal punishment (even beating to near death), regarded sinners as heretics and even Judases, and routinely called for intensive Lenten penitential periods even in congregational settings.[95] The second is Benedict's overall purpose in establishing the monastic community, in which humiliations facilitate humility, which is essential for salvation.

There are three primary questions with which the modern reader must struggle in response to this chapter. They are these:

(1) Are there any moral offenses which can jeopardize our eternal life, and if so, what are they?

(2) What constitutes true repentance, and how can it be embodied and tested?

(3) What process permits forgiveness to flow and be acknowledged by the sinner, so that personal and communal restoration may be effectively received?

Most of these issues are simply ignored in modern times. Consider for a moment the last one particularly. Absolution, that is full restoration, is a concept utterly foreign to the experience of most of us. We frequently express confession in the context of the psychiatrist's couch, but there is no mechanism by which sin can be acknowledged, repented, and removed. One real advantage of Benedict's procedure is that the penitent can fully and joyfully receive the word "Enough"!

Reflection: Two strong images are evoked for me in reflecting on this chapter. The first is a memory of an event that occurred when I was about 11 years old. I had been writing plays (!) which my teacher invited my classmates to perform. One day when I brought a new one in, she stopped me for a moment and said: "Norvene, in each of these plays, you have written in a star character which only you can play. Why not write some in which others can take the lead?" I flushed and momentarily denied that intention, but I knew at once that what she said was true. I think of that as the moment at which I became an adult; my teacher gave me real dignity by treating me as a person capable of choice for my ego or for the community.

The second is a scene from the movie "Mission" in which a man has killed his brother in anger and now wants to die himself. He is restored to new life by a priest who encourages him literally to carry his penance, until the moment when he is freed to weep and laugh as he hears "Enough"!

Prayer/Response:

Chapter 45: Those Who Make Mistakes in the Oratory (entire)

If anyone makes a mistake while reciting a psalm, responsory, antiphon, or lesson and dces not make satisfaction, humbling himself there before all, let him be subjected to greater punishment, as one who would not correct by humility what he did wrong through negligence. But children for such faults are to be whipped.

Comment: Perhaps we are again reminded here of the disciples' words in John 6:60: "This is intolerable language! How could anyone accept it?" In that context, Jesus is talking about giving them his flesh to eat--harsh words indeed. Is there something of redemption also present here in these harsh words of Benedict?

Benedict is drawing here, as he has often in the Rule, on the Rule of the Master, where the rationale for such actions is spelled out more clearly. As regards the whipping of children, the Master says:

> "Young boys up to the age of fifteen, we prescribe, are not to be excommunicated but whipped for their faults. After the age of fifteen, however, it is proper not to whip but to excommunicate them, because then they understand that they must do penance and correct what wrong they do as adults. For it is right that one who sins should repent in his heart, and not be physically whipped for it, because we live under the soul's rule...."[96]

The Master's language illuminates the key issue of this chapter, which is the internalization of the Gospel. This "taking in" of the Gospel is done in obedience to the community's Rule and the abbot, such that the habitual response of the mature Christian to sin becomes self-accusation and spontaneous satisfaction. A small action such as a mispronunciation of the Word of God becomes important because it is a frequent opportunity to train oneself into that spontaneous orientation toward God known as purity of heart.

For children and novices, this training must initially be presented externally, because that is the form in which it is understood. In the *lectio* on Chapter 30, we referred to the contemporary work of Lawrence Kohlberg, which basically is a modern statement of this same point, that at different developmental stages, different behaviors are necessary to influence moral behavior. But the goal of the Rule is the movement toward moral maturity, in which God's law of love is known interiorly as the law of one's very being. (see Chapter 7:68-9)

Reflection: So many questions arise for me. Is there a place (and if so, what sort?) for an "objective" moral standard against which all actions must be measured? Our society is so oriented toward "situational ethics", and I am myself inclined to consider context highly important in the evaluation of moral behavior. Then, too, most of the "strong moralists" I know have such a narrow and dried-up view of acceptable behavior. On the other hand, I am increasingly aware of the terrible loss of a communal framework within which moral choices can be judged. Surely, there is some limit on acceptable behavior, no matter what the context.

Is it really true that corporal punishment (whether self-inflicted or otherwise) is necessary to bring the bodily appetites and willfulness into harmony with the soul's deepest desire? What about the "strategy" of warm affection and loving regard as attracting us toward good, instead of punishment pushing us away from evil? Are both needed at different times? I confess that I am confused and uncertain on these points. Benedict invites me to ponder and pray and study more reflectively in these areas.

Finally, I realize afresh how very difficult humility is. My pride and ego would so much rather ignore the small errors and sins, so I can think highly of myself, than to attend to them and recognize my utter and every-moment dependence on my God.

Prayer/Response:

Chapter 46: Those Who Offend in Other Matters (entire)

If anyone while engaged in any sort of work, whether in the kitchen, the cellar, the office, the bakehouse, or the garden, in any craft, or in any place, shall do anything amiss - break or lose anything, or offend in any way whatever - he must go at once before the Abbot or the community, and of his own accord do penance and confess his fault. But if this becomes known by means of another, let him be subjected to greater punishment.

If, however, the cause of his sin is hidden in his own soul, let him manifest it only to the Abbot or to the spiritual seniors, who know how to heal their own wounds and not to disclose or make public those of others.

Comment: Benedict was a sturdy realist, and he continually makes clear that he does not expect frail human beings to live without error. Why then make such a "production" about repenting for these sins we cannot avoid? First, we are to use these faults to keep us always aware that we are finite creatures, something we prefer not to know, yet something which actually is a source of bonding to our Creator. Second, we are to confess these faults at once, because if kept "secret", they fester in our hearts and do internal damage.

Recall that in Chapter 4, Benedict urges us to "dash down at the feet of Christ your evil thoughts...and lay them open". (verse 50) This chapter is a practical application of that principle. There is a danger to our soul in keeping secrets, even from ourselves. Modern Jungian scholars talk about the negative effects of the undisclosed "shadow" side of our personalities.[97] Benedict is acknowledging a truth about human nature that runs along those lines: the more we allow ourselves to be blind to our true nature, the further we are moving away from God, who is Truth itself. And when one is also trying to hide personal weakness from others, there is a tendency to become self-justifying and proud.

In a sense, then, this routine repentance for normal external and visible faults sets a pattern to guide us in matters of deeper inward sin. Everything is to be brought at once into the daylight, revealed in humility to those who will respond in love. This pattern reveals great wisdom about how the soul's wounds are received and healed. What great freedom there is, always living in the light! No evil is then able to gain strength in darkness, whence it holds our spirit in bondage. A sin once disclosed is deprived of its power to harm.

Notice that Benedict allows such confession to be offered to any of the spiritual elders, rather than reserving this role for the abbot exclusively. This option suggests his recognition that inner healing of the soul is best accomplished in the context of a special human bond of love and regard.

Reflection: Some mornings I wake up under a dark cloud. Who knows why, but it occasionally occurs. Quite often, the "cloud" takes the form of voices accusing me of inadequacy, incompetence, and lack of charity. Sometimes simply noticing the voices as nuisances, like buzzing flies with a monotonous tone, is sufficient to cause them to dissipate. Sometimes that doesn't work. However, I have become aware that if I simply mention to my husband what I am thinking, the specific issue that is bothering me, it quickly fades to realistic proportions that I can handle in some rational way. Taken out of the "darkness" of my inner world and exposed to the context of another, it loses its frightening power to compel me.

From another perspective, I have also noticed that if I fail to care for my children in the manner I expect of myself (however valid the reason for my temporary negligence), I tend to justify myself by mentally finding something that irritates me about them! I can have worked myself into quite a snit before I notice what is happening, and laugh at myself.

Finally, I reflect ruefully that those who know me best--and love me most--have long since been aware of my weaknesses and limitations. I can vividly remember the time I finally had both the insight and the courage to confess an habitual weakness to my husband, who graciously accepted my confession about something he had known for years! It didn't bother him half as much as it bothered me!

Prayer/Response:

Interlude VII:

a note to the reader...

Are you getting discouraged because you seem to be dealing with the same issue over and over?

Perhaps you have noticed that my reflections often seem to repeat the same material. Perhaps you have observed that in your own ponderings. Sometimes it seems like we simply can't get beyond a certain issue. We look at it this way and that; maybe we even understand mentally how to get out of it; but our emotions are blocked and we feel like the interior struggle won't let up.

I have often thought that the message of the Gospel can be told in very few words indeed. It is the learning to live it fully that takes a lifetime.

Each of us brings to Christ specific temperaments and pre-dispositions. Benedict is teaching us concrete ways to practice re-channeling (converting) our dispositions into the mind of Christ. It should not surprise us that, as we undertake those practices, we find ourselves coming up against the same barriers time and again. Because, after all, it is the same self we bring to the process each day. A friend of mine says that confession is not a matter of offering up the "flavor of the month", but rather of offering the same old thing (ourselves) for its gradual redemption.

Two points here deserve special attention. First, the value of the struggle. Second, the importance of release.

During those moments when it seems to us we are deeply involved in interior struggle (perhaps even it feels like we are wrestling with God), we are co-operating with God in the work of interior formation. As long as we are struggling, we need to be struggling. By this, we are keeping tight the tension between what we are and what we are growing to be, and such tension is creative. I have often thought the story of Jacob wrestling all night with the angel of God (Gen 32:24-31) is given to us as a symbol of the creative struggle.

But struggle is not the last word. The freedom of resurrection living comes after breakthrough. A tremendous sense of liberation and wholeness is given as we are able to release our concerns and resistances to God. One major meaning of "consecrated" is that which is offered up. The consecrated gift is one which is offered to God. The consecrated life is one which is daily offered to God. We struggle, we cry, and then we offer. We sing, we celebrate, and then we offer. All things, good and bad, are offered back to God, in the recognition that God is the giver of all.

We are privileged daily to practice this offering of our lives to God.

The Consecration of Mundane Activities

Chapter 47: Announcing the Hours for the Work of God (entire)

Let it be the abbot's care to announce the hour for the Work of God day and night: either by giving the signal himself, or assigning this task to a conscientious brother, so that all things may be done at the fitting times.

The intoning of psalms and antiphons is to be done by each after the Abbot, according to his rank. No one should presume to sing or to read unless he can fulfil this office in a way which edifies his hearers; let this be done with humility, earnestness and reverence, and by the one whom the Abbot has appointed.

Comment: This is a fitting chapter to begin a section called "The Consecration of Mundane Activities". We have already suggested that a central meaning of "consecrated" is something offered to God. Such a definition seems more helpful in understanding Benedictine consecration than that of "set-apart-ness" from the worldly or the mundane. The Rule does not rigidly classify things as holy and unholy, pure and sinful. On the contrary, it always sees them as a continuum, only asking whether we are attentive to the presence of God in their midst. The Rule routinely expresses such a sense of continuity between the sacred and the ordinary that we can best understand its call for consecration as an invitation to offer up the ordinary, so that it reveals God.

This chapter charges the abbot with responsibility to assemble the community for an important occasion. Nowadays when we have standardized hours and individual watches, such a responsibility does not seem as crucial as it was in Benedict's day. Just what is this important occasion, so important that it alone is nominated "the Work of God"? Of course, it is the daily office (see chapters 8-20 above), but let us inquire further.

The daily office establishes a rhythm of corporate prayer which provides the framework for each day. The essential context and reason-for-being of creation is the praise and worship of God. The Rule schedules specific times of prayer and praise, not to suggest that all times are not times of prayer and praise. Rather the purpose of the office is to establish a formative routine which informs all other times. It sets apart special moments, that all moments may increasingly be known as God's.

Reflection: Some days like this morning I awake to the song of the birds and my heart floods over with joy. I long that my own song might be as exquisite. And also, I am simply content, glad to be part of the moment, even as one who only hears.

Some days I wake joyful, and some gloomy. But every morning I say the office. Some days my mind is in harmony with my voice, and some not. (Rule Chapter 19:7) But I think that one of the important benefits of the office is that gradually it forms my heart so that I know the song of the birds is there, even when I don't feel it.

Prayer/Response:

Chapter 48: The Daily Manual Labor, verses 1-13

Idleness is the enemy **of the soul. Therefore the brethren should be occupied at stated times in manual labour and at other fixed hours in sacred reading (*lectio divina*). We think, therefore, that the times for each may be arranged as follows: from Easter to the first of October, on coming out in the morning let them labor at whatever is necessary from the first until about the fourth hour. From the fourth hour until about Sext let them apply themselves to reading (*lectio*). After Sext, when they rise from table, let them rest on their beds in silence; or if anyone wishes to read to himself, let him read so as not to disturb anyone else. Let None be said rather soon, at the middle of the eighth hour; and then let them again work at whatever has to be done until Vespers. If, however, the needs of the place or poverty require them to labor themselves in gathering in the harvest, let them not grieve at that; for then are they truly monks when they live by the labor of their hands, as our Fathers and the Apostles did. But let all things be done in moderation for the sake of the faint-hearted.**

From the first **of October until the beginning of Lent let the brethren devote themselves to reading (*lectio*) until the end of the second hour. At the second hour let Terce be said, after which they shall all labor at their appointed work until None. At the first signal for the hour of None all shall cease from their work, and be ready as soon as the second signal is sounded. After their meal let them occupy themselves in their reading (*lectio*) or with the psalms.**

Comment: This chapter is about the use of time, that is, about the balance of activities within the day. Each day is to include something of several crucial components which together are expressive of the wholeness of human gifts and needs. This is a proposal for the establishment of daily priorities which manifest one's faith.

The rhythms established by this chapter relate both to the year and to the day. The whole year is organized in relationship to Easter and the pattern of the liturgical seasons (as also expressed secondarily but complementarily in the natural seasons), and the daily pattern varies in harmony with those seasonal shifts.

The day itself is set forth to contain a balance of physical work, mental work, and spiritual work, although such distinctions are somewhat sharper in our time than Benedict's. At any rate, Benedict encourages physical labor, based on the example of our Lord and the disciples, and grounded in the practical matter that somebody has to grow the food. He likewise requires mental labor, which is the process in which we have engaged here, the labor of *lectio divina*. Finally, of course, the day is framed by the offices of prayer.

In Chapter 16, we noted that Prime refers to the first hour of daylight and thus the designation Sext (six) refers to about noon, and so forth. The details of Benedict's daily schedule show a design which both (a) maximizes working time available in the fields when the harvesting needs to be done, and (b) gives the earliest and optimum reflective hours of the day to serious study/*lectio* on Scripture.

Reflection: I used to struggle with when (to find time) to pray. Finally, I decided to start the day with prayer, and let other things fall into place as they would. How astonishing to discover that there is always "enough" time left! The best hours can be given to study/prayer and behold! exactly the appropriate hours are left for needed attention to the crops! No doubt this model reflects Benedict's particular genius, but even more does it reveal God's goodness, generosity, and gentle caring built into not only my own physical constitution but also into the way things really are. What an opportunity is thus presented to relax and enjoy what is given!

In pondering the way Benedict has organized the day, I see more ways than one in which it invites relaxation. For not only have I worried about when to find time to pray, I also worry about how to make my work time more like my prayer time. What I sense Benedict might say about that is "be gentle with yourself and your expectations." Everything in the day has its own natural value, its own natural rhythm. There is no need to make work feel the same as prayer; each has its own value and each can be consecrated according to its own inherent qualities.

I see that whatever I can offer to God, God will take. And it is in the momentary offering that the ordinary elements of my life truly become consecrated. I might take a moment when I go to the bathroom or shift from one document to another quickly to offer that moment to God. It almost makes me giggle to think of it, it seems so ordinary, so non-pious. I could take five minutes before lunch to look back on the morning to ask "how's it gone?" (meaning, where was God in it?!). Can everything in my life be given to God?! I think it could! I want to try.

Prayer/Response:

Chapter 48, verses 14-25 (end)

In Lent, however, from the morning until the end of the third hour they should devote themselves to reading, and afterwards work at their appointed tasks until the end of the tenth hour. In this time of Lent let them each receive a book from the library, to be read consecutively and straight through. These books are to be given out at the beginning of Lent.

Above all, let one or two seniors be deputed to make the rounds of monastery at the hours when the brethren are engaged in reading, to see that there is no slothful (*acediosus*) brother giving himself to idleness or to gossip, and not applying himself to his reading; so that he is not only useless to himself, but a distraction to others. If such a one be found (which God forbid!) let him be corrected once and a second time; and if he does not amend, let him be subjected to the chastisement of the Rule, in such a way that the rest may be warned. Moreover, one brother shall not associate with another at unsuitable hours.

On Sunday let them devote themselves to reading except those who are assigned to the various offices. But if anyone is so negligent and slothful as to be unwilling or unable to read or meditate, he must have some work given him that he is not idle.

For weak or delicate brethren let such work or crafts be assigned that they will not be idle, and yet will not be oppressed by heavy labor so as to be driven away. The weakness of such brethren must be taken into account by the Abbot.

Comment: Because the language of this chapter appears to be easily comprehensible, we may at first not realize exactly how extraordinary is the subject of this section. Two words in particular give us a clue. One is *lectio* (reading); the other is *acedia* (apathy/sloth/idleness).

We who have been engaged in this particular reading of the Rule are coming to have a growing appreciation of the work of *lectio*. As we are discovering, it is a profoundly personal and engaging process of allowing oneself to be formed into the mind of Christ through encounter with the living Word, especially in the Scriptures and the Fathers.[98] As such, *lectio* is a strenuous work, requiring great concentration and receptivity. Notice that Benedict treats "reading" in a similar manner to "excommunication" in one respect: it is to be applied primarily to those mature enough to understand it. The weaker or more immature monks must sometimes be challenged with the less complex methods of manual labor (here verse 23) or physical punishment (Rule Chapter 23:4-5).

The opposite of work is idleness, or apathy. In general, our society frantically avoids idleness, but there exists among us (and within each of us, at various periods) a kind of utter boredom, which is oddly enough more like workaholism than like true work. For both idleness and workaholism express a refusal to be engaged with the truth of one's life. Idleness, apathy, and workaholism are ways of avoiding oneself, and God. Very likely they hide the fear either that God does not exist, or that God is not loving. Both apathy and workaholism are the masks of despair.

Reflection: Sometimes I am astonished at how strenuous is the life of faith. It is hard work truly to be engaged, not only with God, but with God-in-the-midst, that is, with my own given life. It is costly to be engaged in open vulnerability, willing time and again to let my assumptions and biases be smashed that I might grow ever more into God's fullness for me. There is often very little to show for it superficially. But what a joy it is to be engaged in such a life!

It's funny, too, how the depth of it "sneaked up" on me. I remember when I first started doing *lectio* on Scripture -- being surprised that a phrase seemed to attract me, and that the phrase seemed directly to speak to something going on in my life. As I continued, it became more and more clear to me that God was in fact speaking to me each day -- in a very ordinary way, nothing spectacular. Nonetheless I felt invited to change my ways in the small, routine daily issues which have emerged so often in these pages.

Then one day I realized how much a miracle this all is -- a startling, life-changing shift in me and in my effect on those around me! Yet it all happened so gradually and so normally that in any given day, it didn't seem like a big deal.

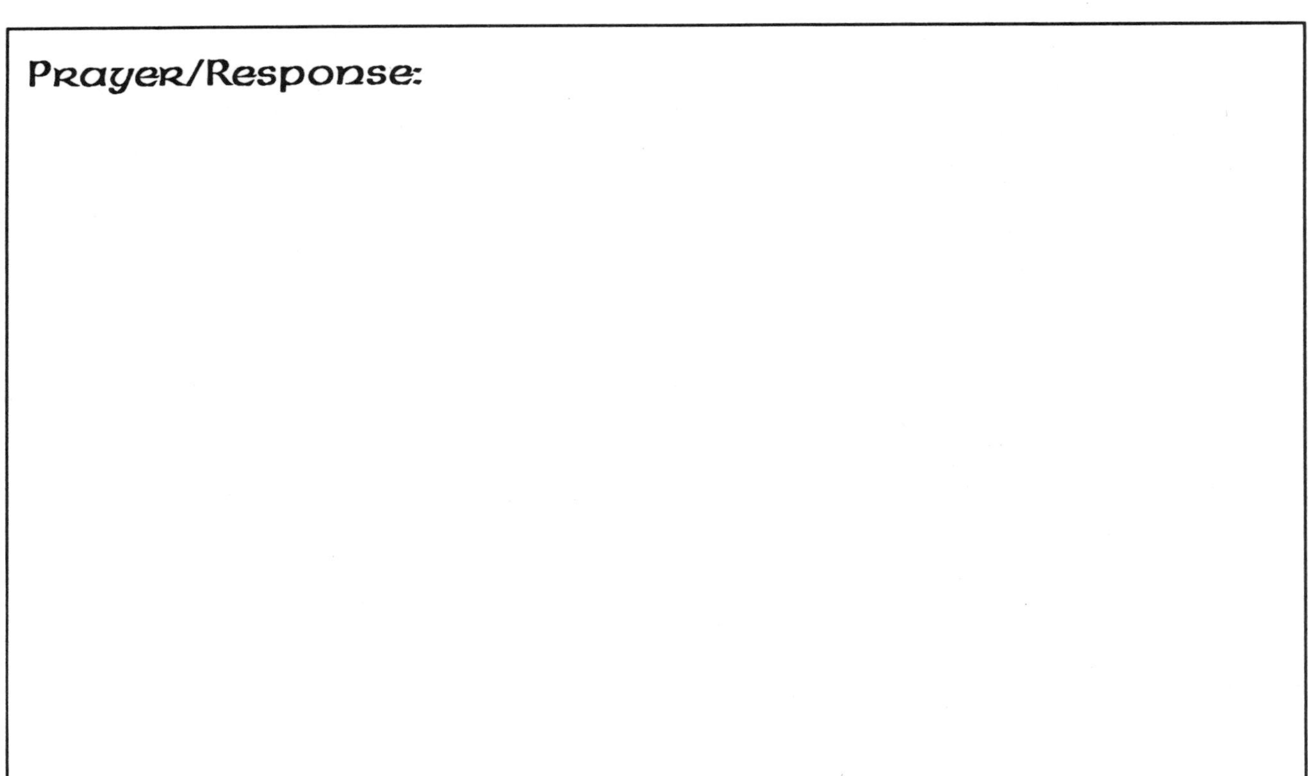
Prayer/Response:

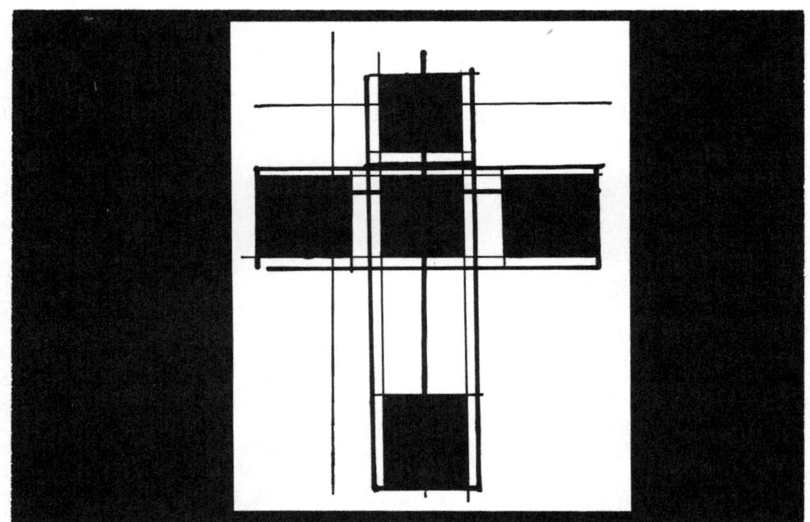

Chapter 49: The Observance of Lent (entire)

Although the life of a monk ought to be a continuous Lenten observance, yet since few have strength enough for this we exhort all, at least during the days of Lent, to keep themselves in all purity of life, and to wash away during that holy season the negligences of other times. This we shall worthily do if we refrain from all sin and give ourselves to prayer with tears, to holy reading, compunction of heart, and abstinence. During these days, then, let us add something to the usual measure of our service: such as private prayers, and abstinence from food and drink, so that everyone of his own Will may offer to God *with joy of the Holy Spirit* (1 Thess 1:6), something beyond the measure appointed him.

In other words, each should withhold from his body something of food, drink, and sleep, refraining from talk and mirth, and awaiting holy Easter with the joy of spiritual longing. Let each one, however, make known to his Abbot what he offers, and let it be done with his blessing and permission: because what is done without leave of the spiritual father shall be attributed to presumption and vainglory, and will merit no reward. Everything, therefore, is to be done with the approval of the Abbot.

Comment: This chapter is one upon which we might fruitfully meditate for many days. Here Benedict presents, in summary, an outline of the ascetical life, the life of Christian discipline.[99] Benedict mentions the strength required for this challenging work, the importance of openness with a spiritual director, the centrality of purity of heart (that single-focused longing for God), and the priority of the goal of salvation. Of interest, too, is his suggestion that the deeper disciplines of Lent, while they involve self-denial, are more fundamentally a matter of self-offering. At their best, disciplines are a means of consecration, that is, ways of deepening our capacity to give ourselves body, mind, and spirit to God.

For Benedict, disciplines are oriented toward joy, toward overflowing celebration of the mystery of Easter.[100] The point of disciplines is to allow expectancy to build in us, that we might more fully apprehend that, in his death and resurrection, Christ makes known to us that we are "loved by God and that (we) have been chosen". (I Thess 1:4)

Reflection: The phrase that touches me in this passage is "everyone may offer to God...something beyond the measure appointed." I have been reminded so often in these pages that consecration means offering that there might seem to be nothing new left in it. But just today, it really touches me that God would want something I might offer. Perhaps God is waiting, eagerly, for my offering.

The offering is to be "beyond the appointed measure". In other words, it's not just the standard, the usual thing. It is to be something perhaps that only I could offer. That means something special from my life, from my self. I suppose the special things could be both those in which I rejoice and those that burden me. I could offer my joy in that wonderful tree which stands just outside my window, so solid and so vital every day of my life. Would God then take it away? Might it come back to me even better? It's all unknown, except in faith, given what I know of my God.

I could offer my pain in that broken friendship, that betrayal of trust. In this case, I hope God would take it away, but perhaps it might be given back! Again, it's a matter of trust: I don't think God plays mean games, so if it was given back apparently still broken, then there must be something else given with it to make it bearable, or to serve some good unknown to me.

It all seems so fragile, so risky. Yet I must say that since I have begun to offer things to God, the overall feel of my life has changed very greatly. I am so much aware of great goodness, and always as undeserved gift. So even if I can't see exactly the "how" of it, I'm glad to be learning this way of offering.

Prayer/Response:

Chapter 50: Brethren Working at a Distance from the Oratory or Traveling (entire) And Chapter 51: Brethren on a Short Journey (entire)

Those brethren who work at a great distance and cannot come to the oratory at the proper time (the Abbot judging such to be the case) should perform the Work of God there where they are working, bending their knees in reverent awe. In the same way the appointed hours should not pass them by who are sent on a journey: but insofar as they can, let them perform them there and not neglect to offer their due service.

(Chapter 51:) A Brother who goes out on any business and expects to return to the monastery on the same day must not presume to eat outside, even though he is asked by someone, unless permission has been given by his Abbot. If he acts otherwise let him be excommunicated.

Comment: At first glance, it appears that Benedict is giving two opposite instructions: (1) do pray when you are away from the monastery, and (2) do not eat when you are away from the monastery. Perhaps we might think this is because prayer is holy, and food is worldly. But as we look deeper, we see it is because of a deep unity between the spiritual and the material, the prayer and the meal. Both instructions are about the nature of the Christian family, which for the monk is the monastery.

The two center points of the family's life together are the prayer hours and the meal. Benedict is making clear that the monks are present in the community's heart and life, whether or not they are physically present. They can lift their voices to join in prayer, crossing space and time and affirming the bond in Christ. But when they eat outside, they break rather than affirm the communal bond expressed in the gathered community.

Whether we are in a monastery or not, it is true for each one of us Christians that we have a particular place of belonging in the whole Christian community. That particular place has an incarnated given-ness, a specific and limited context, while it also transcends any limitations of space and time. Benedict is insisting on the central role of this community/family life in affirming and building the consecrated life of each member. The Rule's emphasis here is an invitation for each one of us to pay attention to what community and/or family has been given us to nurture our growth in Christ, and practice living in fidelity to that family.

Reflection: The mental picture of monks away from home reminds me of a couple of my favorite paintings, although neither one is actually about monks! One is the Angelus, with the farmers stopped in the fields, heads bowed at dusk as the church bells ring, joining their prayers--and their lives--to the whole community's. The other is a sketch of a friar, sitting alongside the road with his donkey beside, saying his rosary as he rests. What for me connects both with the monks is the feeling in the paintings that there is a host of angels and saints filling the air with their songs of praise, since the one who prays seems somehow to be joining a mighty multitude.

Last summer I overhead a conversation between a young mother and a Benedictine nun. The nun was talking about the discipline of arising for the 2am office, and the mother exclaimed: "How good to know there is someone else awake and praying in the dead of the night when I often feel so alone feeding my baby!"

Our community is indeed a giant one. How extraordinary that something which so transcends space and time should also be so localized and situated!

Prayer/Response:

Chapter 52: The Oratory of the Monastery (entire)

Let the oratory be what it is called; and let nothing else be done or kept there. When the Work of God is finished all should go out with the utmost silence and with reverence for God; so that a brother who wishes to pray by himself will not be hindered by another's insensitivity. But if one wishes to pray by himself, he should go in with simplicity and pray, not with a loud voice, but with tears and fervor of heart. And let one who is not similarly occupied not be permitted to remain in the oratory after the Work of God, as has been said, lest another be hindered.

Comment: What is the subject of this chapter? Oratory means "place of prayer", stemming from the verb *orare*, to pray. So the chapter is about the place of prayer, and thus in part about praying. Indeed, many commentators turn to this chapter as one of two in the Rule specifically on private prayer. They point out that from the obvious tone here, Benedict takes it for granted that monks will pray privately as well as during the daily office.

But Benedict has such regard for the variations and inspirations of private prayer, that he leaves those largely to individual development, under the guidance of a spiritual elder. The Rule simply provides a guide to regulate the external life of the community, as well as those individual behaviors which offer a sacramental framework for inner purity of heart. Thus he is here concerned chiefly with those subjects that impinge upon or affect the interactions and relationships among the family. It is fascinating that his expressed concern about the oratory is not primarily the prayer that goes on there, but the "mundane" matters, that is, the way each person's behavior might infringe upon others.

In this connection we note two key words: "insensitivity" and "hindered". As always, Benedict shares responsibility: both the one praying and the one not praying have duties toward one another. The one not praying is to honor the silence of the oratory; the one praying is to keep silence also, even in his tears of devotion. This "humdrum" and "external" matter of everyday thoughtfulness for one another is often where Benedict locates "spiritual" progress. Again, we see the interpenetration of the ordinary and the holy.

Reflection: My reflections tug me in two directions, as perhaps Benedict intends! I often find it difficult to be generous in that practical love of neighbor which is called for, when I feel my "rights" are being infringed upon. Indeed, not infrequently do I want to be "at prayer" in an utterly peaceful and serene setting, when someone else's "agenda" interrupts that. On the other hand, even the noise and flutter of tourists cannot erase the privilege of presence in a "holy place", when it carries centuries of prayer offered there. Several friends observed that the "Way of Sorrows" in Jerusalem today is filled with shouting vendors...and then reflected that it probably was the same way on the day when Jesus carried his cross there.

As I reflect, I glimpse the direct relation between love of neighbor and purity of prayer. The love I receive in prayer is truly the only thing I have to offer my brother and sister in the day to day. I cannot hoard it, for then it disappears; when I give it away, it multiplies! And the wonder of that abundance sends me back to prayer in gratitude for God's goodness enfleshed.

Prayer/Response:

Chapter 53: The Reception of Guests, verses 1-14

All guests who come should be received as Christ, for He will say: *I was a stranger and you took me in* (Matt 25:35). And let fitting honor be shown *to all, especially*, however, *to such as are of the household of the faith* (Gal 6:10) and to pilgrims. When, therefore, a guest is announced, let him be met by the superior and the brethren with all signs of love. Let them first pray together, and thus associate with one another in peace; but the kiss of peace must not be offered until prayer has first been said, on account of the delusions of the devil.

And in the salutation itself let all humility be shown. At the arrival or departure of all guests, by bowing the head or even prostrating the whole body on the ground, let Christ be adored in them, who indeed is received. When the guests have been received let them be led to prayer, and then let the superior or anyone he may appoint sit with them. Let the divine law be read to the guest for his edification; and afterwards let all kindness be shown him. The superior may break his fast for the sake of the guest, unless it happens to be a principal fast which may not be broken. The brothers, however, shall observe their accustomed fast. The Abbot is to pour water on the hands of the guests, and both the Abbot and the whole community are to wash the feet of all guests. When they have been washed let them say this verse: *We have received your mercy, O Lord, in the midst of your temple* (Ps 48:10).

Comment: As for the Jew in the temple of Jerusalem (Ps. 48), so for the Christian in the person of Christ: God is received. The awesome majesty and the sure strength of God is actually received. Benedict takes seriously the words of our Lord that he himself will be received in the stranger; indeed, he regards these words as a promise. By our kindness to the stranger and the sick, in the mundane situations, we do greet Christ.

Hospitality has come to be known as the "fourth vow" of the Benedictines, so seriously do they take this instruction to honor all who present themselves. The monks share the best of their lives with the guest, especially their prayer and the Word of God in Scripture. It is as if they brought out all their treasures in eagerness that the newcomer might appreciate them too. In this way, they honor the guest especially, for they invite him or her to consider and respond to the call God makes to the guest.[101] They offer the guest "all kindness", which no doubt means a meal,[102] and in this and the footwashing ceremony, the liturgical aspect of hospitality is heightened, reinforcing the extent to which the monks are to be aware that they are in fact receiving Christ in this stranger.

Reflection: I confess myself to be mystified and captivated by the implications of finding Christ everywhere. Insofar as Christ is my Lord, when I find him I am to be obedient to him, honoring the power and authority he carries, as well as being strengthened by his presence. So, receiving Christ, I am receiving one who nourishes me. Yet also, I am to serve him and minister to him, as to one in need, the guest or the sick person. In this sense, receiving Christ is receiving one whom I am to nourish. Such a mixture of response is quite beyond my power to imagine, in large part because I want to stay in control, know precisely how things stand, and myself be master of the situation, rather than servant to it.

When I consider this potential for receiving Christ in every situation and every person, I realize that I have been experiencing others only at the most superficial level, given this possibility. How might I begin to see Christ in this very specific human incarnation in front of me? ...who has dirty feet, and is weary and hungry, and maybe foreign clothes and an odd accent and an irritable manner? ...Or, who is so familiar that I see her every day and I know exactly her weaknesses and habits and passions and moods?

I see that it begins by being open to the possibility of true relationship with this person now before me. There is no room for categories (this is a such-and-such type!) and none for preoccupation (how will I ever manage to prepare for tomorrow's schedule?). It involves allowing myself to be moved by the impulses of love and joy which burst from Christ's indwelling in me, rather than by the more constrained impulses of my own ego-safety. Such relationship means openness to the possibility that I will be changed, essentially, by something this other might do or say. It involves being willing to encounter irresistible grace and power in this person who carries Christ. I think such openness, such relationship must be the work of a lifetime...as well as a spontaneous response to the sufficiency of grace presented now!

Prayer/Response:

Chapter 53, verses 15-24 (end)

Special care and thoughtfulness should be shown in the reception of the poor and of pilgrims, because in them Christ is more especially received. For the very awe we have of the rich assures them of respect. The kitchen for the Abbot and guests should be set apart by itself so that guests, who are never lacking in a monastery, may not disturb the brethren when they arrive at uncertain hours. Let two brothers who are able to fulfill this duty well be placed in this kitchen for the year. If they need it, let help be offered them, so that they may serve without murmuring. On the other hand, when they do not have much to occupy them let them go out to other work, wherever they are assigned. And not only with regard to them, but also in all the offices of the monastery let this consideration be shown: that when [the monks] need help it is given to them; and again, when they are less busy they should do whatever is assigned them.

Moreover, let a brother whose soul is possessed by the fear of the Lord have the guest-house assigned to his care. There should be sufficient beds provided there And let the house of God be wisely governed by wise men.

Those who are not required to do so should on no account associate or converse with guests. But if (a monk) happens to meet or to see guests, he should, after humbly greeting them as we have said, ask their blessing, and then pass on, explaining that he is not permitted to talk with a guest.

Comment: The second half of this chapter is a great surprise. Considering that the principle articulated in the first half is that guests are to be received as Christ, most of us moderns would interpret that in an "absolute" way; we would give ourselves unstintingly until we exhausted ourselves in the service of the needy who carry Christ.

But Benedict takes the incarnation more seriously than that, both positively and negatively. He knows how seductive "worldly" things can be, if they are not placed in their proper context through prayer, reverence, and silence. So he limits contact between the guests and the monks in general. But this has the effect not only of protecting the monks against worldly influences, but also of protecting them against their own misguided instincts: no one is to exhaust himself. Flesh is to be cared for, according to its requirements. A sufficient number of people are to be assigned so that the work of care-taking can be accomplished within the context of the normal daily routines of the office, the *lectio*, and other matters.

The overall rhythms of the House of God which the Holy Spirit has shown to be essential are to be honored, as well as the guests, for in both is Christ revealed. And unless the daily rhythms which teach us how to see Christ in the ordinary are sustained, then we will lose touch with him in both places. No person can truly serve Christ, unless he or she is also continuously nourished by Christ in prayer, silence, community life, and regularity of food, rest, and study.

Reflection: What a difficult lesson this is for me! How easily I slip into a pattern of exhausting myself in constant busyness, rather than following that pattern of harmonious stewardship of self which involves balance and rest. In a sense, I suppose, what is usually happening for me is the opposite of consecration, of offering up: what I am usually doing is holding on!

If consecration is to be meaningful in a whole life, it must be possible to offer things up when I don't feel like it, when demands become excessive, when I seem to be very far from God. How might I go about that?

It seems to me that Benedict suggests here that I need to honor my own limitations. If I have developed certain rhythmic patterns for the day, knowing that those patterns are beneficial for me, then it is well to stay with those patterns even and especially in times of crisis. Obviously, there will be moments when I must let them go, but I need to return to them as soon as possible, knowing that without them, my strength is limited.

Whatever helps I have found from the Rule, I need to be faithful to them. Maybe it is daily "silence breaks", maybe morning and evening prayer, maybe a time for *lectio*: whatever is found to be valuable is to be honored. Indeed, *lectio* is a good example. If I leave my *lectio* with a prayer word or phrase, I might take that phrase into the day, using it to bless everyone and everything all day long.

All this is a reminder that I am not Christ, all by myself. I can begin to bring Christ and receive Christ, only insofar as I am rooted in those daily patterns which in fact enable me to offer whatever I encounter in the press of the day.

Prayer/Response:

Chapter 54: Letters or Gifts for Monks (entire)

On no account is it allowed for a monk to receive, either from his parents or anyone else, or from his brethren, letters, tokens, or any little gifts whatsoever; nor may he give them to others, without the permission of his Abbot. And if anything is sent to him, even by his parents, he should not presume to receive it, unless it has first been made known to the Abbot.

If [the abbot] orders it to be received, it remains in the Abbot's power to decide to whom it shall be given; nor should this grieve the brother to whom it has been sent, *lest occasion be given to the devil* (Eph 4:27; 1 Tim 5:14). Should anyone, however, presume to act otherwise, let him be subjected to the discipline of the Rule.

Comment: This seems at first an unnecessarily cruel chapter, condemning as it does the "harmless" human habit of sharing gifts as an expression of special relationship. Let us note in passing that such restraint was a standard practice in monasteries of the time,[103] and then turn to the question of its general relevance.

The principle behind this instruction can be found both in the cited Scripture and the Rule's Chapter 33 on the evil practice of private ownership. The procedures of the Rule are intended to build a solid center for the soul, a keen awareness of the Source and Course of one's whole life (Gal 5:25) that penetrates every moment. This is the positive pulse. The negative pulse is the devil's effort to distract us from this awareness of God, generally by misdirecting our own good instincts. Benedict is convinced that pride of ownership is one of the main reasons we abandon God, and thus every impulse to say "this is mine" is to be rooted out.

For example, as this chapter follows immediately after the one on guests, we can imagine that a rich visitor, who had been well-served on a recent stay at the monastery by one of the brothers assigned to the guesthouse, might offer a costly token of affection as thanks. If the brother were to accept such a gift and keep it secret, silently telling himself what a fine chap he is, he would be beginning to build a small wall between himself and his brothers though his own sense of superiority. Whereas, if he offers it at once to the abbot, it might be sold and the funds used to improve the irrigation system, so that all might eat better. This example is overdrawn, perhaps, but one that nonetheless shows the danger to the soul of a spirit of separation.

Even gifts from parents can be a major cause of separatism, for Benedict sought to build an integrated community, without reference to the rigid class system then prevailing in the countryside.[104] Costly gifts from some parents could be a major stumbling block to such an integrated community of faith.

Reflection: I don't like it. I rebel against such a narrow-minded, tight-fisted view of acceptable behavior! And having said that, I realize just how deeply ingrained is that spirit of pride in me which wants to see myself as better than my brothers and sisters. I realize how tied I am to certain possessions which give definition to my personality. It is not easy to know myself to be precious and loved, apart from these external forms. And yet, very often I know the external forms don't convey genuine care at all. Such a muddle!

It occurs to me that there is a place for the offering up, or the consecration, even of anger. It does make me angry to think that gifts might endanger my soul. And I realize as I gently probe my anger that I cannot altogether sort out exactly why I am angry, or what is the remedy. So, there is nothing I can do today to "fix things", whatever that might mean in this context. But what I can do is to offer to God all this: that I am angry, that I am confused, that I can't find a solution. And then I can trust that because this offering really comes from the center of my concerns at this moment, God will be pleased to accept this offering.

Again it is the psalms which help me believe in the value of my anger-offering. Frequently the psalmist seems to shake his fist at God! In the psalms, it seems to be more important that any concern is offered to God, than whether the concern is "appropriate". It's interesting, too, that treating concerns this way seems different than psychotherapy primarily in that, when I have finished analyzing things as far as I can, I release the whole thing. I give up my concerns; I give it all back to God.

Prayer/Response:

Chapter 55: The Clothing and Footwear of the Brethren, verses 1-12

The clothing given to the brethren should be suitable to the nature and climate of the place where they live; for in cold regions more is required and in warm regions less. It is the Abbot's duty, therefore, to consider this. We think, however, that in temperate climates a cowl and a tunic should suffice for each monk: the cowl to be of thick wool in winter, but in summer worn and thin: likewise a scapular for work, and sandals and shoes to cover their feet.

Concerning all these things, as well as their color or coarseness, the monks should not complain; rather they should use whatever can be easily obtained in the region where they live, or can be bought cheaply. The Abbot should be careful about the measurements, so that these garments are not too short for those who wear them, but fit well.

When they receive new clothes they should always return the old ones at once, to be stored in the clothes-room for the poor. For it is sufficient for a monk to have two tunics and two cowls, to provide both night wear and convenience in washing. Anything beyond this is superfluous and ought to be taken away. In the same way let them give back their sandals and whatever else is worn out when they receive new ones.

Comment: At first we are surprised that the Rule should concern itself with such apparently minute and unimportant matters. But, again, we see that the "mundane" reveals Benedict's spiritual theology.

As we note the care to be given to clothing--in terms of attention, careful cleaning and storing for the poor, etc--we are reminded of the principle set forth in the Rule's Chapter 31: everything is to be regarded as is a consecrated vessel of the altar; nothing is to be neglected. And yet again, this realization of the sacramental quality of the material world is balanced by awareness of the sometimes exaggerated attraction of things in themselves.

It is well to be attentive to the things immediately in front of us. We are to reverence them and give them care according to their nature. The specific form of things is important and not accidental, for God is creator. But we are not to stop at the surface level. The form is like a window opening up onto a beautiful vista. If we spend all our time looking at the window frame, what joy we miss! We are to let our enjoyment of things be a lesson in joy, leading us even further in, to the very fullness of Joy Itself.

And Benedict says all this as he talks about clothing, and dishwashing, and care of the sick, and greeting visitors, and the like. In all things, may God be glorified (Chapter 57:9), even in the matter of daily dress.

Reflection: Esther de Waal remarks of the Rule's guidance that it is utterly simple (beyond the reach of no one), and yet utterly demanding (requiring the most strenuous and continuous discipline).[105] This chapter on clothing is a good example of that. It makes me realize how far I am from being aware that every single thing I do has the potential to glorify God or not. It is not a hard thing to remember, in the sense of complexity. But it is so hard, in the sense of difficulty. I'm dumbstruck at how far I am from loving God with my whole heart.

For Benedict, the mundane reveals God. It's such a paradox. I have always thought of God as being apart from the earthy, the ordinary. It's hard to make this shift to seeing everything as a prism which shows forth something of God. And yet, when I can see it this way, how lovely it is! A simple dish becomes a precious vessel, an ordinary hand becomes a thing of wonder, my life itself becomes full of glory.

One of my favorite meditations is to imagine young Mary of Nazareth, sweeping the floor on a hot day, hearing the sound of flies buzzing, and suddenly having the sense that the whole small house was filled up with the amazing presence of Gabriel, whose next words will change not only her life but the course of the world! I have recently discovered a modern novelist[106] whose books convey that same sense of potency inherent in every encounter. Something like that is what Benedict communicates to me in this careful stewardship even of clothing. Something like that must be what consecration means.

Prayer/Response:

Chapter 55, verses 13-22 (end)

Those who are sent on a journey should receive underclothing from the clothes-room, and on their return, return them washed. Let their cowls and tunics also be a little better than those they usually wear; they are to receive these from the clothes-room when setting out on their journey, and restore them on their return.

For their bedding let a mattress, blanket, coverlet, and pillow suffice. These beds must be frequently inspected by the Abbot because of private property - lest it be found there. If anyone is found with anything he has not received from the Abbot, he is to be subjected to the most severe discipline. In order that this vice of private ownership may be cut off by the roots let the Abbot supply all things that are necessary: that is, cowl, tunic, sandals, shoes, belt, knife, stylus, needle, handkerchief, and writing tablets; so that any excuse of necessity may be taken away.

Yet the Abbot must always be mindful of those words in the Acts of the Apostles: *Distribution was made to everyone according to his need* (Acts 4:35). Let him, therefore, consider the infirmities of those in want, and not the ill-will of the envious. Nevertheless, in all his decisions, let him reflect on the judgment of God.

Comment: For the second time, Benedict speaks severely of the "vice of private ownership" (compare RB 33:1), and immediately thereafter quotes Acts in the description of the first Christian community in Jerusalem (see RB 33:6, 34:1).

Careful reading of that whole section of Acts (4:23 to 5:16) reveals a Christian community empowered by the Holy Spirit, a community filled with awe and wonder and love and thanksgiving and praise -- a community whose life was wholly turned in gratitude toward God the Savior. Thus, the sharing of goods in common was not so much a discipline for its own sake, as rather the natural expression of hearts so full they could not contain their love. Benedict's discipline of common ownership is intended to work backwards toward the goal of the disposition of charity. His intention is to establish a framework for practicing charity day in and day out in small things, whereby one's heart is gradually opened to the fullness of True Charity which transforms the whole personality from within.

Reflection: I am drawn by the phrase "any excuse...(will) be taken away" (verse 19 above). A friend of mine argues that was the main purpose of the life-death-resurrection of Jesus: to take away our excuses that we can't be good enough for God. That's where I "live"! I know myself to be flawed, and I keep insisting I need this or that improvement before I can really give myself to God. All of which talk simply turns out to be an excuse not to risk myself to the awesome out-of-controlness that involves abandoning myself to the glory of divine providence.

And the wonder of it is that abandonment can take place in such ordinary, workaday environments! Perhaps until now I have avoided seeing the simplicity of this because it does make abandonment/offering to God so remarkably easy. I can do it while making beds, washing clothes, buying shoes, taking out a handkerchief. I can, of course, even do it while thinking how much "better" I need to be before I am suitable for God. Everything can be offered, any time and any place.

And the truth is that all along and anyway, I am upheld even in my very breathing -- much less everything else I "possess" -- only by that loving Providence. What joy when I can truly rest in that!

Prayer/Response:

Chapter 56: The Abbot's Table (entire)

The Abbot's table should always be with guests and pilgrims. But when there are few guests, it is within his power to invite any of the brothers he wishes. Let him take care, however, always to leave one or two seniors with the brethren, for the sake of discipline.

Comment: We recall from Chapter 51 that the table is a symbol of monastic (Christian) unity, second only in importance to the oratory (chapel). So, despite its great brevity, this chapter reveals important principles.

First, the abbot is to welcome and receive as those-who-belong the strangers and guests of the community. The abbot joins the guests, as a sign that they are also brothers and sisters, that is, also children and co-heirs of God.

Second, the abbot is free to share his bread with every member of the monastic community, much like the family in which young and old freely interact. This viewpoint is particularly apparent in Benedict by comparison with his main source, where only senior monks and "those who know the psalter" are privileged to share the abbot's table.[107] Wherever possible, Benedict emphasizes the affirmative motivation: that our lives are a joyful response to God's love, rather than primarily a fearful avoidance of punishment. The abbot may invite monks to share his meal, out of care for each person as one specially loved by God. Such privileges need not be reserved as a special reward for "good behavior". Each one of us can share and receive the daily love of God in such concrete events of daily life.

Reflection: Who are the people I encounter in a day? Often I stay at the most superficial level, making judgments on the basis of dress or manner or behavior, distinguishing between them and myself. I have been slow to learn the deep joy that comes from recognizing and responding to the spirit in every person. The sacramental awareness of things can be extended to a sacramental awareness of people. I'm learning to be very attentive to the person as he or she is externally, while also open to his or her deeper inner reality. As I let the Spirit guide my knowing of persons, I am privileged to see great beauty.

I am learning to see Christ in those who are given to me. And as I have begun to appreciate that gift, I have come to a startling realization. I can see Christ in others far better than they can in themselves. The reverse is also true: others can see Christ in me better than I can in myself. So one of the great gifts of belonging to the community, the Body of Christ, is that others can help me have faith in Christ dwelling in me, especially at those moments when I have completely lost sight of that possibility. When we hold out this vision to one another, in some way we help bring the Kingdom into being. It's like that image of heaven as a long banquet table, piled high with food, with forks three feet long. So the only way to eat is for everyone to feed the neighbor across the table. We are esssential to one another in order that together we become Christ's whole Body.

What does Christ's Body look like? Sometimes on Sunday mornings I watch people coming back from the communion rail, saying to myself: "This is Christ's Body; these are God's people." They are in some ways as strange to me as an earlobe might be to an elbow; and in some ways as familiar as one human cell to another.

Prayer/Response:

Chapter 57: The Artisans of the Monastery (entire)

If there are craftsmen in the monastery, let them practice their crafts in all humility, provided the Abbot gives permission. But if one of them becomes conceited on account of his knowledge of his craft, believing that he thereby confers some benefit on the monastery, he is to be taken from it and not permitted to exercise it again, unless having humbled himself, the Abbot bids him resume.

If any of the work of the craftsmen is to be sold, let those through whose hands the business has to pass not presume to commit any fraud. Let them remember Ananias and Sapphira (Acts 5:1-11), lest perchance they and all who deal fraudulently with the goods of the monastery should suffer in their souls the death which these incurred in the body.

In the the establishing of prices the vice of avarice must not creep in; rather, the goods should always be sold a little cheaper than by those living in the world, *that God may be glorified in all things* (1 Pet 4:11).

Comment: This chapter is a reflection on giftedness and stewardship. The passage is I Peter here quoted begins with these words:

"Each one of you has received a special grace, so, like good stewards responsible for all these different graces of God, put yourselves at the service of others...that in everything God may receive the glory."

This whole section has been concerned with the fact that the mundane and the ordinary elements of each day are in fact gifts of God. It is when we see them and treat them in that way, that we become God's stewards and co-participants in the bringing forth of the Kingdom.

In particular, the artisan--or one who works skillfully in a craft--is one gifted by God. The gift is not his or hers to possess, hoard, or exploit, but rather is something given by God for the purpose of extending God's creation. The reference to Ananias and Sapphira is a reminder that all things are God's gift--physical possessions such as land, property, and money, no less than personal skills. When God gives, it is for use and enjoyment, but God also expects a return on the investment (Luke 19:11-23): stewardship, offering and thanksgiving are the appropriate responses to gifts. Fundamental to the consecration of life is awareness of all life as gifted: we are offering back to God that which originally was given to us from God.

All this is congruent with the overall tone of the Rule about possessions in common (Chapter 33), service of one another (Chapter 35) and reverence for the ordinary as filled with the holy (Chapter 31). This chapter is a fitting summary of this section on the consecration of the mundane: everything is to be done that God may be glorified!

Reflection: Conceptually, who would disagree with Benedict? But again, I see a great gulf between what I know and what I do. I see how important it is to practice what I believe in my daily life experience.

Recently I have thought frequently about the place where my husband and I live. It is a kind of wooded haven, which is entered by an ambiguously public/private street, thus often inviting the curiosity of strangers. Regularly people drive or stroll down our driveway, sometimes cutting through a dirt pathway to the street above our canyon, sometimes turning around sheepishly to drive out the way they came. Recently a small commercial outfit wanted to use our place to film an advertisement, and our outraged neighbor insisted they compensate us financially for the use of our "private property". My first instinct is to assert ownership and drive out the stranger, but then I wonder if the truth is not rather that we are simply stewards of a gift which rightfully belongs to many besides us.

Perhaps this is a model for me of the process of consecration. Our home is such a rich blessing, for which I am daily thankful and to which I give daily care. But underneath both care and thanksgiving is offering up of everything I have, acknowledging regularly to myself that all of it was first a gift.

Prayer/Response:

Interlude VIII:

A Note to the Reader...

Do you sometimes wish for a deeper and more complete interaction with the material than these brief *lectio* meditations offer?

Perhaps you have been doing this process mentally, and have never actually written down your responses. Perhaps even if you have written, you have stayed within the confines of this book, or your regular limited *lectio* time. And occasionally, that's just not enough.

You might like to start a separate "spiritual journal", where you can explore at more leisure some of the themes you have noticed during your *lectio*. A spiritual journal is as unique and flexible as your own personality. The only required elements are paper and pencil, your reflections, and actually writing them down. Like so much in the spiritual life, it sounds so simple, and yet it is capable of producing much fruit.

From your *lectio*, you already know how to start the reflection process, and that is the key to good journaling. You pay attention to what is going on in your life, and then you reflect on it. In the reflection, you look at it from different points of view, so as to deepen your awareness.

First, write down a life incident, of any sort: a dream, a personal encounter, something you noticed that bothered or attracted you, a nagging feeling of dissatisfaction about something. Then, if you can, try to find a metaphor for it. Say to yourself, "It feels like ____________." Fill in the blank. It feels like a bud about to open. It feels like clinging to a tiny branch above a deep canyon. Or, to use an example we cited earlier, it feels like wrestling with God.

Then, let the metaphor lead you into other perspectives. What image does the metaphor evoke for you from Scripture? from the culture? from your own opinions and beliefs? For example, the bud about to open suggests to me Mary and the Angel Gabriel. It also suggests to me the eager hopefulness in the Philippines a few years ago when people brought a new democratic government to birth. Oddly, perhaps, it also evokes in me Grandma's favorite phrase about nipping fleshly desires in the bud.

In other words, bring to bear on your life incident the additional perspectives of Scripture, culture, and personal values, journaling about whatever seems pertinent. Let these additional perspectives expand your reflection on how God might be speaking to you in this present situation. The point is to become more deeply aware of our own perspectives, so that we can more fully offer all that we are to God. It doesn't matter how formally or informally we do that, so long as we are seeking to let the Light penetrate into our inmost being, that it might bring healing, transformation, wholeness and love.

Membership and Governance Within the Community

Chapter 58: The Procedure for Receiving Brothers,

verses 1-8

To those who are beginners in this way of life an easy entrance should not be granted; rather, as the Apostle says, *Try the spirits whether they are of God* (1 John 4:1). If, therefore, the one who comes perseveres in knocking, and after four or five days seems patiently to endure the wrongs done to him and the difficulty made about his entrance; and if he persists in his petition, let entrance be granted him, and let him stay in the guest-house for a few days. Afterwards let him stay in the novitiate, where he is to meditate, eat, and sleep.

There should be assigned to him a senior monk skilled in winning souls who will watch him with the utmost care, considering carefully whether he truly seeks God, and is zealous for the Work of God, for obedience, and for humiliations. It should be clearly laid out for him how hard and rugged are the ways by which we walk towards God.

Comment: With this chapter, Benedict shifts attention to matters of membership within the community and its governance. This chapter in particular, dealing as it does with the primary process for admission to the community, provides a marvelous image or metaphor for the initial steps of the consecrated Christian life.

The phrase "perseveres in knocking" appears to be taken from Luke 11:8, where Jesus is teaching about perseverance in prayer, which is certainly a crucial ingredient of consecration. Hardships all along the way are a test and a strengthening of our endurance. Endurance, or perseverance, is a primary method by which our many desires become purified into the one central desire for God. Deeper and more fundamental than the many spirits is the one of Christ, and our waiting and our longing will ultimately bring us to him.

But it is by no means the case that all the endeavor is solely on the part of the individual seeking God. As the person refines his or her intention, the community lends all its support, wisdom, and skill, eagerly to assist the new arrival.[108] This interdependence between the arrival and the community is suggestive of the way God is present here, supporting every impulse of love as the Kingdom is built by many hands.

Above all, we should not miss the language of verse 8. There will be many hard and rugged ways. But that is not the point. The point is that by them "we walk **towards God**". Within the community of faith and the tradition of prayer, hardship is known as a natural part of the path to Life.

Reflection: However long we have been Christians, it seems to me that we are always encountering new beginnings, new life, deeper conversion. These "initial stages" do indeed seem to have certain patterns, though I seldom notice them at the time. One regular pattern is the appearance of a period during which I know there is a new step to take, but I haven't quite decided with my whole being to take it. (My longing needs to intensify first!) Oddly enough, at this point, if someone tries to help me along, I'll have a thousand reasons "why not now". The first step has to be taken by me alone, and only when I am ready.

After that step has been taken, there is often an initial period of intense and joy-filled awareness of God. But not too soon thereafter follows a time of frustration and difficulty. This period seems to be characterized by a superficial sense of God's absence while yet also a peculiar certainty that I am being faithful to my own particular call. Eventually, there seems to occur an internal synthesis in which I experience a deepened awareness of God's presence and love. But, how very important it has been for me to have a spiritual friend or director as I negotiate that middle passage. Otherwise, I convince myself that I am being totally untrue, not only to God but to myself, and I abandon that difficult and "blind" work of purification. I can read books about this middle stage, but it has been essential to me to supplement such impersonal knowledge with the help of one who knows me.

Prayer/Response:

Chapter 58, verse 7 (same passage)

It should be considered carefully whether he (the novice) truly seeks God, and is zealous for the Work of God, for obedience, and for humiliations.

Comment: It seems worth breaking our usual pattern to dwell formally two days on this rich text about initial steps in the consecrated Christian life, particularly this verse 7.

Here Benedict is advising the novice master and the community on those qualities which are the marks of one likely to endure in the monastic commitment, one likely to strengthen and contribute to the monastic community. What qualities does he emphasize?

(1) "truly seeks God". This is a frequent theme not only in the patristic literature generally but also in Scripture. For example, it is keenly expressed in Psalm 27:

> "One thing I seek: to live in the house of Yahweh all the days of my life." "My heart has said of you, 'seek his face'." "This I believe: I shall see the goodness of Yahweh, in the land of the living" (verses 4,8,13).

Benedict is unquestionably familiar with the patristic thought on this phrase, as well as considering it in his own prayer. The phrase is a short-hand expression for a specific longer meaning. That meaning is implicit in the Rule's Prologue (verses 14-18) where we are reminded that it is God who seeks us.[109] Thus the one who truly seeks God is one who has simply heard and responded with his or her whole heart to the voice already calling.

(2) "is zealous for the Work of God". This phrase "Work of God" refers specifically to the daily office, as we have previously noted. The monk is one who finds his or her life rooted in regular prayer. The prayer is a source of nurture and also a formative influence; one is open to the prayer in such a way as to become docile to God's Spirit in and through it. The prayer with the community shapes one's whole life with the community. (See for example, Chapter 13:12-14; 19:3-7.)

(3) "is zealous for...obedience". Such language almost seems a contradiction in terms to us, but it probably means something like this: the novice is to show evidence of awareness of the limits of his or her own knowledge and an eagerness to be taught. Learning involves life skills and not just mental knowledge. Learning involves sometimes not understanding the purpose of certain practices, but willingness to consent cheerfully nonetheless.

(4) "is zealous for...humiliations". "Humiliations" - that wonderful source of humility! Here the issues might be framed like this: Does the novice have a "chip on the shoulder", or a neurotic need to be right all the time or in control all the time? Is there in this person some recognition that life often brings hardships which cannot be prevented, and a patience to bear with them? Is there a sense of humor which can laugh at and bear with one's own foolishness, receiving mistakes gratefully as good teachers?

Most of us don't have the opportunity to be objectively tested by such questions in modern lay life. Even marriage and family settings are often a way to avoid rather than face these issues in ourselves. Yet how important these matters are for our psychological health, not to mention spiritual! And if we have eyes to see and ears to hear, many ordinary opportunities give us the chance to practice simplicity of heart.

Reflection: As I reflect on this list, it seems to me that these are qualities needed for the Body of Christ, wherever and however it is incarnated. When I lived alone, I could fool myself in many ways about my charitable disposition. If I live with others but refuse them permission to confront me with these issues, I can still be blind to the truth about myself. But if I really long to live in loving Christian community, then these true tests of intimacy are a wonderful gift to me, as they wear away my pride.

Benedict's list includes no consideration of like-mindedness or common table manners etc. This suggests that it doesn't really matter whether or not I am attracted to, agree with, or feel friendly toward a fellow Christian. What matters is that we both earnestly seek God and try to live in faithfulness to God. How seldom I look at my brothers and sisters in that pure light!

Prayer/Response:

If he promises to persevere in his stability, after the lapse of two months let this Rule be read to him straight through, then let him be told: "Behold the law under which you choose to fight: if you can keep it, enter; if you cannot, freely depart." If he still stands firm, let him be taken to the aforementioned novitiate, and again tried in all patience. After the lapse of six months, let the Rule be read to him again, that he may know what it is he is entering. Should he still stand firm, after four months let the same Rule be read to him once more. And if, having deliberated within himself, he promise to keep all these things and to observe everything that is commanded him, then let him be received into the community, knowing that it is decreed by the law of the Rule that from that day forward he may not depart from the monastery nor shake off from his neck the yoke of the Rule, which after such prolonged deliberation he was free either to refuse or to accept.

Comment: Another extraordinarily rich passage! Here Benedict is dealing with the root issues of longing, freedom, and obedience, of human Will enfolded in God's Will.

The evident tension which Benedict presents here is that expressed by Paul in the seventh chapter of Romans: that for which I most long is that which in isolation I am utterly unable effectively to choose. And yet I can choose with that part of me which carries my deepest intention, that is, where the gift of my strong longing attracts me to my God. And I can then back this choice up with perseverance and self-acceptance. It is this choice which God's grace (mediated by the Scripture, prayer, community, abbot and rule) rewards richly. But it is well to know at the start that it will require both patience and grace. (Compare Prologue 41)

Presenting the opportunity for acceptance three times is reminiscent of Jesus' questions to Peter in John 21:15f: "Simon, son of John, do you love me?" That is the question: do we love God? And it is the question we need to be asked again and again, until we realize how paltry is our love, and how richly and helpfully God knows that. We are told that Peter was grieved that Jesus asked the third time, for he knew the limits of his own love, but he also knew that Jesus knew them as well. And therein lies the hope which enables any true commitment.

Reflection: I notice especially that Benedict encourages and indeed requires a "prolonged deliberation" to inform this important commitment. Just so do I realize newly how important this daily process of reflection is -- laying side by side both my aspirations and my behavior, and discovering therein ever freshly both that longing and that humility which keep me eager for sweet dependence upon my God.

Reflection helps me to get more deeply in touch with who I am and what I do long for. Several years ago I was irritated and then amused when someone asked me, "who are you?" and after I had answered, he asked me again! After the second answer, the question was posed yet a third time. At first, I thought I was not being heard, but then I realized the repeated question was intended to evoke deeper and deeper reflection, until I was able to hear myself at a vastly more authentic level than at first.

My life with God is always going on at those deeper levels, but sometimes I lose awareness of it by failure to reflect.

Prayer/Response:

The one to be received is to make in the oratory before all, a promise of stability, faithfulness to monastic life (*conversatione morum suorum*), and obedience. This is done in the presence of God and His saints, so that, if he should ever act otherwise, he will know that he will be condemned by Him whom he mocks.

Comment: Benedict is emphasizing that the monk's promise contains three elements: stability, "conversatione" and obedience.

These "are not to be understood to be three distinct vows, as the vows of religious life later came to be understood. Rather, the phrase describes the content of the monk's promise."[110]

We can understand this content as a commitment to the whole way of life spelled out in the Rule. Special emphases of this life embodied in this promise are these:

(1) stability: This is not running away from oneself or God. It is staying put and allowing oneself to be purified in the fire of God's life growing within.

(2) obedience: This is simple obedience to the Rule, the abbot, and one's brothers, in the context of the deeper obedience of attentive listening to all of life for the face of Christ there revealed.

(3) *conversatio*: This is ongoing conversion to God, as expressed in the whole monastic manner of life (simplicity and humility, for example) and deepened formation of the heart toward virtue and grace.[111]

Benedict also clarifies that the monk's promise is made in the presence of the community, but to God. The word "mock" is the same word used in Gal 6:7, as follows:

"Don't delude yourselves into thinking God can be cheated (mocked): where (one) sows, there he reaps."

Thus we see the great seriousness of the promise, the great importance of the commitment. We understand that here is one who has solemnly declared, in the presence of God, the angels and saints, and human brothers and sisters, that he or she is committed each day to listen to the voice that calls out: "do not harden your heart!" (Prologue, verse 9-10)

Reflection: What touches me is the wonderment whether, in the life of the laity, there is such a solemn moment as this. Is there a point at which, supported by a community of peers, we declare our intention to love God with all our heart and mind and soul and strength? Certainly it is implicit in baptism, for this monastic commitment is an intentional living out in full of the baptismal covenant promise. Perhaps for many young people and adults it is brought to some degree of solemnity and personal commitment in adult baptism and/or confirmation.

Yet even if the moment itself is not given as such, for me there was a growing conviction, a growing longing, which more and more found its expression in the daily self-offering of my life to God. And even though there was a special time of consecration, it seems to need daily renewal. Also for me, the evolving consecration typical of my life needs to be nourished among a community of fellow disciples, even if we be only three friends who meet regularly in prayer, or a director and a directee, or a Bible study group at church. How much I need the presence of others who are also trying to live out this daily self-offering to God! For me, it is largely in the context of life together with a few others that I am empowered to deepen my personal discovery that God still does call, and still does provide the resources necessary for my generous daily response.

Prayer/Response:

Chapter 58, verses 19-29 (end)

Concerning this promise of his, he is to make a petition in the name of the saints whose relics are there, and of the Abbot who is present. He is to write this petition with his own hand; or at least, if he is illiterate let another write it at his request, and let the novice place his mark on it and place it with his own hand upon the altar. When he has placed it there, the novice himself is to begin this verse: *Uphold me,* Lord, *according to your word, and I shall live; let not my hope be put to shame* (Ps 119:116). The whole community is to repeat this verse three times, adding to it the *Gloria Patri.* Then the brother novice is to cast himself at the feet of all, that they may pray for him; and from that day let him be counted as one of the community.

If he has any posessions he should either first bestow them on the poor, or by a solemn deed of gift donate them to the monastery, keeping nothing for himself; knowing that from that day forward he will have no power, even over his own body. Immediately afterwards in the oratory he is to be stripped of his own garments which he is wearing, and be clothed in those of the monastery. Those garments which are taken from him are to be placed in the clothes-room to be kept there, so that if ever by the persuasion of the devil he consents (God forbid!) to leave the monastery, he may be stripped of the things of the monastery and cast forth. The petition, however, which the Abbot received on the altar will not be given back to him, but will be kept in the monastery.

Comment: Here Benedict directs certain physical actions to express specific theological convictions.

(1) Body of Christ: The new monk expresses his awareness that trust and interdependence are essential to salvation, as he offers the prayer from the Psalms, which the community joins, and asks for their prayers to support his promise.

(2) Baptism and Christian life as a dying-and-rising with Christ: The monk offers his whole self and indeed is stripped of his clothes and possessions, only to be robed with the new clothes symbolizing new membership in this communion of God's people.

(3) God's grace in everything: Even when things go wrong, they are not beyond God's mercy. The provision to retain the monk's pledge paper is an ironic form of reassurance that even when the devil tricks us into believing we have passed beyond God's mercy, there is grace enduring beyond our flight. (See Chapter 29.)

Reflection: I am so drawn to the words of the prayer of consecration! "Uphold me, Lord, according to your word, and I shall live; let not my hope be put to shame". I make the promise to the community and to God with all my heart and soul. Yet even as I do so, I know it is beyond my power to keep. How shall I turn toward God in every moment, when I know I can't do it more than five minutes in 24 hours?! How shall I be humble at all times, when I know the power of my pride?! Even with the prayers and support of the community, it is beyond my power to keep this promise.

So, what is it that I am doing in this promise? I am asking to be received. I am asking God to take me into the divine life. I am, in short, expressing that hope which is my deepest longing. And I place my faith in that longing and in my God, and not in any power of my own.

Prayer/Response:

Chapter 59: The Offering of Sons by The Noble or the Poor (entire)

If a nobleman offers his son to God in the monastery, and the boy is not old enough, the parents are to make out the petition of which we spoke before. And, together with the offerings, let them wrap that petition and the hand of the child in the altar-cloth, and so offer him.

With regard to their property they must in the same petition promise under oath that they will never, either directly, through an intermediary, or in any way whatever, give him anything or the means of having anything. Or else, if they are unwilling to do this and desire to give something for their advantage as an offering to the monastery, let them make a donation to the monastery of the property which they wish to give, reserving to themselves, if they so wish the revenues. And so let every way be blocked, that the child will have no sort of expectation by which he might be misled and perish (which God forbid!), as we have learned by experience may happen.

Those who are poorer are to do the same. But those who have nothing whatever shall simply make the petition, and offer their son along with the offerings and before witnesses.

Comment: The last chapter and this one set forth the two major methods of entrance into monastic life, and in a sense form a parallel to adult baptism/confirmation and infant baptism, the latter involving a parental commitment on behalf of the child.

The context of entrance is set by the phrase "together with the offerings", referring to that moment in the Eucharistic celebration known as the oblation, or offering. The Eucharistic oblation is the offering to God for consecration of the ordinary elements of daily life--bread and wine. Indeed, even as ordinary things, they are gifts of God. We offer them back to God in thanks; God returns them to us transformed. In this exchange we are given the necessary nourishment for true life.

This offertory exchange is a metaphor for monastic profession. A life is offered to God, which in the first place was God's own gift. In God's hands that life is transformed. It is received yet again, filled with God's own presence and guiding care. This offering is not once only, but daily re-enacted. This is the method of consecration.

This metaphor suggests why it is so important not to presume to possess anything. The awareness that all is gift lies at the heart of the consecrated life. Nothing is possessed; in all that is important, the Christian is receptive. Any hint of ownership or entitlement is a basic refusal of this essential disposition toward the Giver of Life.

Reflection: I ponder what seems to be Benedict's formula of consecration:

(1) receive life as gifted;

(2) offer the gift in return to God;

(3) receive the transformed gift, which carries the presence and nourishment of the Giver;

(4) repeat the process each day, with everything.

This formal description of a moment of consecration serves as a model for the daily process of consecration seen so often in the Rule's section on "Consecration of Mundane Activities". Yet taken so straightforwardly, it seems much easier to say the formula than to live it.

As I try to practice consecration in daily life, I encounter resistances in myself. Pondering that resistance, I realize that I prefer to have something I can claim as my own, something well defined and "reliable", something I can possess and manage comfortably. At first, it feels very frightening to become aware that the only "constant" is ongoing relationship (not material possession in any of its forms). Yet as I practice, gradually I sense the release of fear and a growing sense of comfort with One who is trustworthy. I realize that I do not need to cling to my ideas of God, nor even my ideas of myself. Certainty lies not in those static pictures, but only in the dynamism of the love we share. As this becomes real for me, how free I am to enjoy everything!

Prayer/Response:

Chapter 60: Priests who Wish to Live in The Monastery (entire)

If anyone ordained to the priesthood asks to be received into the monastery, assent should not be granted him too quickly; but if he persists strongly in this request, he should know that he must keep all the discipline of the Rule, and that nothing will be relaxed in his favor, for it is written: *Friend, for what have you come* (Matt 26:50)? Nevertheless, it may be granted him to stand next to the Abbot, to give the blessing, and to celebrate Mass, if the Abbot asks him to do so. Otherwise, he should not presume to do anything, knowing that he is subject to the discipline of the Rule; but rather let him give an example of humility to all. Should there arise a question of an appointment or other matter in the monastery, he is to expect the position due to him according to the time of his entrance, and not that which was granted to him out of reverence for the priesthood.

Clerics who similarly desire to be admitted into the monastery are to be placed in a middle rank: but this only if they promise observance of the Rule and stability.

Comment: Perhaps in our time this whole chapter seems odd, since we are familiar with monasteries composed chiefly of ordained persons. However, in Benedict's time the monastery was a lay community, and we believe Benedict himself to have been a layman.[112]

The emphasis on the importance of being subject to the Rule, and observing humility and stability, is a reminder that the Rule is designed to facilitate a certain kind and depth of Christian formation, which is not necessarily found even in priestly formation! Even today, with the emphasis on academic qualifications in seminaries, many priests are hungry for solid spiritual formation. However, if the entering priest is one who has deeply integrated say, the steps of humility (above in Chapter 7), then he will have no difficulty entering harmoniously into the community life. But if he has not previously had some such training, then the monastery will become for him what he ought to be seeking there--a way of breaking the arrogance of pride against the Rule's daily disciplines of finding Christ in all.

It may seem strange that Benedict cites this specific Scripture from Matthew, which of course is the question Jesus poses in Gethsemane to Judas, who has come to betray him. Yet again does Benedict reveal his even-handedness. He honors the priest as one who carries Christ, especially in his capacity to consecrate the bread and wine; even while he warns that same priest that the call of every Christian is to enter fully into that mind of Christ which finds expression in the Rule's guidance. Exemptions from this call are granted neither for any weakness nor for any strength. Those closest to Christ may yet betray him, if they trust primarily in their own self-will.

Reflection: What a hard word this is! My need is so great for security and comfort. I want so much to be able to say, "Well, I know I am a disciple; I've been with Jesus and I understand his mind; I am able and deserving of God's generosity." It's interesting that this happens for me especially with the issue of ordination. Occasionally, I will be overwhelmed by an impulse to seek ordination. Every time, when I track it down, I discover it to be an impulse for certainty and for security. Sometimes I want a tidy little box, which will give me a "code-word" I can use for others and myself to "verify" that I'm alright-with-God. Yet I'm always brought back to the realization that ordination describes a function and not a relationship. The relationship may or may not co-exist with the function, but they are separate issues. And ordination is no assurance of relationship; often in fact it's a distraction from it.

My call, like the monks of old, is to be a consecrated layperson. It's an unsettling call, which never fits into any tidy categories, and which must be renewed each day. A friend of mine says: "Each morning when I wake, I must reaffirm my vocation to be a monk." That's what it's like for me; each day I must reaffirm my self-offering in response to God's call. It involves a deepening realization that I have an important relationship with One who loves me, and that alone is my secure point of reference in good times and bad.

Prayer/Response:

Chapter 61: How Visiting Monks are Received, verses 1-4

If any visiting monk comes from a distant place and wishes to remain in the monastery as a guest, and if he is content with the customs of the place as he finds them and does not trouble the monastery with any unreasonable requests, but is simply content with what he finds; he should be received for as long a time as he wishes. Indeed, if he offers criticism or makes suggestions reasonably and with humble love, the Abbot should consider the matter prudently; for perhaps God sent him for this very reason.

Comment: One of the main ways in which balance is expressed in the Rule is by the complementary obligations which Benedict places on co-participants in any situation.[113] For example, in Chapter 36 the monks are instructed to care for the sick, and then the sick are instructed not to make excessive demands on their caretakers. A similar complementarity is expressed in this chapter. Guests are to be received by the monks as Christ (see Chapter 53:1-2), but guests themselves are admonished to be "content with the customs of the place as he finds them and does not trouble the monastery with any unreasonable requests". To deepen this complementarity, Benedict also invites the abbot to be aware that sometimes discomfort and disagreement express a point of view we really need to hear.

Perhaps we find it odd to have contentment stressed as a Christian virtue, as Benedict does with visiting monks. Ordinarily we may think of contentment as an expression of lukewarmness, which Benedict emphasizes is at odds with the Gospel. But we may better understand contentment as the opposite of that discontent so typical of our age. Our discontent is like that *acedia* mentioned in Chapter 48, which is an idleness of spirit, revealing fundamental inability to be present to the moment before us. Thus, the virtue of contentment expresses attentive presence, the ability to see God in the midst of things as they are. It is a receiving of that which is offered to us, as a necessary prelude to offering it back to God. It is, of course, this contentment which enables the abbot to be receptive to the criticisms and observations of strangers.

Reflection: I wonder if contentment is really a virtue? Like balance, it can so easily slip over into lukewarmness or fence-straddling. And I know there are times, say when tempers get hot at a party, that I am glad to be neutral about a particularly distressing issue. Yet surely contentment must be more than merely indifference.

Again, I think it is my prayer that begins to teach me about this. I find that the more seriously I pray, the less easily am I able to be opinionated about issues. The more keenly do I listen to both sides of an argument, and hear the wisdom represented in each. In fact, I often think it was a great deal easier to know what I thought and what I wanted, before I began to take prayer seriously. Oddly, though, today my sympathy is much more keenly drawn into situations of suffering of all types, and my intercession in "hopeless" cases much more fervent.

I've begun to realize that this "middle place" may not just be a temporary stop on the way to a fixed opinion. It may be indeed that it is right for me to feel constantly tugged between two competing points of view, now closer to one and now another. I think in fact that the thing I must hold fast to in all this is the sense of tension.

One clear example for me is that I am called at this moment both to love the monastic life and to be an active layperson in the world. At first, it seemed to me that the tension was unbearable, and that I should "fish or cut bait"! I ought to choose between one and the other, and give up the longing/desire for the unchosen one. Yet I was unable to choose, and gradually I began to see that at the moment, God calls me to have a foot on both sides. It may look like fence-straddling to some, but to me it feels like a bridge, a conduit through which communication becomes possible in a way it would not, were there not persons like myself who become content being "mixed". The tension continues, but the contentment predominates.

Prayer/Response:

If after some time he wishes to fix his stability [in the monastery] this desire should not be denied, especially since his manner of life could be well ascertained during the time he was a guest. But if during that time he was found extreme or prone to vice, not only should he be refused admission as a member of the community, but he should even be told courteously to depart, lest others be corrupted by his misery.

If, however, he is not the sort who deserves to be sent away, he should not merely be received as a member of the community on his own request; rather, he should be persuaded to stay so that others may be taught by his example, and because in every place we serve one Lord and fight under one King. And if the Abbot perceives that he is a man of this kind, he may put him in a somewhat higher place. Not only a monk, but also any of the aforesaid priests or clerics may be put by the Abbot in a higher place than they would be accorded by the time of their entrance, if he perceives that their lives merit it.

But the Abbot must take care never to receive permanently a monk from any known monastery without the consent of the monk's own Abbot and letters of recommendation; because it is written: *What you would not have done to yourself, do not do to another* (Tob 4:16).

Comment: Benedict is suggesting that the quality of life of the visitor also affects the community in very deep ways. The "presence" of this newcomer may be beneficial or toxic. If we who serve the same Lord are members of one another, then the persons we are have a profound mutual influence for good or evil. Therefore it behooves us to develop the discernment to recognize those who are negative influences and those who are positive ones, and respond accordingly.

This is not the same as refusing the company of sinners; it is awareness that among the self-proclaimed righteous, some will be life-giving and some will be death-bringing for this specific human community.

How interesting that Benedict chooses to cite the negative form of the Golden Rule from Tobit rather than the positive form of it in Matthew (7:12). Perhaps he does so to heighten the teaching of Jesus in Matthew that this rule of life-wisdom is one (even) he has received from the tradition.

Reflection: What do I want done to myself? Well, I really appreciate beneficial presences, and I really suffer from "toxic" persons. So I would like to be a beneficial presence. I imagine that sometimes I am, and that sometimes I'm pretty toxic. How do I become more beneficial and less toxic?

I suspect that all these elements Benedict has emphasized in these recent chapters contribute. It apparently begins with giving attention to what is actually going on around me, really to receive what is given in the here and now, both good and bad. That's a big first step. It must involve a kind of allowing things to be what they are, while also recognizing God in the midst of them.

But a crucial question is, what kind of God is in the midst? I was quite astonished recently by the statement "it is of far more consequence what kind of a God than whether a God or not".[114] But in a sense that's one of the main elements I hear Benedict emphasizing in these sections on membership in Christ's Body. God is love. Maybe I have a distorted or inadequate idea of what God is, or of what love is, but as I really pay attention to what is in front of me, looking for God there, then my whole self--perspectives, values, behaviors--begins to be shaped by Love Itself. Conflict, differences, inadequacy: all these are grist for the mill of God's redeeming love. My own presence becomes beneficial as I allow myself to be formed by the beneficient Presence in the heart of all things.

I remember that benefit means to "make good" or "do good". The goodness is God inside things, groaning to be freed. I've begun to wonder if my main task is not simply to notice that goodness. My paying attention, actually looking for God in the midst, somehow helps to release the goodness ready to emerge. Is such a simple vision close to the truth? I don't know, but I will try it and watch.

Prayer/Response:

Chapter 62: Concerning the Priests of the Monastery (entire)

If any Abbot wishes to have a priest or deacon ordained for himself, he should choose from among his monks one who is worthy to fulfill the priestly office. Let the one who is ordained beware of arrogance and pride, and not presume to do anything that has not been commanded by the Abbot, knowing that he is now all the more subject to the discipline of the Rule. His priesthood must not become the cause of his forgetting the obedience and discipline of the Rule; rather he should advance ever more and more in the Lord.

He is always to keep the place due to him according to his entrance into the monastery, except with regard to the duties of the altar, or if the choice of the community and the will of the Abbot should promote him on account of the merit of his life. Nevertheless, he is to know that he must keep the rules for deans and priors. Should he presume to do otherwise he must be considered not as a priest, but as a rebel; and if after frequent admonition he does not amend, the bishop is to be brought in as a witness. If even then he does not amend and his guilt is obvious, he must be expelled from the monastery; only, however, if his insolence is such that he will not submit or obey the Rule.

Comment: Benedict is inviting us to consider, what is our own model of personal holiness? Do we have an image of what a holy person is like? How do we go about assessing the spiritual quality of our own lives, and assisting others in their spiritual journey? These are the questions Benedict is considering here, as he speaks of some who are more "worthy" than others, and of those who "advance ever more" in God. It is ironic that our culture praises many kinds of advancement, but has very little notion of movement toward God! Yet this notion of an increase in holiness is basic to the whole concept of monastic life.[115] Indeed, here Benedict clearly associates spiritual advancement with the three elements defining cenobitic life (Chapter 1:2): obedience to the abbot and to the Rule, and belonging to the community. The point here is that the priest must move more deeply into the faith and practice which has made him worthy of this honor, and not draw away from it at this critical juncture.

At first, it may seem paradoxical that Benedict should speak of advancement in the spiritual life in the same chapter with flagrant violation of its principles. It is clear that Benedict has encountered problems of this sort again and again, for the tone of this and several subsequent chapters has the feel of long-suffering. The problem is captured in the words "arrogance" and "presume". All too often when we see ourselves as spiritually adept, pride begins to presume on the relationship with God, and arrogance replaces humility. It is well to be aware of particularly dangerous points in the spiritual journey; Benedict emphasizes that "promotion" due to spiritual "worth" is always a dangerous moment.

Far from being dismayed at Benedict's attention to such problems, we should find comfort in it. Even for one with Benedict's vision, the spiritual life in community is hard work. There are many "pot-holes", especially for those who are "advanced", into which we all fall from time to time. It is simple prudence to be aware of these dangers, and increase rather than decrease our reliance on God. If we are willing to acknowledge our probable vulnerability, the remedy of humility is readily available.

Reflection: I find it extraordinary for Benedict to suggest in verse 6 that the whole community (as well as the abbot) might choose to give a priest/monk a higher place among them! This is such a strong statement of communal discernment, and I seldom have experienced even the possibility of a community so "in tune" with itself and God that such could be considered. Yet as I ponder this, I see that in some sense it is a logical outgrowth of the idea (in the last chapter) that the quality of each life does very much influence others. As a practical matter, that suggests to me the importance both of attention to my own call from God, as well as accepting help and strength from others who are attending to theirs. The holiness of each affects the holiness of all, in indirect ways I'll never fully understand. But I can begin to live into this awareness.

"Advance toward holiness" is such an awesome phrase. I realize that as I think about such a thing in my own life, almost immediately I become muddled. How do I know when I am becoming more holy? And what do I do with it when I do know?

It seems to me that Benedict has given me two good tests. One is, how is my relationship with God? Do I feel near to God or far from God (or indifferent)? The quality of intimacy in that relationship is a far better test than any personal assessment of holiness.

The second test from Benedict lies in community life. While it does have its ups and downs, as Benedict knows only too well, there is something sacramental about a community in which Christ is at the center. It is strange how difficult it is to see that from inside the community; just as it is difficult to see Christ inside myself for myself. In both cases, loving "outsiders" can often see with greater clarity. Even from inside, however, when I begin to act as if Christ were (invisibly) present, remarkable things happen.

So holiness does seem intimately connected with relationships, with life in community. Seldom in the past have I thought of it so. I must watch for it now, and co-operate with it....

Prayer/Response:

Chapter 63: Rank in the Community, verses 1-9

They are to observe their rank in the monastery which the time of their entry and the merit of their lives determines, or as the Abbot shall appoint. The Abbot is not to disturb the flock committed to him, nor by the use of arbitrary power establish anything unjustly; but let him ever bear in mind that he will have to give an account to God of all his judgments and of all his deeds.

Therefore, in that order which [the Abbot] has appointed or which they hold themselves, the brethren approach to receive the kiss of peace and Communion; and in the same order they intone psalms and stand in choir. And in absolutely every place, age is not to decide the order or be prejudicial to it; for Samuel and Daniel when but children judged the elders (1 Sam 3; Dan 13:44-62).

Excepting, therefore, those whom (as we have said) the Abbot has promoted for very good causes or degraded for solid reasons, let all the rest take the order of their entry; so that, for example, he who enters the monastery at the second hour of the day must know that he is junior to him who came at the first hour, whatever may be his age and dignity. But children are to be kept under discipline in all matters and by everyone.

Comment: A discussion of this passage could go in many directions. But since the responsibilities of the abbot and disciplinary procedures have been discussed elsewhere, let us concentrate on what Benedict reveals in this chapter about the constitution of the community. The issue of rank may be seen as one of hierarchical order, or it may be seen as one of relationships among persons. Let us take the latter view as one which has considerable relevance to the Christian life in general. From such a perspective, the question of this chapter is one of fraternal relations, that is, how to relate to one's peers.

Benedict deliberately turns his back on two ranking methods common in his time. He mentions and discards age. He does not mention social class except indirectly ("dignity"), but obviously he has also declined to use social rank as a governing factor in the monastic community.

What does "order of entry" suggest about Benedict's basic yardstick for rank? It suggests precisely a choice for monastic standards and a turning away from worldly standards. It reminds us of Jesus' language in Matthew 20:26. Jesus advises his disciples that when they look at the way worldly people order their relationships, they should be aware that "it shall not be so among you". The standard which governs relationships among monks can only be that all are one in Christ. (Chapter 2:20) Granted that there are many differences of temperament and giftedness; relationships are to be arranged fundamentally on the basis of kinship in Christ.

Like the abbot, each of us does have the power to do as we wish, but it may conflict with our commitment to God. From the day upon which we make our first decision to give our whole selves to Christ, we give up that power. But we are given the opportunity to choose Christ again and again, each day, in the way that we relate to one another. Again, it is not a complex choice, but it is insistent and quite ordinary.

Reflection: What standard governs my relationships with others? I'm afraid that all too often it is exactly the same as the world's, that is, very superficial. Perhaps I judge based on how people feed my ego, that is, how similar to me they are, or how helpful to me. But there is another way: the daily recognition that we are all one in Christ. How might that look?

I am privileged to have a close friend who is indeed a beneficial presence. Recently I observed with interest the way in which he dealt with an important relationship with a colleague. The colleague had been coldly furious with him, actually because of a misunderstanding. But, before it was cleared up, a great many harsh words had been directed at my friend. The next day, I overheard him speaking about that colleague, gently concerned that "Joe" might recover speedily from a bad cold. I reflected on this vignette with amazement, because I was aware that my friend had made a deliberate choice not to be drawn into the whirlpool of anger and accusation. Rather, he had intentionally turned his emotional energy to those matters in which he could be loving to that one who had hurt him. He is not naive about "the way things are", but he is utterly convinced that Christ is everywhere to be found. In such ordinary matters, he makes the choice to seek him. And, wonderfully, in many contexts, his gentle presence has indeed revealed the Christ in themselves to many people.

Prayer/Response:

Let the younger brothers, then, reverence their elders, and the elder love the younger. In calling each other by name, no one is to address another by his simple name; but the elders are to call the younger brethren "brother", and the younger call their elders *Nonnus*, which means "reverend father". But the Abbot, since he is considered to represent Christ, is to be called "Lord" and "Abbot"; not that he receives this himself, but out of honor and love of Christ. Let him reflect on this, and act so as to be worthy of such honor.

Wherever the brothers meet one another the younger are to ask a blessing of the elder. And when an elder passes by, the younger is to rise and give him a place to sit down. Nor should the younger presume to sit unless his senior bids him, that it may be as was written: *seek to outdo one another in showing honor* (Rom 12:10).

Young children and boys are to be kept under discipline to their rank in the oratory or at table. In other places, too, wherever they may be, they are to be kept under custody and discipline until they reach the age of reason.

Comment: Here Benedict asks us to consider, what's in a name? How do we understand the relationship between the inner and the outer, between the spirit and the law? If you whistle in the dark, do you gain courage? If you address your brother and sister with respect, do you gain love?

Somewhere Martin Buber has said that education is to establish law and hope that it will become inward order. That is the theme of the 119th Psalm. That is what Benedict means about children being disciplined physically until they "reach the age of reason" (understanding). That is why we practice exterior, virtuous behavior, hoping that in time our heart will be formed by our practice and our prayer. But the external practice must be congruent with inner intent, or we have only hypocrisy. However, when external practice is congruent with inner expectancy, we have the transforming power of sacrament.

In these few words of guidance about the names we call each other, Benedict has set forth his vision of Christian community.[116] That vision is rooted in the conviction that we are all one in Christ. The essence of Christian community is the growing recognition that we are the Body of Christ in our relationships with each other, that Christ is revealed among and within the "joints", as it were, of our human interactions. Thus we are called in a special way to become Christ's Body in our daily intercourse.

Reflection: I think about how I use names. In my Southern California world of flexible titles, I am sometimes surprised to hear myself spontaneously address a priest as "father" when my heart has learned respect and regard for the beauty of that person. Perhaps it might also work the other way. I suppose I could practice speaking to all those in my immediate environment with respect, thus teaching myself that they are children of God deserving of my regard. At first, it might seem contrived, as does any new exercise of this sort. But Benedict is inviting me to consider new possibilities for practical ways of seeking God in my actual present environment.

His invitation sounds to me something like this:

(1) Everything that is given is a gift of God.

(2) The task set for me is to learn to receive the present moment fully, with all its dynamics, as a gift containing Godself. Among other things, that means receiving my sister and my neighbor that way.

(3) If I treat the moment and the person as a sacrament, that is, as a precious outer sign bearing that inner gift of Christ, I predispose myself to see something new/transforming in the present situation.

(4) I also invite the other to see that something new in themselves and the situation.

(5) Often I will feel very foolish. Occasionally, I will feel high and lifted up, for glory will indeed break through into the ordinary.

Am I willing to try that? What can I lose?

Prayer/Response:

Chapter 64: The Appointment of the Abbot, verses 1-6

In the appointment of an Abbot this principle is always to be observed: he is to be selected Abbot who is chosen by the whole community unanimously in the fear of God, or by a part [of the community], however small, which possesses sounder counsel. The one who is to be appointed should be chosen for the merit of his life and the wisdom of his teaching, even though he should be the last in community rank.

But even if the whole community (which God forbid) should elect a person who condones their evil ways, and this somehow comes to the attention of the bishop to whose diocese the place belongs, or to the attention of the Abbots or neighboring Christians; they are to prevent the agreement of these wicked men from prevailing, and are to appoint a worthy steward over the house of God, knowing that for this they will receive a good reward if they do it with a pure intention and for the love of God; on the other hand, they will sin if they neglect to do it.

Comment: These words are clear enough. There may be two modes of selection, either by a unanimous vote of the whole community or a smaller group of sound judgment, with the backup possibility that the bishop or neighboring Christians might intervene if the community selects an unworthy abbot. But if one were to try to implement this as a formal procedure in an ordinary community of Christians, hundreds of questions would arise. And indeed, today "there is no agreement about the precise meaning" of this passage![117]

The problem arises from Benedict's primary concern in this process, which is that the abbot (like the prophets and kings of the Old Testament and the disciples in the New) is one chosen and called by God, and it is the community's responsibility to be open and responsive to this divine intention. However, since any discernment of the concrete will of God in any specific situation depends greatly on the depth of the ongoing relationship one has with God, the details of the abbot's selection are less important than overall obedience to the Rule in which the monks' hearts are continuously formed in Christ's Spirit.

In the context of human frailty and lukewarmness (which is the one we are always given), much can go wrong, and apparently Benedict has experienced several variations on just how wrong things can go. It is a comfort to realize that even Benedict sometimes can't see the next step clearly, for we are so often in that position ourselves. It is nonetheless a sobering thought that Benedict suggests there will be occasions when true discernment occurs more effectively through the ordinary common sense of those in the neighborhood, than through the monks themselves. However little Benedict trusts his own principles, or their implementation by monks, he has great confidence that God's purpose will eventually work itself out, through whatever resources are open to God's ways.

Reflection: I notice especially that Benedict says "which God forbid" that the community act in self-will. His language implies that God intends and desires to enable the community to choose God's Will. He seems to see God as always present and helping to carry out beneficial purposes. So the issue of discernment becomes not so much a matter of trying to figure out "right" what God has already "decided", but is rather that of relying on the ever-present help now available in the situation.

Strangely, Benedict's muddling around here, even to the point of throwing up his hands and suggesting that help might come from the unlikely source of the neighbors, gives me comfort. So often I look at a situation from all sides, and feel utterly stuck. I can't see any way out of the mess, the brokenness, the terrible hurt that all parties are feeling. I feel quite blind to God's presence and Will, wherever it is at the moment! But Benedict's confidence that even beyond the usual boundaries of our awareness, God's beneficial presence is making itself known, gives me confidence. I realize that I can offer up my burden of lonely responsibility. I can relax and simply do my best, only watching for what wants to emerge.

Prayer/Response:

Let the one who has been appointed Abbot always bear in mind what a burden he has undertaken, and to whom he will have *to give an account of his stewardship* (Luke 16:2); and he must know that it is more fitting for him to profit his brethren than to preside over them. He must, therefore, be learned in the law of God, that he may know how to *bring forth new things and old* (Matt 13:52).

He must be chaste, sober, merciful, and always *exalt mercy above judgment* (Jas 2:13) that he himself may obtain the same. Let him hate sin and love the brethren. And in correcting others he should act prudently, not going to excess, lest in seeking too eagerly to scrape off the rust, he breaks the vessel. Let him keep his own frailty ever before his eyes, and remember that *the bruised reed must not be broken* (Isa 42:3).

By this we do not mean that he should permit vices to grow up: on the contrary, he should cut them off prudently and with charity as he sees best for each, as we have said. Let him seek to be loved rather than feared.

Comment: As we have noticed before, it is often the case when Benedict is trying to lay a theoretical framework that his mind turns to Scripture. As his spirit flows freely through that holy book which he knows by heart, he offers one image after another, so that there is almost an embarrassment of riches rather than a systematic and explicit presentation.

Here he is trying to explain what the abbot should be. Another way to consider this theme is to inquire what "merit of life and wisdom" (verse 2) looks like in a mature Christian. In order to explore his conclusions, we are best advised ourselves to turn to the Scriptures he cites, and read the verses leading up to and following his quotations, allowing our minds and hearts to resonate to them. This is one possible paraphrase:

•For every gift we receive, we are responsible to Another for its care; this is no less true of our relationships than of our skills or possessions. (Luke 16)

•Key to this care is knowledge of the ways of God, so that we are no longer limited to a narrow and singular view; with God, we may choose old or new, selecting that which is best to reveal the previously hidden, the Kingdom in our midst. (Matt 13)

•Justice is born of harmony. Harmony with all creation occurs when we constantly recall that we too are created, we too will be judged, and that we too are frail as a bruised reed. (Isa 42 and James 2)

All through this section on membership and governance in the community, there is continuous emphasis on awareness of who God is and how God works. In concrete details, Benedict reminds us that God is love, and he helps us to see how that is so. Benedict takes seriously the goal of salvation. Yet he knows a salvation which is filled with joy, which is governed by One whose desire is to be loved rather than feared. Obviously, in this behavior the abbot is imitating the one whose name he carries, the Abba.

Reflection: My eyes fill with tears as I think how much the goal of being loved rather than feared expresses my deepest longing. Over and over in these chapters, Benedict has reminded me of the basic questions: do I love God? and does God love me?

At some level of my psyche, it is so much easier to believe in a mean and stern God, who wants to punish me for my shortfalls, than it is to believe in a God of care, a God who really loves me more than I can ask or imagine. The God of love is still largely a God of my mind, and not yet one of my heart. I lack the innocence simply to reach out to God in trust and faith. But again and again I see that innocence, in practical expression, in Benedict. I am deeply moved by his trust and it strengthens my own.

Prayer/Response:

He must not be violent and anxious, nor exacting and headstrong, nor jealous and too prone to suspicion; for otherwise he will never be at rest. In his commands, whether they concern God or the world, he should be prudent and considerate. Let him be discreet and moderate in the tasks which he imposes, bearing in mind the discretion of holy Jacob, who said: *If I cause my flocks to be overdriven, they will all die in one day* (Gen 33:13). Therefore, taking this and other examples of discretion, the mother of virtue, let him balance everything so that the strong have something to strive after and the weak are not dismayed.

And he must especially keep this Rule in all things, so that, having ministered well, he may hear from the Lord what the good servant heard, who gave grain to his fellow-servants in due season: *Truly I say unto you, he shall place him over all his possessions* (Matt 24:27).

Comment: In every respect, Benedict is drawing a portrait of the "faithful and wise servant" of Matthew 24, the one whom the Master has set over the household, to give them their food at the proper time.

Notice two things especially about this servant. First, he is the one whom the Master has appointed. The authority of the abbot comes from God, and this is not less true, but more true, because he has been selected by the community. It is the community's act to express the choice of God. This is because the abbot's selection is a sacramental act: an outward sign manifesting the invisible grace of Christ's presence among the community.

Second, notice the abbot is to be a man "at rest" (verse 16). It is true of our age that we believe responsible servants are overworked. Such a view might seem to be reinforced by the language of Chapter 48:1: "Idleness is the enemy of the soul". But this chapter adds to that picture the awareness that the soul is also endangered when never at rest. The abbot is to model for the community that fundamental being "at rest" which can only come from singleness of heart. The soul at rest is focused on the One Thing necessary. From this perspective, the multiple concerns of the world fall into their natural order.

Reflection: I am attracted to the passage Benedict cites about Jacob, taken from the chapter in Genesis showing the moving reconciliation of those long-separated brothers, Jacob and Esau. In such a context, "not causing the flock to be overdriven" is clearly a gentle symbol of reconciliation. If I take this symbol for my own, it is a reminder not to push myself too hard, to be gentle with myself and patient with the development of events around me. This is important not just for my own peace of mind (though that is a good reason), but also because "not pushing" becomes a basic method by which I participate in God's reconciling power in the world.

I know many Christians who act as if they had to re-do the crucifixion in their own lives. Usually they are so caring and giving that they are very attractive persons. But I weep for their way of understanding God and Christ, for it seems to me they believe the whole redemption of the world rests on their self-immolation. And it seems to me that Benedict rightly points to another, more true, vision of the Shepherd whose own gift of life now provides gentle care for the weakness of his flock in a restoration of wholeness for each beloved lamb.

Prayer/Response:

Chapter 65: The Prior of the Monastery, verses 1-10

It happens very often that the appointment of the Prior causes grave scandals to arise in monasteries: for there are some who, puffed up by the evil spirit of pride and deeming themselves to be second Abbots, take upon themselves a usurped power, and so foster scandals and cause dissensions in the Community. This occurs especially in those places where the Prior is appointed by the same Bishop or the same Abbots as appoint the Abbot himself. How foolish this custom is may easily be seen: for from the first moment of entering upon his office he is given an incentive to pride, his thoughts suggesting to him that he is free from the authority of his Abbot since he has been appointed by the very same persons.

Hence are stirred up envy, quarrels, backbiting, dissensions, jealousy, and disorders. And while the Abbot and Prior are in conflict with one another, it necessarily follows that their souls are endangered through their dissension; and those who are their subjects, favouring one side or the other, run along to their destruction. The blame for this perilous evil falls on the head of those who by their actions originated such disorders.

Comment: In certain respects, this seems one of the most time-bound chapters of the Rule, for it is clear that Benedict is angrily resisting a common monastic practice of his time. Yet Christ's anger in the temple revealed a situation common to human experience which symbolized "saying no" to God. In a similar way, this matter of concern to Benedict reveals basic human truths.

Basil Hume comments that the Rule almost seems to have been intentionally "written for a monastery that functioned imperfectly....(It) almost seems to assume that there will be misbehavior."[118] Time after time the Rule conveys a realistic appreciation of human nature. In this chapter, we see such a great familiarity with the ways of human rationalization that the "internal voices" in the prior's head (telling him what a fine fellow he is) are given almost as a quotation!

It is a central principle for Benedict that those in authority have a responsibility to create conditions and environments which will minimize "legitimate" eruptions of pride and self-will. Benedict does not call for, nor assume, the "destruction of self-will; he takes it for granted it is always alive, and he celebrates that as a marvelous vehicle for ascetical discipline."[119] Instead, he creates a setting in which self-will is minimized and constructively channeled. Thus his anger is here directed at those who set up a system bound to evoke pride; those in authority should have a better appreciation of human nature than that!

Benedict understands that we can refuse the offer of divine goodness in two main ways. We can refuse to respond in joy to the call of God to live as the beloved. But we can equally well refuse God, by ignoring the evident willful tendencies of our human nature and pretending we will be able to be gods ourselves.

Reflection: What am I personally invited to do, by the suggestion that I not ignore my own willful tendencies? Well, for one thing, I can pay attention to patterns which are likely to evoke negative reactions in me. Recently, my husband asked me if I would try to let him know when I was becoming tired, rather than buck up bravely until the last possible moment, and then collapse in an hysterical heap all at once! Or sometimes when I am feeling particularly tired, I insist on our trying to make major long-term decisions, even when I know that an argument is the likely outcome.

It occurs to me, too, that there are situations out of my control which are likely to bring out my worst self. Clearly, those are not the times to expect optimum behavior from myself, and then punish myself for not achieving it. Honestly, the most life-giving thing to do would be to be as patient as I can, both with the situation and with myself.

What brings life? What evokes love? Yet again Benedict invites me to look clearly at the nature of God in the midst, and to give myself to that reality.

Prayer/Response:

Chapter 65, verses 11-22 (end)

We foresee, therefore, that it is advisable for the preservation of peace and charity, that the management of the monastery depends upon the will of the Abbot. If possible, let all the affairs of the monastery be attended to (as we have already arranged) by Deans whom the Abbot may appoint; thus, the same office being shared by many, no one person will become proud.

But if the needs of the place require it and the community ask for it reasonably and with humility, and the Abbot judges it expedient, let the Abbot himself appoint a Prior - whomever he chooses, having taken counsel with God-fearing brothers.

The Prior is to perform reverently whatever the Abbot asks him to do, and nothing against [the Abbot's] command; for the more he is elevated above the rest, the more carefully he ought to observe the precepts of the Rule.

If the Prior is found to have serious failings, or is deceived by the haughtiness of pride, or proves to have contempt for the holy Rule, let him be verbally admonished up to four times; and then if he does not amend, let him be corrected by the discipline of the Rule. But if even then he does not amend, let him be deposed from the office of Prior and another who is worthy be substituted in his place. If afterwards he is not quiet and obedient in the community, he is to be expelled from the monastery. Nevertheless, let the Abbot bear in mind that he must give an account to God of all his judgments, lest the flame of envy or jealousy be kindled in his soul.

Comment: Benedict obviously had very negative experience with troublesome priors, and prefers to abolish the office altogether. Yet he does not quite do that. Why not?

One of the most notable characteristics of the Rule is its balance, and this chapter is a good example of that balance at work. We notice that in the last verse Benedict acknowledges the psychological wisdom that whenever there is severe conflict, both parties are likely to have something at stake in the issue. Under such circumstances, each party is well served by an examination of conscience (and consciousness) both about his or her contribution to the problem, and about his or her benefit from keeping it unresolved.

Benedict applies this principle to his abbot. But Benedict is gracious enough also to apply the principle to himself. He allows the possibility that his own blindness prevents him from seeing a case where a prior might be a helpful community asset. Thus he offers his successors freedom to make that independent judgment within their own setting.[120] Undoubtedly it is such flexibility that has enabled the Rule to be such an effective Christian guide for so many centuries.

Ultimately, Benedict's confidence does not rest in all these "arrangements", even though he has worked hard at them, and they reflect the best of his wisdom. His confidence rests in assurance that all is in God's hands, and thus peace and love are the basic conditions of equilibrium to which things (and people) are predisposed to return. His humility is such that he is able to acknowledge the value of his work, even when he is sure he will sometimes be wrong, for even his work is in God's hands. Thus this rule he writes can be "holy" (verse 18), because it belongs to the whole community of faith secure in the hands of God.

Reflection: I am in awe of Benedict's confidence in God's vital presence. It involves the courage to act boldly, based on what I see, with the liberty to let all my visions go, in confidence of a truer One.

I am deeply impressed by Benedict's balance. He is so comfortable with the possibility (even probability) of "backsliding" in faith and action. Obviously, this is not just theoretical for him; he is comfortable with his own errors and weaknesses. By comfortable, I don't mean that he wallows in his sinfulness. But I mean he doesn't unduly punish himself, and he isn't particularly surprised when he falls short. He is genuinely repentant, meaning he "confesses and accepts his faults with the specific desire to change, in a spirit of peace and tranquillity rather than in fear and guilt."[121] In contrast, whenever I get in touch with my faults, I am so overwhelmed by a sense of blackness and ugliness that it is hard for me to do anything other than beat myself. But Benedict helps me see that such an attitude is not genuine repentance, for it separates me from a sense of God's love, and hinders my ability to grow in faith and charity.

How moved I am by Benedict's way of repentance, which seems to permit him always to stay within the governing reality of God's love for him, as well as aware of his continuing challenge to respond to God! I realize how hungry I am for the wholeness of life Benedict models. And hunger itself is a gift, for which I am grateful.

Prayer/Response:

Chapter 66: The Monastery Porter (entire)

At the gate of the monastery let there be placed a wise old man, who knows how to give and receive an answer, and whose maturity keeps him from wandering. This porter ought to have his room near the gate, so that those who arrive will always find someone at hand to give them an answer. As soon as anyone knocks or a poor man calls to him, he should answer, *Thanks be to God!*, or *Please give me your blessing!* Then with all gentleness in the fear of God, he is to answer quickly in the fervor of love. If the porter needs assistance, let him have one of the younger brothers with him.

The monastery ought, if possible, to be so constructed that all necessities, such as water, a mill, a garden, a bakery, and the various crafts may be contained within it; thus there will be no need for the monks to wander outside, for this is not good at all for their souls.

We wish this Rule to be frequently read in the community, so that none of the brethren may excuse themselves on account of ignorance.

Comment: Several themes are interwoven in this short chapter, and they center around familiarity and routine, that is, stability. The old man will stay put; the monks should not roam; the Rule is to be read again and again.

What do we imagine is the value of stability? Do we believe it "breeds contempt" or even boredom? What positive benefits might stability carry? Why on earth (or heaven) would we give ourselves to one place and one group of people for the rest of our lives? Is this not a narrowing, a denial of the giftedness of all God's creation?

We know that stability is a crucial element in the promise the monk makes upon joining the community (Chapter 58:17). Stability was a particular contribution of Benedict to the monastic vocation; it was his insight that it was central. Stability as a virtue is rooted in the concept of a sacramental world. It is based upon the view that outer reality (any created outer reality) is a sign of inward grace, if deeply attended to with "all gentleness in the fear of God".

But we humans cannot give this kind of attention to anything at all, if we are trying to give it to everything. We must concentrate, and focus, and be centered rather than fragmented. We must be able to wait patiently, with expectancy and love, for Christ to reveal himself in that which we behold. Stability is a precondition for attentive listening to the sacramental reality built into the structure of the world.

The monastic community is a setting designed to offer this kind of stability. In every respect, Benedict has tried to create a routine and an environment which facilitates sacramental presence. This whole section on membership and governance has been an extraordinarily complex and fruitful one, for Benedict has presented a number of the basic theological assumptions upon which he founds the consecrated life, as always in the context of the ordinary daily experience.

The consecrated person is one who seeks God, that is, one who responds to God's seeking him or her. The continuing questions with which such a one deals are "do I love God?" and "(how) does God love me?" As these questions are asked within the context of daily experience, certain perceptions emerge. One learns to accept the present as gifted and then to offer it back to God. This acceptance and offering is undertaken with the limitations imposed by the specific setting and one's own human nature. Yet the daily practice of such behavior, with inner expectancy to meet Christ, gradually reveals God's Kingdom come.

Probably the two most lovingly drawn portraits within the Rule are those of the cellarer and the porter. This chapter contains a powerful vignette of an "old" monk, who has begun to taste the "unspeakable sweetness of love" (Prologue verse 49) promised to those who progress in this way of life and faith. How well and yet how subtly is this shown in the porter's greeting to the unknown stranger: "Please give me your blessing". For, "it is indisputable that a blessing is given by a superior to an inferior." (Hebrews 7:7) The porter has the great freedom to know himself inferior to whomever might pass, for the stranger for him truly carries Christ.

Reflection: I am reminded of one of my favorite quotations from C.S. Lewis:

"The world is crowded with God. He walks everywhere incognito. And the incognito is not always hard to penetrate. The real labour is to remember, to attend. In fact, to come awake."[122]

How similar this quotation is to Benedict's prologue comment that it is time now for us to rise from sleep! (Prologue verse 8). Am I awake or asleep? I guess probably mostly asleep, but how glorious are the moments of wakefulness!

As I have begun to practice stability, I find it brings great gentleness to my life. I have begun to notice and enjoy the way the sunlight shifts not only from one hour of the day to another, but from one season to another. I delight in the gradual unfolding of a new philodendron leaf. I watch with awe the slow healing of a cut on my finger. I even enjoy the predictable outbursts of adolescent rebellion in my children. I come to know things better in their true context, of ebbs and flows, of death and life, of care in the hands of the Creator.

Prayer/Response:

Interlude IX:

a note to the reader...

What have you learned in faithfulness to this daily process of *lectio?*

Perhaps you have realized how much less stress affects you in every area of your life, because you have set aside a few moments of peace and quiet regularly in your week. Perhaps you notice that your mind and spirit seem more rested and less irritable, as you attend to them regularly. Perhaps as you have reflected on the Rule, you have recognized certain disciplines which you know to be helpful in keeping your own life centered.

Before you finish this particular process, you might want to honor it specifically by taking time to reflect on what you have discovered about what nurtures you. Then you might wish to make that discovery somewhat more formal by drafting a simple "Rule of Life" for you personally. Benedict's Rule is a community rule. It is appropriate to supplement that by a personal rule, adopted generally for about a year at a time, to guide your own unique journey.

A personal rule always should be considered within the context of the communal Christian experience, and it may articulate or assume the corporate framework. Generally, there will always be membership in a worshipping community, involving regular commitments of time, money, and energy to that community.

But specifically, what regular patterns of faithfulness has the Spirit pointed out are nurturing for your spiritual life? What practices powerfully enable your deepened responsiveness to God's presence in your life? What is good for you? These are the questions a personal rule is intended to answer.

Practical considerations might involve daily, weekly, monthly, and annual rhythms. Look at not only the "spiritual" matters, such as times for prayer, Scripture and *lectio*, but also at "ordinary" matters, such as regular physical exercise and mental stimulation. Don't forget the practice of charity, and simple courtesy to those who are given to you as family and friends.

A rule should be selective, containing a few important elements, rather than so many items you will be burdened with "oughts". A good way to choose the important ones is to ask, what helps me to develop the Spirit's dispositions of love, joy, peace, gentleness, kindness, etc? (Gal. 5:22f) Another way to ask this question is to inquire, what nurtures me? Pick one or two things and give them to yourself, as a way of valuing the person you are in God's eyes. Then, watch with awe.

A Few Final Guidelines for the Consecrated Life

Chapter 67: Brothers Who are Sent on a Journey (entire)

Brothers who are about to be sent on a journey should commend themselves to the prayers of all the brethren and of the Abbot; and always, at the last prayer of the Work of God, all the absent should be remembered. The brethren who return from a journey should, on the very day they come back, lie prostrate on the floor of the oratory at all the canonical Hours at the ending of the Work of God; they request the prayers of all on account of their transgressions, in case they have seen or heard anything evil on their journey, or have fallen into idle talk.

No one may presume to tell others what he may have seen or heard outside the monastery, for from this comes great destruction. If any so presumes, he is to be subjected to the punishment of the Rule. Also, he shall undergo a like penalty who presumes to leave the enclosure of the monastery, to go anywhere or do anything however small, without permission of the Abbot.

Comment: There is some evidence that Chapter 66 was a primitive conclusion of the Rule. However, it is generally agreed that these final chapters are also the work of Benedict, perhaps as an "afterthought" to add a few final notes. Thus, these last chapters are Benedict's reminders of important points he has neglected so far or wishes to emphasize. They can also be read as succinct summaries-by-example of some foundational elements in monastic life.

This chapter is a deepening lesson about the value of stability. It emphasizes that stability involves not only not wandering with the body, but also not wandering with the eyes or ears, the memory or the imagination. There is here an important distinction between the quality of the created order as such, and the problem of the human spirit's response to multiplicity.

The created order is God's and therefore essentially good. Because this is so, brothers may be sent into the world for reasonable and important matters, and strangers from the world may be welcomed into the monastery. There is a natural interface, and indeed interdependence, between the whole created world and the committed Christian. But the Christian's primary goal is to seek God and to respond to God, as God is revealed in creation and elsewhere. Such seeking and responding must set the context and order one's relationships within the material world.

It is the long experience of those who seek God that the ear or eye which takes in everything, finds nothing. Discovery of the sacrament within is a matter of discipline and discernment: it involves allowing one's deepest longing to become central so that peripheral or superficial longings may drop away. A sacramental presence involves a deliberate decision not to be captured in the merely superficial, in favor of a commitment to union with the ultimate. Such decisions are most effectively made within the stability of a community sharing that commitment.

Reflection: I so often allow my curiosity to draw me away from my center. Oddly enough, "the news" is one major source of temptation to me. I was reflecting this morning on how little of the "morning TV news" is about anything at all real. There is so little context given from which to understand events; there is so little time for sacramental attention to situations. I often find too large a dose of 30-second news disorienting.

Another way in which my curiosity pulls me away from my center is gossip. I realize there are many times when I ask about people simply to be titillated by random details. Usually this is true of the media folk-heros, but often enough it is true about people in my parish or my club. "Is Jane still going around with that terrible fellow?" is seldom a question I ask out of prayerful concern. These discrepancies become more severe as I am privileged to know what it is to meet the world and persons in it from the vantage point of deep prayer.

Prayer/Response:

Chapter 68, Brothers Who are Commanded to do the Impossible (entire)

If a brother is commanded things that are hard or impossible, he should accept the order of his superior with all gentleness and obedience. But if he sees that the burden completely exceeds his strength, he should lay before his superior the reasons for his incapacity, patiently and at a fitting time, without showing pride, resistance, or contradiction. If, however, after these explanations the superior still persists in his command, the subject must know that this is best for him; and he is to obey out of love, trusting in the help of God.

Comment: This chapter (exploring obedience and humility in a specific context) is surely one of the strongest and most important chapters in the Rule, for it makes utterly clear the radical nature of the consecrated life. Radical means "at the root" and we see here that the Christian's transformation is to extend to the deepest center of his or her being.

The monk is to do "the impossible". He is to accept it, meaning to undertake it, in the same way implied by the Hebrew verb "to hear", meaning already-to-be-in-response. Truly to accept is already to be doing.

And yet in the doing, one discovers that one has passed beyond one's strength. In a sense, this is the proto-typical Christian situation. Always do we find ourselves acting as if transformation were implicit, ready to be released in ourselves and others, as we sense that we are being utter fools for Christ: we have no true personal power to do that which we intend and desire. And yet there is also a deep sense of the rightness of this action; it is best for us in some mysterious way. How are we to proceed?

Benedict gives us a summary model of how to be obedient in difficult situations:

First, listen. Listen to our superior -- to whatever has been given us to do. Listen to the situation -- to the nature of the environment in which the task is set. Listen to our selves -- to what information is provided by our bodies and our psyches.

Next, state clearly and fairly how we see the situation. Honor ourselves enough to recognize the value of what we have heard from these sources, and present our view with clarity and openness. The actual statement or presentation may be made only to ourselves (and God) in a journal, or to a spiritual director, or may actually be made to our superior. In any case, at some point, we need to face clearly how we see things and seek to make whatever adjustments seem appropriate.

Finally, accept and submit to what is required! Generally in our modern culture, we tend to omit either step two or step three. Seldom do we consider combining them. Among other things, step three seems unfair and unjust, against "democratic principles" or whatever. But this combination of elements contains a fundamental insight of Benedict's about when God's power is most effectively released into the world: when a just man goes to the cross. Or when "(we) obey out of love" in the life situation given us this day.

Reflection: I resonate with the image suggested by the Latin word translated "gentleness". The word is *mansuetudine*, meaning "accustomed to the hand" and is used literally of training wild animals.[123] I have a vivid sense of a small colt, standing shivering in cold and excitement as an attentive trainer approaches and gently caresses. So do I often feel in the presence of God: fearful and shivering both with anxiety and eagerness, but willing myself to do all I can to respond, which is often simply not to run away. Instead I tremble, and await the hand which touches me in love.

Perhaps this is often the way of obedience....

Prayer/Response:

Chapter 69: Monks May Not Presume to Defend One Another in the Monastery And Chapter 70: Monks May Not Presume to Strike One Another At Will

The greatest care must be taken that no one in the monastery presumes for any reason to defend another or to take his part, even if they are closely related to one another by ties of blood. The monks must not presume to do this in any way whatsoever, because the most grievous occasions of scandals may arise from this. If anyone transgresses this rule, let him be very severely punished.

(Chapter 70:) In order that in the monastery every occasion of presumption may be avoided, we ordain and decree that it is not lawful for anyone to excommunicate or strike any of his brothers, unless he is given power do to so by the Abbot. *Those who sin shall be reproved before all, that the rest may have fear.* (I Tim. 5:20)

Children, however, are to be kept under diligent and watchful discipline by all until their fifteenth year: yet this too is to be done with all measure and discretion. For if anyone presumes, without permission of the Abbot, to chastise those who are above that age, or shows undue severity even to the children, he is to be subjected to the discipline of the Rule; for it is written: *Do not do to another what you would not have done to yourself* (Tob 4:16).

Comment: These two chapters reveal an essential element of monastic (Christian) formation. They convey an important image about one of the central dynamics of life in Christ: conversion of heart.

As always, the first level of awareness is the material or physical. The chapters go hand in hand, and in combination make clear the instruction: neither take the side of, nor take the side against, one of your brothers and sisters in Christ, in any matter of conflict. Neither defend nor strike.

Why not? In part, because it is the abbot's prerogative, but more deeply because the abbot stands in the place of Christ, who is drawing that person daily toward deeper union with God. The bystander's observation of the issues involved may be quite wrong; indeed it may seem things are directly opposed to what is needed for one's friend's health at that moment.

The inward reality is that each person stands naked before God, in the essential particularity and uniqueness of their relationship at that moment. The Christian life is to facilitate that relationship with God in Christ. The abbot and the person himself/herself are the only ones close enough to understand how the relationship with Christ will best be deepened at this moment. No one else can take the essential steps of the spiritual life for us. No one can "carry the lamp oil" for us (Matt 25:1-13). No one dare take away from us the good portion we have chosen (Luke 10:42).

Benedict cites Tobit for the third time in the Rule (see also Chapter 4:9 and 61:4). We may perhaps see his intention best by noting its context in Chapter 4, where it immediately follows the phrase: "honor everyone". The intention of the quotation is to emphasize that we are to have the deepest regard for each person's life in Christ. We are to be aware that for each of us, life in Christ is the fountain of *conversatione*/the monastic way of life/ongoing conversion of heart. Above all Christ in us is to be cherished, that our life might be daily recreated in him.

Reflection: One of my earliest memories is desiring to defend my baby brother from what I thought was unjust criticism. Not too many years later, I was forced strictly to cease reading to him, for he had not needed to learn to read himself. I love my brother deeply, and we are very close, but I think in both instances I was "stealing" from him the chance to be his own person in experiences which tested and strengthened him. I still struggle with the great desire to "do for" others what rightly they can only do for themselves.

This is a twin-headed monster. On the one hand, in my supposed love and care I am denying others their opportunities to interact creatively with their own life: to develop their own strength, to realize the value of their own weaknesses, to undertake their own privileged response of formation. Benedict teaches me that conflicts or difficulties or sufferings are always opportunities to choose Christ. Thus I see that it is a privilege to respond to them, a privilege on which I as an outsider have no right to intrude.

On the other hand, I realize too that my preoccupation with other people's issues is a neat way to avoid my own. By directing all my energies outside me, I can pretend that I have no issues or problems of my own which are giving me the opportunity to choose Christ in my life. Even if I am aware of the need to deal with my interior issues, I may manage never to have the time, because I am always busy in the care of others.

It is not easy to learn emotionally how to "be with" others. I hope to be vulnerable and interdependent, as a member of Christ's Body. Like everyone, I do need the love and care of others, their support and the assistance of their strengths. But I also need to do the work given to me to do, and let others proceed to do theirs at their own pace. That way, each of us learns, not only to do our own work, but also to ask for help as we discover it is needed. To be human is to be utterly alone and unique, while also to be wonderfully connected and supported. I suspect it takes a lifetime of trial and error to manage a contentment in the midst of tension with those two apparently distinct realities.

Prayer/Response:

Chapter 71: They Should Obey One Another (entire)

Not only is the blessing of obedience to be shown by all to the Abbot; the brethren must also obey one another, knowing that by this path of obedience they go to God. The commands, therefore, of the Abbot or the superiors appointed by him (to which we allow no unofficial orders to be preferred) are to be given precedence. For the rest let all the younger brothers obey their elders with all love and courtesy. Anyone who is found to be quarrelsome is to be corrected.

If anyone is rebuked by the Abbot or by any superior in any way for however small a cause, or if he comes to believe that any superior is angered or perplexed about him, however trivially; he should immediately and without delay cast himself on the ground at his feet, remaining there to do penance until the turmoil is healed by the other's blessing. But if any one is too haughty to do this, he should be subjected to corporal punishment: if he remains unyielding, he must be expelled from the monastery.

Comment: Is it true that we are all one in Christ? (Chapter 2:20, Gal 3:28) Is it true that Christ is to be found in each one of our brothers and sisters, and that when we truly listen to each other we are listening to God? (Chapter 5:6,15) Benedict is making clear here, what he has suggested throughout the Rule, that not only is Christ found in the abbot, but Christ is found in all our brothers and sisters. This is a radical extension of the thought in Benedict's time; it is a startling idea in our own. Yet, as we consider it, we realize it flows naturally from the sacramental orientation toward the world: the outer form of created life always and everywhere reveals and leads to a deeper inner reality which is God.

If this is true-- that Christ is present in all our brothers and sisters-- then what would our attitude be toward them? Obedience. Deep, attentive listening. Expectancy. Obedience to one another is an important way to God, because as we listen attentively to one another, God is revealed in our interaction.

But to say Christ is present in all is not just to say Christ is present in everyone else. It is also to acknowledge Christ present within ourselves. Each of us is called to deepen our participation in the mind of Christ, who dwells in us. This is what enables us to cast ourselves at another's feet, even as Jesus humbled himself utterly before us (even us!) (Phil 2:5-11)

True, it takes considerable humility for the young monk to cast himself at the feet of an elder he may have offended. But we can be sure that Benedict is not unaware of the humility required from the "offended one" who is subsequently obliged to allow himself to be sufficiently calmed to offer his blessing with generous heart. In such humble exchanges we are privileged to see with greater clarity the radiance of Christ shining forth.

Reflection: Early in our marriage, my husband taught me about seeing the emerging beauty in another person. He "taught" me by the way in which he did that for me. He listened carefully to me, and then he marveled at the growth of loveliness in me, which I was ironically often less able to see than he was! It was not that he saw his own "agenda" being fulfilled in me; it was that he genuinely saw and responded to an emergent beauty in me, in a way that helped me be more faithful to that beauty in myself. What a glorious gift that was to me.

I think this sort of thing is what obedience to another person must mean. I see that obedience in this sense is a powerful way to release reconciliation and transformation into our human experience of brokenness. I pray that I shall more and more learn to give and receive this gift of seeing and releasing Christ in ordinary people.

Prayer/Response:

Chapter 72: The Good Zeal Which Monks Ought to Have (entire)

Just as there is an evil zeal of bitterness which separates from God and leads to hell, so there is a good zeal which separates from vices and leads to God and to life everlasting. This zeal then, should be practiced by monks with the most fervent love. That is: *they should outdo one another in showing honor.* (Rom 12:10) Let them most patiently endure one another's infirmities, whether of body or of character. Let them compete in showing obedience to one another. None should follow what he judges useful for himself, but rather what is better for another: they should practice fraternal charity with a pure love, to God offering loving reverence, loving their Abbot with sincere and humble affection, preferring nothing whatever to Christ; and may He bring us all together to life everlasting. Amen.

Comment: Substantively, this is the last chapter of the Rule, the next and final one having the quality of a postscript on the author's purpose. So here are Benedict's final words to us on the consecrated life, his summary of what we are about.

It is often as interesting what Benedict does not say, as what he does. If we were to set forth a statement of the "good zeal", that is, the eager and earnest desire of our hearts which will lead us to God, what might we say? Very likely, we would frame some statement such as, loving God with our whole beings. Unquestionably that is what Benedict intends, but he understands it to be lived by showing respect for one another. Yet again, Benedict directs our thought to something that seems very simple, but which is profoundly transforming if we begin to live it.

For Benedict, God "bring(s) us all together" to everlasting life; salvation is not an individual project, but one which we undertake with and among our brothers and sisters in Christ. We work out our salvation not only in fear and trembling, but also in community. It is in our care for, and interaction with, one another that we become the Body of Christ, now and forever. That is why Romans 12:10 and the other ethical portions of Paul's letters and Matthew's Gospel and the Old Testament "wisdom literature" are so central to Benedict's thought and the Rule. Salvation is near at hand! Our goal as Christians is the daily growth into seeing and responding to Christ present in the midst of us.

That is why preferring Christ is something we are able to do, in hundreds of ways, each and every day, no matter what our setting. We are given daily choices to accept the love present implicitly in every portion of the created world, by abandoning our self-will in favor of that purity of heart which knows itself everywhere the recipient of God. The movement toward Christ, in heart and mind and soul and spirit, within the daily round--that is the whole goal and the whole longing of the Rule.

Reflection: Yet again the simplicity and accessibility of the Rule causes me to catch my breath in wonder. Benedict helps me to see that living the Gospel life is something I can do today, within the setting and among the persons right in front of me. Christ present in the situation draws me; Christ present in my heart and soul helps me respond.

Sometimes I have wished he would make it more difficult than this, so I could have better excuses for not doing today the simple thing which is possible for me to do. But by and large I am thrilled and delighted with the discovery that the little details of my life matter so very much, and that I can respond to such a worthy calling, simply by taking up my day today, supported by my brothers and sisters in Christ.

Prayer/Response:

Chapter 73: The Whole of Observance is Not Contained in This Rule (entire)

We have written this Rule in order that, observing it in monasteries, we may show that in some measure we have goodness of virtue and a beginning of monastic life. But for those who are hastening to the perfection of monastic life there are the teachings of the holy Fathers, the observance of which brings one to the heights of perfection. For what page or what word is there in the divinely inspired books of the Old and New Testaments that is not a most accurate rule for human life? Or what book of the holy Catholic Fathers does not loudly proclaim how we may by a straight course reach our Creator? Moreover, the *Conferences of the Fathers*, their *Institutes* and their *Lives*, and the Rule of our holy Father Basil - what else are these but examples for observant and obedient monks, and instruments of virtue? But to us who are slothful, unobservant and negligent, they bring the blush of shame.

Whoever, therefore, you are who hasten towards your heavenly country, fulfil with the aid of Christ this little Rule for beginners which we have set forth; and then at last you shall arrive, under God's protection, at the lofty summits of doctrine and virtue of which we have spoken here. Amen

Comment: For some time we have been engaged with this Rule, and have found it an intense and earnest manual for the practical living out of a life consecrated to God. We cannot help but wonder if Benedict is not being somewhat coy here by describing the Rule as "only a beginning". But perhaps we can discover his meaning by way of these considerations:

(1) Much of the Rule is synthesized from other sources. Benedict did not intend to do a "new thing" or make an "original" creation in the Rule. His primary intent was synthetic in the best sense of that word. He sought to gather ideas from the Fathers, Scripture and tradition, into a simple presentation to guide daily life. His goal was always to be pointing elsewhere and onward, to fix the monastic's eyes on Christ. In a sense, he is emphasizing that goal here: inviting the monastic to go on from this "secondary" sourcebook to the originals, perusing them in greater depth for the work of his heart.

(2) In the Rule, Benedict describes aspects of a quality of life summarized in the phrase "some degree of virtue."[124] The phrase refers to that formation into the mind of Christ which is a life-long process, enabled by lived familiarity with formal disciplines, and involving ever more whole-hearted inner receptiveness and response to God's Spirit. It is not like a race track, which one simply completes a circuit to finish. It is an ongoing and ever deepening work. The Rule began with an exhortation earnestly to engage in such a life, and that exhortation is renewed here at the end.

Even the words of this chapter are both echoes of and invitations to deepen the words of the Prologue: "Today if you hear his voice, harden not your hearts" (verse 10). Whole observance, as used in the title of this chapter, means something like "fullness of justice", and evokes another Prologue phrase: the one who may dwell in the Lord's temple is the one who "works justice" (verse 25). Or yet again, the phrase from this chapter "you who hasten towards your heavenly country" is a recalling of the Prologue's discussion of "resting on the holy mountain" (verse 22).

So, the work of the consecrated life is like that of a spiral, ever returning to the beginning to enter more fully into the habitation of the Lord. In that sense, no matter where we are, we are always just beginning in the journey with Christ.

Reflection: I am reminded of a meditative exercise in which one slowly counts from one to ten, with a full inhalation and exhalation for each number. It is intended as an exercise in concentration, so that the meditator is advised that each time any other thought enters one's mind than the present number, he or she is to go back and begin again at the number one. But it becomes a spiritual exercise when the meditator realizes that the purpose is not to reach the number ten, but to be willing to begin over and over at number one.

So in my life with Christ, I must begin again and again: that is my work. But the great miracle is that I do not do it alone. Each time I begin again with humility and generosity, Christ rises up to greet me in a new and radically transforming way. And by some miracle not of my own making, I pray I will at last arrive at my heavenly home. Amen.

Prayer/Response:

The End; The Beginning

An Afterword

If you have completed the journey, travelled by this book, then you will have been both encouraged and challenged as you followed the way. Encouraged by the nearness of Christ which the Rule points us towards - indeed God is everywhere and all is holy - but challenged in that to be lived rightly, the Christian life is fulfilled in the relationships upon which the community depends. God both confronts us in everything and cries out for our response in everybody.

6th century wisdom, compiled for the good order and discipline of religious in community, is shown as wisdom indeed when its elements are extended to the wider relevance of any Christian's ordinary way of life. The clue to this discovery is the ancient, and yet largely forgotten art, of *lectio divina*. This book is in itself a wonderful and effective example of this method. Use *lectio divina* now in your own daily life.

The "text" is before you - in the one you love, in the hurt you suffer, in the joy which lifts you, in the disappointment which drains you. Of such things is the "text" of life comprised.

"Read" the text, in the face of others, in the world of nature, and in the circumstances which build up around you. Having "read", proceed to the applied work of understanding. Your "comment" will be formed by the perspectives that informed understanding gives. Then you will be rightly placed to "reflect" - with God, to relate what is before you to yourself personally. From that relationship flows your "response", presented to God in the affirming openess of your prayer. It is a "response" which will become increasingly wordless and still, in a simple, contemplative statement of yourself.

Texts from the Psalms and the Gospels and the Epistles bubble up all around us as we read the Rule. They indicate to us how behind the one "text" lies another - that of Holy Scripture. Extended Biblical study will show up "texts" behind that. The Rule is a rich deposit, laid down in the evolution of practical, spiritual wisdom.

Norvene Vest's very special contribution has been to give us a stepping stone, itself very richly made up of clues and understandings. This stepping stone we can use to bring ourselves within a sustaining tradition which represents a way of Christian life characterised by realism and balance. The stepping stone is one which we can use in two directions. We can step backwards into the Rule itself or we can step forwards into is enlightening of our own day-to-day growth.

There is, of course, the originally intended setting in which we can find the Rule being worked through and realized - that of a Benedictine community itself. We can go to those communities as visitors and retreatants, to find some space for ourselves. We can "belong", as members in the world, by becoming oblates. Such a step carries with it formalised obligations and commitment - things we all need anyway as we face up to the journey of life which follows the steps of our Lord and Master.

That of course is not for all. But anyone who has worked this book to the end will have been touched by the Rule indelibly. Again and again we will come back to it - we will come back, as well, to the wealth of exposition Norvene Vest has given us.

Listen, carefully, my son to the master's instructions, and attend to them with the ear of your heart... (RB Prologue 1)

Peter Brett
Canon Residentiary
of Canterbury Cathedral

References

Introduction

[1]In the text of this book, Rule is not italicized, and *lectio divina* is simply called *lectio*. Throughout the text the term "monk" is used to embrace **both** sexes, since it is not inherently gender-specific, and since the words "nun" and "sister" are normally used to **separate** the contemplative and active dimensions of life, **both** of which are central to the Rule.

Prologue

[2]Throughout the commentary, we have not sought to discuss and compare sources, so there is no effort, for example, to attribute certain sections of the Rule of Benedict to the Rule of the Master. Other sources deal with that subject far more fully than would be appropriate for this treatment. We note here simply that most contemporary scholarship assumes that Benedict chose to take much of his prologue directly from the so-called Rule of the Master, translated by Luke Eberle, OSB (Kalamazoo, Michigan: Cistercian Publications, 1977), and yet abbreviated the RM substantially. I suggest it was because of Benedict's practical interest that he selected what RM calls "the performance of our service" as his primary concern in the RB prologue.

[3]For other references to salvation in the Rule, see RB 4:46, 5:3, 25:3-4, and elsewhere.

[4]See indications of good desires in RB 49:6 and 61:5.

[5]C.S. Lewis, *The Problem of Pain* (London: Collins Fontana Books, 1957), p. 64.

[6]See Jean Leclerq, OSB, *The Love of Learning and the Desire for God*, translated by Catharine Misrahi (London: SPCK, 1978), especially Chapter 5, "Sacred Learning" for a deeper discussion of this method of "scripture by heart".

[7]See *RB 1980: The Rule of St. Benedict in Latin and English with Notes* (henceforth called simply *RB 1980*), edited by Timothy Fry, OSB (Collegeville, Minn: The Liturgical Press, 1981), for more detail on the importance of this phrase "to see God" in shaping monastic life, especially pp. 34-40 and footnote on pp. 160-1.

[8]Indeed, Benedict is so conscious of the recent Arian controversy that he never uses the name "Jesus" without adding "Christ" or "Lord". See Jean Leclerq, OSB, "The Problem of Social Class and Christology in Saint Benedict", *Word and Spirit*, Volume 2 (Still River: St. Bede's Publications, 1981), especially pages 33 and 42f.

[9]At first it may seem repugnant to think of being used by anyone, even God. But the word is curiously apt, if we understand it as rooted in its earliest agricultural meaning. The Latin, *utor*, was a term that originally would have been applied to a fertile field, where the soil was rich and the crops would be abundant. So, that which is "used" is fecund, fruitful, and capable of being enjoyed by one who has need of it.

Foundational Matters (Ch. 1-4)

[10]*RB 1980* (*ibid.*, see footnote 7), Appendix 1: "Monastic Terminology: Monk, Cenobite, Nun", p. 319.

[11]A good modern interpretation of this "battle" is presented in Tad Dunne's extrapolation of the methods of St. Ignatius of Loyola in *Review for Religious*, Vol 45: No.5 (Sept/Oct, 1986), p. 709ff.

[12]Wilfred Tunink, *Vision of Peace* (New York: Farrar, Strauss, & Co., 1963), pp. 307-8.

[13]For details on this shift in the tradition and in Benedict's treatment of it, see RB 1980 (*ibid.*, footnote 7), pp. 356-363.

[14]Compare this with St. Paul's thought in I Cor. 4:15-6.

[15]For elaboration of this point, see *RB 1980*, pp. 325-6.

[16]George MacDonald, *The Marquis' Secret*, edited by Michael Phillips (Minneapolis: Bethany House Publishers, 1982), pp. 143-145.

[17]Notice too that Benedict has not included the Fifth Commandment: honor thy Father and Mother, but has instead added at the end the phrase from I Peter, translated "honor everyone". The family here has become greatly extended, because in Benedict's family everyone is kindred in Christ.

[18]This wonderful definition of fasting is from Dr. Paul Ford, in a presentation made at St. Andrew's Priory on July 12, 1989, during the Benedictine Spirituality for Laity workshop on "Work and Prayer".

[19]There is an excellent modern psychological treatment of this daily "training of the will" presented in Roberto Assagioli's work, especially *Psychosynthesis* (New York: Penguin Books, 1965), "Exercise of the Will in Daily Life", pp. 133-6.

[20]In addition to these two main citations, the preference for the love of Christ occurs another time in Chapter 4 (verse 72: "pray for your enemies out of love for Christ"); in Chapter 7 on Humility (verse 69: "no longer out of fear of hell, but out of love for Christ"); in Chapter 63 (verse 13: the abbot is called father "out of honor and love for Christ"); and indirectly in Chapter 5 on Obedience (verse 1:

"...obedience, which comes naturally to those who cherish Christ above all"). Meditation on these citations might help give deeper dimension to Benedict's meaning in "preferring Christ".

[21]Benedict refers to Christ as "Lord" at least 37 times in the Rule. For a further discussion of Christ's titles in the Rule, see the Thematic Index in *RB 1980* (*ibid.*, see footnote 7), p. 560.

[22]C.S. Lewis, *Perelandra* (New York: Macmillan Publishing Co., Inc., 1944), pp. 68-9: "One joy was expected and another is given....You could refuse the real good; you could make the real fruit taste insipid by thinking of the other."

[23]Eschatology is the doctrine of the last things, traditionally considered to be sin, death, hell and judgment.

[24]See also RB 19:1 and 7:13 for explicit acknowledgment of this principle.

[25]The term is used here as by William James in *Varieties of Religious Experience* (New York: Collier Books, 1961), meaning those souls whose basic experience of life tends to be tragic. See especially his chapters 6 and 7, and page 80 for the terminology once- and twice-born.

[26]Pope St. Gregory the Great, *Life and Miracles of St. Benedict* (Book Two of the *Dialogues*), translated by Odo J. Zimmermann, OSB, and Benedict R. Avery, OSB (Collegeville, Minn: The Liturgical Press), pp. 46-7.

[27]Leclerq, *The Love of Learning and the Desire for God*, *ibid* (see Footnote 6), p. 94.

[28]For example, there is the suggestion that the beautiful Song of Zechariah (Luke 1:68-79), used daily in the morning office of Lauds, was made possible because of the enforced silence and contemplation required of Zechariah between the visit from the angel Gabriel and the birth of his son John. Patrick O'Connell, "Worth Pondering", *Living Prayer*, Vol 20: No.6 (Nov/Dec, 1987), p. 13.

[29]An excellent study of silence and word in the Rule is that of Ambrose G. Wathen, OSB, *Silence: The Meaning of Silence in the Rule of St. Benedict* (Washington D.C: Cistercian Publications Consortium Press, 1973). See especially pages 195-7 and 230 on the matter of normal discourse among monks.

Monastic Virtues (Ch. 5-7)

[30]The earlier citations can be found in the Prologue and in Chapter Two (*lectio* segments on Prologue, verses 1-2, and Chapter Two, verses 6-10).

[31]See *RB 1980* (*ibid.*, footnote 7) note on page 187.

[32]See also the *lectio* segment on Chapter Four, verses 59-61.

[33]Benedict does allow some specific checks on obedience: those of the abbot's own accountability to Christ, as noted in Chapter Two, and the importance of the Rule as known by all the monks as a countervailing influence to the abbot's power. In addition, Benedict omits the passage from the Rule of the Master 2:36-7, which allows monks to impute all actions done under obedience to their superior, at the last judgment. See *RB 1980*, p. 187.

[34]John Cassian (died 435) wrote the *Institutes* and the *Conferences*, cited by Benedict in RB Chapter 73. (See notes 57 and 124 for citation.) Dom Cuthbert Butler indicates that we "must look to Cassian for Benedict's 'system' of the spiritual life." (*Benedictine Monachism*, London: Longmans, Green and Co., 1919), p. 47.

[35]As cited earlier, one modern psychologist has done some fascinating work on the will, as the "unknown and neglected factor in modern psychology, (even though)...the will is the function which is most directly related to the (authentic) self." His description of the training of the will sounds like a page taken out of Benedict's Rule! Assagioli, *Psychosynthesis, ibid.* (see footnote 19), especially pages 125-136.

[36]See *lectio* segment on Chapter Four, verses 39-40.

[37]Wathen, *Silence*, *ibid.*, (footnote 29).

[38]See in particular *RB 1980* (*ibid.*,footnote 7) notes on pages 186 and 193. Another good source is Emmanuel Heufelder, OSB, *The Way to God, According to the Rule of Saint Benedict*, translated by Luke Eberle, OSB (Kalamazoo, Michigan: Cistercian Publications, 1983) who uses Chapter 7 of the Rule as the basis for his entire commentary on the Rule. See especially his pages 116-7 on this point.

[39]Note, too, that tradition associates this Psalm (114) with David's sorrow as his first child of Bathsheba, conceived in sin, is dying after Nathan's prophecy to David and his admission of guilt.

[40]Benedict has taken this quotation from the Rule of the Master, whose source was the *Acta Anastasiae* 17.

[41]For a more full exploration of this "inner necessity" in modern terms, see Paul Ricoeur, *Phenomenology of Will and Action* (Pittsburgh, PA: Duquesne University Press, 1967).

[42]See *lectio* segment on Chapter Four, verses 59-61, and Chapter 5, verses 1-9.

[43]See footnote in *RB 1980* (*ibid.*,footnote 7), p. 198.

[44]Carl Sagan, *Contact* (New York: Pocketbooks, 1985), pp. 209-210.

[45]The phrases "dark night of the spirit" and "dark night of the soul" are, of course, taken from the work of St. John of the Cross. They seem to have been appropriated willy-nilly in modern language to refer to any opacity in understanding or experience.

[46]Jim Wallis, *The Call to Conversion* (San Francisco, CA: Harper & Row, 1981), see pages 100-107.

The Daily Office (Ch. 8-20)

[47]Ernest Becker, *The Denial of Death* (New York: The Free Press/Macmillan Publishing Co., 1973), pp. 3-34, 51, 58.

[48]Throughout the text, I have used the Hebrew numbering of the Psalms, which is the normal usage in most modern Bibles. In contrast, Benedict and the *RB 1980*, for example, generally use the Vulgate numbering. So the reader who meditates these psalms along with Benedict will have to check the normal usage in his or her own devotional source.

[49]David Parry, OSB, *Households of God* (London: Darton, Longman, and Todd, 1980), p. 56.

[50]In order to see how the hours for the offices are established from this "timetable", see the footnote below for RB Chapter 16 (note #55). For additional detail on this and other elements of the daily office, see the helpful appendix entitled "The Liturgical Code in the Rule of Benedict" in *RB 1980* (*ibid.*, footnote 7), especially pages 409-10.

[51]*RB 1980*, p. 388. The Syrian manual called the *Apostolic Constitutions* invites and exhorts the faithful to this celebration with these words: "...give praise to God, who made the universe through Jesus, sent him to us, permitted him to suffer and raised him from the dead. For what excuse will a person make to God if he fails to assemble on that day to hear the saving word concerning the resurrection?"

[52]Charles Cummings, OCSO, *Monastic Practices* (Kalamazoo, Michigan: Cistercian Publications, 1986), p. 39.

[53]Much of the analysis which follows here is suggested by Parry, *Households of God*, (*ibid.*, footnote 49), pp. 60-61.

[54]Parry, *Households of God*, his commentary on Chapter 15 of the RB.

[55]As mentioned in the *lectio* segment for Chapter 10, in Benedict's time the secular day was divided into two twelve hour periods, from sundown to sunup, and sunup to sundown. "Prime" (or first) refers to the first hour of the day period (or just after sunup), "terce" (or third) to the third hour, and so on for the other Latin designations. Thus, the "actual" hours of the daily offices were approximately as follows:

Vigils (2am)	**Sext** (noon)
Lauds (shortly after Vigils)	**None** (about 3pm)
Prime (about 6am; at dawn)	**Vespers** (dusk)
Terce (about 9am)	**Compline** (before bed)

[56]The source here is Parry, *Households of God*, his commentary on Chapter 16 of the RB.

[57]Benedict's key source, Cassian, has a lengthy dialogue on the power of the short prayer from Psalm 70:1: "Lord, come to my assistance". See John Cassian, *Conferences* (New York: Paulist Press, 1985), especially Conference Ten with Abba Isaac, p. 132. Predecessors of the "Jesus Prayer" ("Jesus/Lord, have mercy") were also well known to the desert fathers, tending to be more highly developed in the eastern church, as in the *Philokalia*. A more recent discussion of this prayer and its use is presented in *The Way of a Pilgrim* (New York: Doubleday/Image, 1978).

[58]Francis de Sales, *Introduction to the Devout Life* (New York: Doubleday/Image, 1950), p. 56f.

[59]Parry, *Households of God* (*ibid.*, footnote 49), his commentary on Chapter 19 of the RB.

[60]Discipline can mean a variety of things in the Rule, prominent among which is the forming of interior disposition. For a study of these and related themes in the Rule, see *RB 1980*'s Thematic Index under "Discipline", p. 561f. As a helpful supplementary study and devotional guide to the Rule, the Thematic Index of *RB 1980* is a marvelous resource.

[61]Heufelder, *The Way to God* (*ibid.*, footnote 38), pp. 153-4.

[62]See Parry, Households of God, in his commentary on Chapter 20, and Butler, *Benedictine Monachism* (*ibid.*, footnote 34) especially Chapter VI, "Benedict's Teaching on Prayer", pp. 58ff.

[63]It may be that Benedict is recollecting a moment like this while he writes this chapter, thus accounting for the almost poetic cadences of the Latin text. See *RB 1980* (*ibid.*, footnote 7), p. 100.

Disciplines of Community (Ch. 21-30)

[64]For further details on these origins, see *RB 1980*, especially footnotes on pp. 216-7.

[65]See Cummings, *Monastic Practices* (*ibid.*, footnote 52), Chapter XI, "The Monastic Cell", beginning on page 154, and his cited footnote of John Baptist Hasbrouck, pp. 214-5.

[66]See for example the *Episcopal Book of Common Prayer*, pages 99 and 123-4, as well as the Compline service in that book on page 133. As noted earlier, this document is solidly rooted in the Benedictine influences on the English Church.

[67]The wonderment was initially expressed by Adalbert de Vogue', *The Rule of Saint Benedict* (Kalamazoo, Michigan: Cistercian Publications, 1983) in his chapter XI, p. 185. In something of an overreaction, an alternative position is well presented by Julian Stead, OSB, "The Penal Code of St. Benedict", *Word and Spirit* Volume 6 (Still River, Mass: St. Bede's Publications, 1984), pages 58-68.

[68]On this point, see Dom Justin McCann, *St. Benedict* (London: Sheed and Ward, 1938), p. 139.

[69]See Stead, "The Penal Code..." (*ibid.*, footnote 67), p. 59.

[70]See the discussion in *RB 1980* (*ibid.*, footnote 7) on Benedict's theory of excommunication and salvation as rooted in many of the Pauline letters, pages 421-6.

[71]See Stead, "The Penal Code..." (*ibid.*, footnote 67), p. 65 especially.

[72]For reference, see the earlier *lectio* segments on Chapter 4:41-3, :74, and Chapter 7:49-50, :62-6.

[73]Stead, "The Penal Code..." (*ibid.*), p. 67.

[74]See *RB 1980*, pp. 100-1.

[75]See *RB 1980*, p. 430.

[76]See *RB 1980*, p. 225.

[77]Compare, for interest's sake, the stages of moral development outlined in such modern authors as Kohlberg. In particular, notice his Preconventional Level, Stage I Compliance category, in which response to authority is chiefly on the basis of force, or simple rewards and punishments. Lawrence Kohlberg, *Essays in Moral Development* (San Francisco: Harper & Row, 1984).

[78]See for example the Rule of the Master (*ibid.*, footnote 2), Chapter XIV, verses 78-87. The Rule of the Master was Benedict's major textual source, as we have noted, and this brief passage should in no way be construed as characterizing its whole tone and direction.

Domestic Arrangements (Ch. 31-42)

[79]*RB 1980* (*ibid.*, footnote 7), p. 226.

[80]Very possibly Benedict's thought on this passage was shaped in part by Augustine's (see his *Epist* 211: 5 and 9), *RB 1980*, p. 604.

[81]For support of this statement, see Daniel Rees *et. al.*, *Consider Your Call* (Kalamazoo, Michigan: Cistercian Publications, 1980), pages 59-60f and *RB 1980*, p. 167. For an opposing view, see de Vogue', *The Rule of Saint Benedict* (*ibid.*, footnote 67), his pages 65-6f.

[82]For a particularly good brief discussion of the monastic custom of dishwashing as a sacrament, see Cummings, *Monastic Practices* (*ibid.*, footnote 52), pages 82-3.

[83]See the *lectio* segments on Chapters 17 and 18.

[84]See also Benedict's Chapter 4:15-16 and Chapter 53:1.

[85]See especially Matthew 5:46, 6:1f, 7:11 and so forth.

[86]For more discussion of these practices, see Wilfred Tunink, OSB, *Vision of Peace* (*ibid.*, footnote 12), p. 104; as well as Dom David Knowles, *The Monastic Order in England* (Cambridge: University Press, 1949), p. 688; and Basil Hume, OSB, *Searching for God* (London: Hodder and Stoughton, 1977), p. 150.

[87]See Wathen, *Silence* (*ibid.*, footnote 29), especially pages 165-172.

[88]Eucharist is seldom mentioned in the Rule, probably because it was assumed. There were not necessarily any priests in the monastery, so Mass itself might be infrequent, but daily Communion was probably the norm. For more detail on this point, see *RB 1980* (*ibid.*, footnote 7), pages 410-12 especially.

[89]"We read" apparently refers to the *Lives of the Fathers*. See *RB 1980*, p. 241.

[90]Esther de Waal, *Seeking God* (Collegeville, Minn: The Liturgical Press, 1984), p. 72. This book is a very fine introduction to Benedict's thought for the contemporary lay person.

[91]Wathen, *Silence* (*ibid.*, footnote 29), particularly his pages 30, 97, 168, and 179.

Lukewarmness and its Remedies (Ch. 43-46)

[92]Parry, *Households of God* (*ibid.*, footnote 49) in his introduction to these chapters of the Rule.

[93]See especially Augustine's *The Lord's Sermon on the Mount* (translated by John J. Jepson, Westminster, MD: Newman Press,, 1948), page 43 in which he sets forth three steps in the commission of sin: suggestion, pleasure and consent. Benedict may well have been familiar with this thinking of Augustine, who is a source on whom he often draws.

[94]*RB 1980* (*ibid.*, footnote 7), p. 435.

[95]See *RB 1980*, Appendix 4: "Disciplinary Measures in the Rule of Benedict", p. 415f.

[96] The Rule of the Master, (see footnote 2) Chapter XIV, verses 78-82, p. 158.

[97]See for example M. Esther Harding, *The I and the Not I: A Study in the Development of Consciousness* (Princeton: Bollingen Series, Princeton University Press, 1965).

The Consecration of Mundane Activities (Ch. 47-57)

[98]Some authors suggest the lenten "books" referred to here are sections of the Bible. See *RB 1980*, note on page 251, for example.

[99]There is some evidence that indeed this chapter is the fruit of Benedict's own long reflection on the sermons of Pope St. Leo (39-50) on Lent. *RB 1980*, p. 253.

[100]For elaboration of this point, see Heufelder, *The Way to God*, (*ibid.*, footnote 38), pages 161-4.

[101]On this point, see de Vogue' *The Rule of Saint Benedict* (*ibid.*, footnote 67), page 263.

[102]See *RB 1980*, note on page 257.

[103]This practice is also provided for in the Rules of Augustine, the Master, Pachomius, and Caesarius of Arles. See *RB 1980*, (*ibid.*, footnote 7), notes on pages 258-9.

[104]Leclerq, "The Problem of Social Class..." (*ibid.*, footnote 8), pages 35-42 especially.

[105]de Waal, *Seeking God* (*ibid.*, footnote 90), her page 152.

[106]namely, Iris Murdoch.

[107]The Rule of the Master, (*ibid.*, footnote 2), Chapter 84, page 250.

Membership and Governance (Ch. 58-66)

[108]Verse 7, which is also the subject of the next *lectio* segment, describes "careful consideration", suggesting that the whole community, as well as the novice master, is lending its prayers and presence to this process. See *RB 1980*, note on page 267 and text on page 447.

[109]See Parry, *Households of God*, (*ibid.*, footnote 49), page 158.

[110]*RB 1980*, (*ibid.*, footnote 7), p. 268. For detail on the various interpretations of these vows, see the Appendix on "Monastic Formation and Profession", especially pages 458-466.

[111]Numerous texts discuss this promise in detail. For lay use, see especially de Waal, *Seeking God* (*ibid.*, footnote 90).

[112]Indeed, the Master's Rule always considers priests and deacons as "outsiders" to the monastic community. See *RB 1980*, note on page 273.

[113]I am indebted for this idea to Martin Cawley, OSCO, "Four Themes in the Rule of St. Benedict", *Word and Spirit*, Volume 2 (Still River, Mass: St. Bede's Publications, 1981), especially page 97.

[114]George MacDonald, *The Musician's Quest*, edited by Michael Phillips (Minneapolis, Minn: Bethany House Publishers, 1984), p. 128.

[115]See *RB 1980*, note on pages 276-7 and text on pages 34-41.

[116]The brief reference to Romans 12 suggests these verses may be the fruit of Benedict's reflection on the vision of community set forth by St. Paul there.

[117]See *RB 1980*, appendix on "The Abbot", page 372f.

[118]Cardinal Basil Hume, OSB, *In Praise of Benedict* (London: Hodder and Stoughton, 1981), p. 18.

[119]Butler, *Benedictine Monachism*, (*ibid.*, footnote 34), p. 50. This statement is presented in an excellent chapter on "Benedict's Teaching on the Spiritual Life" (Chapter V).

[120]See also Chapter 18:22 of the Rule for a similar example of Benedict's humility.

[121]Adele M. Millette, "Searching for the God of My Heart", *Living Prayer*, Vol 21: No.1 (Jan/Feb, 1988), page 12.

[122]C. S. Lewis, *Letters to Malcolm: Chiefly on Prayer* (New York: Harvest/HBJ, 1963), p. 75.

A Few Final Guidelines (Ch. 67-73)

[123]*RB 1980*, (*ibid.*, footnote 7), note on page 288.

[124]This phrase was culled from the patristic and monastic literature, and might be particularly well traced from Cassian's *Conferences* and *Institutes* as well as Basil's Rules. We have previously given one reference for Cassian's *Conferences* (footnote 57); another for both of his books is the Eerdmans Series on the *Nicene and Post-Nicene Fathers of the Christian Church*, editorial supervision by Philip Schaff and Henry Wace, *Volume XI: Sulpitius Severus, Vincent of Lerins, and John Cassian* (Grand Rapids, Michigan: Wm. B. Eerdmans Publishing Company, 1986). A convenient English translation of Basil's "Long Rules" has recently been re-published by the Daughters of St. Paul in pamphlet form (50 St. Paul's Avenue, Jam Pl., Boston 30, Massachusetts).